Bridging our Differences

Gerry S. M. Hughes

 New Generation Publishing

Dedication

For my Mum and Dad

Acknowledgements

'...the easy things are not worth doing. Where is the satisfaction from achievement? It is the difficult things we take on that bring us pride and is real achievement.'

Sir Robin Knox Johnston (personal email written to Gerry Hughes on rounding Cape Horn).

There are so many people who have helped and supported me through my life that it is impossible to name them all, but there are some people who really influenced the course of my life.

First, Sir Robin Knox Johnston. Robin Knox Johnston (he wasn't Sir Robin at the time) allowed me to use his name for insurance on my circumnavigation of the British Isles with Matthew Jackson. Without that, I would never have achieved any of my sailing ambitions. Sir Robin has been a great support to me since then – always believing that deafness was not a barrier to me achieving my sailing ambitions.

Dr Mary Brennan was a linguistics researcher at Moray House College of Education, University of Edinburgh. Mary gave me a position as a research associate in her BSL Linguistics Research Team. Mary changed my life. It was through researching the linguistics of BSL that I found my true identity as a Deaf BSL user. I never looked back. Mary's research was the foundation for the creation of recognised qualifications in British Sign Language and, eventually, the British Sign Language (Scotland) Act 2015. Thank you, Dr Mary.

There are a number of people who supported me over the years I spent campaigning to the General Teaching Council to be allowed access to teacher training college. Thank you to Bridget Hill for being a great colleague and for supporting me through those difficult times. Thanks also to Professor Peter B. Watson BA LLB SSC for challenging the General Teaching Council's rules on admitting deaf people into the teaching profession. I would also like to say thank you to Professor Bart McGettrick. Bart was the Principal of St Andrews College, Glasgow when I was accepted into teacher training. I know that Bart argued my case and that it was not easy. Bart's decision to accept me into St Andrews College meant that, for the first time since the Milan Convention of 1880, a deaf BSL user was allowed to train to teach in Scotland. This has opened the door for other deaf people who aim to become teachers. Thanks to Bart also for commenting on draft chapters of this book and his ongoing support.

It would have been impossible to complete my solo circumnavigation without a leave of absence from teaching at St Roch's Secondary School. Thank you to Gerry McGuigan (former Head Teacher) and Tommy Donnelly (Deputy Head) for supporting my application for a leave of absence.

Stephen Bennie at Troon marina provided invaluable support by offering me a reduced berth fee for *Quest III* for my round the word project. This allowed me to complete the modifications to it. Thank you to Stephen and all the staff at Troon marina for making me, my family, and my friends so welcome. Of course, I must also mention Bill MacKay who recommended a Beneteau 42s7 for sailing round the world. Thanks also to Duncan Yacht Chandlers, Saturn Sails, Mast and Rigging Services (Scotland) and Robert Hogg at Autofreeze, Cambuslang. I must make special mention of the Clyde Cruising Club. The Clyde Cruising Club made me a lifetime honorary member and awarded me the Todrick Trophy for my round the world log. That was the catalyst for writing this book.

I also want to acknowledge the support I have received from Raymond Williams FRSAMD, former Lord Dean of the Guild of the Merchants House of Glasgow. Raymond invited me to give the after-dinner speech at the Merchants House annual dinner in 2014. I was so honoured when he announced that I was to be made an honorary member of the Merchants House of Glasgow. Raymond has been a good friend to me since I first met him and he has shown a keen interest in the deaf community. I want to thank him for encouraging me to write this book and for commenting on the draft manuscript.

Thanks also to Dr Elizabeth Mooney, BSc, PhD, FRGS who worked as a designated interpreter on this project. Elizabeth is a geographer and registered sign language interpreter. English is my second language so we worked together on the manuscript refining my written English until I was happy with it.

Thanks to Jim Colhoun and Demi Stevenson for all the support you gave me and my family during my round the world voyage. Jim corresponded with me regularly during my voyage, keeping me up to date with news and helped me keep up my spirits when the going was really tough.

Thank you also to the admin team of the Gerry Hughes *Quest III* Facebook Page for keeping the world up to date with news about my adventures with

Quest III, and all the work they did in the background to support me throughout my voyage. I must also give heartfelt thanks to the *Quest III* Fan Club for all the support they gave my family while I was at sea. And to all the people and organisations who donated money and organised fundraising events to help me recoup the money I spent on my solo circumnavigation – thank you so much.

Most important of all, I want to say thank you to my wife Kay Hughes and our two daughters Nicola and Ashley. Kay, Nicola and Ashley have unending faith in me and my skills as a yachtsman. Thank you for your love, support and for being so brave when I was at sea. Sailing can be very dangerous. There were times when I was very frightened, but knowing that you believed in me and were waiting for me to come home kept me going.

Contents

Chapter 1: The Seeds of a Dream

Decision must be made now, barometer continue to drop, 978.8mb,
Deep depression is on way, series drogue on standby
Quest III hammered by fierce waves, bracing myself, need run before
the storm. Should we alter course go up north or go south?
This is my last chance of survival. I fear for worse to come.
1346 NM to Cape Horn.

(Gerry's logbook, 22nd February, 2013)

My name is Gerry Hughes. I am a yachtsman. I have loved the feel of the southwestly wind, and the smell of seaweed in the low tides of Kyles of Bute and Firth of Clyde, for as long as I can remember.

I was born in Glasgow. It was a very difficult birth. Twice within a few months of being born, my parents were told I was unlikely to survive. Each time, the priest was called and I was given the last rites. But to the doctors' surprise I pulled through.

Shortly afterwards, I became seriously ill again. I had problem in my oesophagus that caused difficulty swallowing, and I was sick when eating. I also had a restriction of the diaphragm that created problems with my lungs. The doctors informed my parents that exploratory surgery was the only option. Sick with worry, my father contacted his family in Ireland for advice. They told him about a specialist hospital for the children in Dublin that had a good reputation. So instead of agreeing to surgery, my parents bundled me up, and flew to Dublin.

My father's cousins met us at the airport and took us to the hospital. After a few days of tests, my parents were delighted when the doctors told them that I would not need surgery. My oesophagus would heal, but for a while I would need to sleep upright and be fed through a tube in my nose. But there was another shock in store for my mum and dad. The doctor asked 'Do you realise your son is profoundly deaf?'

In those days there was no screening available of new-born babies and it was common for children to be diagnosed as deaf several years after they were born. My parents had no experience of deafness, but they knew raising a deaf child would not be easy. At age two and half, I was enrolled as a day pupil at St Vincent's School for the Deaf in Glasgow.

My dad was in the Royal Navy and served on HMS Sparrow. When he left the Navy, he trained to be an accountant, but he never lost his love of the sea. He had a GP14 dinghy called 'Wee G' and, from the age of two, my dad would take me sailing in that wee dinghy. From that very first moment until now, I have always been drawn to the sea. Even as a small child I was keen to make the most of any opportunity to spend time with the sea.

Once, while visiting family in Largs, I slipped off while nobody was looking. I was about five years old. I had been playing in the garden with the big black Labrador dog that lived on the house. Mum was distraught. The family set out to find me: splitting themselves between the north and south beaches. Eventually, I was found two miles away on the beach at a local landmark: The Pencil. I was happily playing with my pals (the wee crabs), completely unaware of the panic I had caused.

A few years later, I did my disappearing again. This time I was on a family holiday with my cousins in Belgium. I managed to slip out of the hotel early in the morning, before my mum and dad woke up. Despite the panic, my dad knew that I would be heading for the sea. He scoured the beach looking for me. He had almost given up all hope when he heard the chatter of different languages. There was a group of people, standing in a circle looking down at the ground. My dad was terrified. He feared for the worse. But then he realised that the people in the crowd were trying to talk to someone. There I was, sitting on the beach, busy playing with the sand and the wee crabs. I was given strict instructions never, ever, to leave the house without asking first!

When I think back to my early childhood, I was always impatient to get back to our boat. I have very few memories of those early days, or how my dad and I communicated with each other, but we must have created our own signs. My most vivid memory is my dad explaining to me when we would be back at sea on the boat. He would sign 'two sleeps', 'three sleeps' etc. – in other words, two days or three days.

By the time I was about eight years old, Dad and I would spend every weekend and most of the summer at sea. By that time, Dad owned a Norweigh wooden keel boat. I loved that boat: I loved the smell of the varnished wood and feel of the toe rail against my hand. She was moored at Rhu, Helensburgh but we later moved her to a mooring at Largs.

Although I was only eight, I was very ambitious and wanted to be involved in sailing as much as I could. I remember trying to pull sheets, but my dad was very cautious about the strength need for pulling the jib so he gave me another sheet in attempt to keep me happy. I was so annoyed with him – I wanted to sail the boat! My dad would explain the sea to me by pointing to the waves and demonstrating to me that the waves would splash over the deck. I jumped below to avoid getting soaked, and we laughed together as the waves drenched us. From that, I learned to read the waves and began to regularly push Dad away from the tiller to avoid the big waves. In the late afternoons, I loved to examine the changing clouds, knowing that they were a sign to expect a strong breeze and that the boat would soon be heeling down very fast.

Like many Glasgow families, our holidays were on the Isle of Bute. That was my favourite part of summer. I was a regular customer at the local cycle hire shop. Early in the morning, as soon as I woke, I would hide my hearing aid in the bedroom, and cycle to the bakery, where I could get rolls for Mum and Dad's breakfast.

After breakfast, I would jump on my bike and cycle for miles and miles around the island. I loved the feel of the drizzling rain, and the force of the wind against my ears, as I sped along the country roads next to the rocky coastline.

Sometimes, I would secure my fishing rod, wee stove and frying pan to my bike and cycle south past Craigmore for a morning of fishing. I loved to cook the fish once I had caught them. After a morning of fishing, I swam in swimming in the pool near the Glenburn Hotel.

On other days, I would row out the sea early in the morning. I loved the smell of low tide coming. Sometimes, I would nip through the back garden, climb over the wall, and walk up to the top of the hill overlooking Kilchattan Bay. I always carried a knife in my belt like a scout. In those days, there were only two to three trees on the hill, so knowing that it was very likely I would be back the following year, I buried my knife under my favourite tree (I was planning to retrieve it when I returned). I never got the chance to look for it again.

A few years ago, I sailed past Kilchattan Bay, with my Deaf pals crewing for me. I pointed to the hill, telling them the story about my knife. The hill is covered in trees now. I don't think I would be able to find that knife.

One day, while I was out at sea in Kilchattan Bay, rowing a wooden dinghy, my dad appeared at the shore and waved to me to come in to shore. I couldn't understand why he was there. The sun was still high in the sky, so I knew it was far too early for dinner. I knew it must be something important because he was waving frantically, so I rowed to the shore.

We climbed the stairs to our one-bedroom holiday flat. A black and white TV was flickering in the living room and I stared at the screen in awe. A man had landed on the moon! I watched very, very, closely as my dad tried to explain to me what was what happening. I signed to my dad: 'same moon at night?' I was sure he did not understand my question because he nodded 'yes'.

From that day on, my mind was full of questions. I would fall asleep gazing at the moon and stars overlooking the bay and ask myself: *How could someone get to the moon? How does the wind blow? Why does the sea go low? How do trees grow?* I became more and more interested in trying to figure out how things worked. I fell in love with space and spent hours and hours trying to figure out how people managed to land on the moon.

A few weeks after returning from that holiday, we visited a model shop in Glasgow City Centre. Using my pocket money, I bought a model kit for Space Rocket Apollo 11 and lunar module. I would build these during those rainy days in Bute, when it was too wet to go outside.

The family holidays in Bute were full of adventures. Looking back, I don't think I ever had any fear of water. My Uncle Cyril, Aunt Pat and their five children (Michael, Claire, Mark, Paul and Brian) would holiday in Bute as well. Claire's family had a motor cruiser and my dad had a Westerly Centaur 26ft yacht.

Once, when both boats were alongside each other in Rhu, Mum, Dad and I joined our uncle on his motor cruiser. Our parents were down below talking and I was walking along the deck. The deck was narrow and there was only enough room for one person, but Claire was walking along for the opposite direction and wanted to get past. I held the toe rail to let her pass but must have lost my footing because suddenly I splashed overboard. I could feel myself drifting out to sea on the ebb tides. The motor cruiser seemed to be getting smaller and smaller and I could see people waving to me, rushing about, picking up ropes, fishing rods and the long pole. My dad was at the stern of the boat and signing 'swim and you will get a medal'. So, that's what I did. I swam as fast and strong as I could towards the boat and Uncle Cyril lifted out of the water using a long wooden rod. Dad hugged me tightly to him. I stood shivering, but I was also smiling. My dad was delighted that I was safe, but I could also see that he was very, very, proud of me for staying calm and swimming to the boat.

It was those early sailing experiences that led my father to make a decision that would change the course of my life. I can't remember exactly what happened, but my mum later explained the story to me in detail.

One day, my Mum, Dad and me, were on a family sail in the Firth of Clyde. It was a beautiful, peaceful day and we were sailing under full sails. For some reason, I wanted my dad to change course, and tried to explain to him by pointing to the bay where we had dropped anchor. I was getting more and more frustrated because Dad seemed to be ignoring me. Instead of changing course, he continued smoking his cigarette and listening to his favourite opera music. So I grabbed the tiller to take control of the boat and my dad and I then battled with each other over the tiller.

Eventually, my dad succeeded in pushing me away. I let go of the jib and caught a tight hold of the tiller to make sure I could steer us to the bay. My dad was furious. He could not understand why I was behaving like that. Mum and Dad had a chat and agreed it was best to alter course in an attempt to calm the situation.

It was one of those days when darkness arrives in the early evening. After checking the sky, Mum and Dad dropped anchor for the night. I climbed into my bunk and fell asleep. As usual, my dad switched on the radio to listen to the shipping forecast. He could not believe his ears. A warning was issued to all ships in the area to prepare for a severe storm, one of the worst experienced to date. My dad looked across at me sleeping peacefully while the boat was rocking and the force of the wind pulled on the anchor.

Dad climbed on deck to add more chains to stabilise the boat. Far in the distance, the sky was lit up by flashes of light from distress flares set off by other yachts as they signalled for help from the coastguard and lifeboats. At that moment, Dad began to worry about the quality of my education. He knew I could easily follow charts and navigate and now he realised that I could anticipate changes in the weather by reading the sky and the waves. But I could not read or write. Although I could speak, I didn't even know the name of the street in which our family lived.

I loved our family holidays in Bute, but the best holiday was in the summer of 1970 when Mum and Dad invited John Church (a deaf boy who lived nearby and attended St Vincent's school) to join us in Port Bannatyne. John and I communicated in sign language for the whole holiday and I loved it! I didn't need my hearing aid. My holiday was very different. Suddenly I felt alive and part of something. Every morning, I would take John out to explore the island. We investigated the beaches (examining the stones and rock pools), visited the pier to watch the ferries and the fishing boats, and bought chips on our way home.

Very early one morning, the light went on in the bedroom. It was dark, and without saying anything, I pulled on my clothes. John did the same and we were bundled into the car. John did not have a clue what was happening and began to get very anxious. Dad switched on the car headlamps and drove towards the shore.

When we arrived at the shore, we scrambled into the dinghy and slipped out to sea. Dad quietly pulled up the sails, and told John we were going to do some fishing. We caught many mackerel that morning as we waited for the sun to rise. When we returned to our mooring, my dad took out a few fish and wrapped them in paper. He handed the wrapped fish to John and asked him to place them in the cockpit of the other boat. My dad left a wee note on the wrapper: *this is for your breakfast*.

It was very hot that summer so, in the late afternoon, John and I would cool off by swimming in the sea between Wemyss Bay and Bute. John liked to wear flippers when he was swimming. On one very calm day, John and I were swimming around the boat, when John realised that one of his flippers had fallen off.

John signed to me: 'one of my flipper fall. I go dive, get it'.

We both held our breath and dived down into the sea chasing after the flipper. Through the light of the sun rays glistening in the green water, we could see the flipper zig-zagging down towards the sea floor and falling deeper in to the blackness where the light could not reach. We both stopped and our eyes met, then we watched the flipper slowly descending into the darkness below.

We were struggling to hold our breath. There were bubbles coming out of our noses and covering our faces, and we were out of easy reach from the surface of the sea. We had no option but to raise our arms straight above our heads to let the buoyancy of the water lift us towards the surface. But we moved very, very, slowly and our eyes grew wider and wider with concern as we began to worry how much longer we could hold our breath.

Finally, we broke the surface and gasped for air. I looked around, wondering where my dad was. His boat was far away in the distance. I couldn't believe how far from the boat we had travelled.

6

That particular holiday in Bute was the best holiday I had ever experienced. Eventually, the holiday came to an end and it was time for John to go home, but I knew it would not be too long before we would meet up again at school.

I said goodbye to John: 'See you at St Vincent's soon.'
'Aye, see you there,' he replied.

My family stayed on in Port Bannatyne for a few weeks before returning home to Glasgow. I was sure it must be time to go back to school, but no, I was still on holiday. Then, one day, my mum started to pack a case.

'Where are we going?' I asked in sign language.

She ignored me. I couldn't understand it so I rushed to my dad, asking him the same question. At first, I thought we might be going to the boat, but there was something different about the luggage: it was hard, not like the waterproof luggage used for sailing.

My neighbours at the time were Dr Willie, Trish and my mate Alan Moyes from across the road. Alan was not deaf so attended a different school, but we loved to play football together on their driveway after school. His mum gave me a wee book about the same size as a cigarette packet: *Collins Gem Dictionary of Synonyms and Antonyms*. Then Aunt Edith arrived. I assumed they had just come long to say 'cheerio' but they all looked so upset and tearful. I could not understand why they were upset.

We got into the car and set off. I sat in the back, looking at Mum and Dad, wondering what was going on. Mum was very, very, quiet: she did not say a word. My dad drove in silence, smoking one cigarette after another.

It was a beautiful day. The sun shone so brightly that I had to shield my eyes as I gazed out of the window, trying to figure out where we were going. I remember thinking, *it can't be Bute because this is not the route you take to get to Bute and catch the ferry'*.

We drove for miles and miles through the countryside. I sat in the back seat, watching the fields with trees and cows munching grass, but I knew something was wrong. I examined my dad's eyes in the rear-view mirror. He was fully concentrating on driving, and as far as I could tell, he did not say a single word to my mum.

Eventually, we stopped at the entrance to a huge building. We got out of the car. There were two nuns standing at a heavy oak door that smelled of wood polish. I looked at my dad and asked via my facial expression: *what is happening?*

My dad's face was firm and steady: 'Go do what Sister Barbara, the head teacher, asks you to do.'

We walked through the long corridors. I had my hearing aid on, so I could hear that Sister Barbara and my parents were talking, but I could not follow their conversation.

We arrived at a classroom with six pupils sitting at desks arranged in a horseshoe shape. Nobody said 'Hello'. The teacher was wearing a microphone. Each pupil was wearing a set of large headphones on their head so they could listen to the teacher's voice. There was one empty chair. I was instructed to sit down and put the headphones on.

Immediately, the teacher began checking the volume: 'one, two, three, four…' I turned to look at Mum and Dad. They had vanished! All I could see was the large white door that was slowly closing.

My heart was racing as I looked around at the other pupils, trying to work out what was happening. But they couldn't see me because they were busy focusing on the teacher, lipreading to understand what the teacher was saying.

I could feel myself getting more and more upset, but I knew I had to behave myself and try to stay calm. At break time, one of the boys in the class was given the job of showing me the school, but I shot out of the classroom, frantically running through the corridors, trying to remember the route back to the entrance of the building. *Where am I? Where are my mum and dad?* At last, I found my way to the main door and looked out. My dad's car had disappeared.

I stood at the door, gazing at the large statue in front of the school building and the brilliant green lawn. The air smelled so different from home: it was so dry. The walls of the school buildings and local houses were made of limestone (completely different from the stone walls in Glasgow). I looked up to the sky. The clouds were different and moving in a different direction. I did not have a clue where I was, but I knew I was a long way from home, and completely on my own. I was lost. I slumped down and sobbed.

For about a month after that day, I was very ill. I lost my appetite and left my food on my plate. I stayed in bed whenever I could. I felt lost and alone and had given up hope. I must have been very unwell because one of the nuns, Sister Maria, was allocated to look after me. She would keep watch over me during the day, and I vaguely remember her sitting by my bed through the blue dim of the night.

I cried myself to sleep every night. The sisters changed the sheets to help me feel dry and comfortable. By November of that year, I was moved to another room to share with four other boys. And my recovery slowly began.

The school was St John's School for the Deaf, Boston Spa, Yorkshire. I was thirteen. I could not read or write. I could say words and copy them from a blackboard or a book, but I did not understand their meaning. Unknown to me at the time, my dad had recognised that I had potential to achieve more in education. He could see that I was skilled at sailing and that I could read charts and observe and understand the weather. He also knew that, despite not knowing the name of the street in which we lived, I could easily find my way around the local area. He decided that he had no choice but to move me to a new school for special educational needs, in the hope that I would be able to learn to read and write. But he would need to pay for this out of his own pocket.

Perhaps, you are wondering how I could get to the age of thirteen without being a being able read or write? It is worth just taking some time to explain a little about the education of deaf children. In 1880, sign language was banned from being used in schools by the International Congress in Milan[1]. Across the world, deaf teachers lost their jobs and a new model of teaching was introduced in schools for deaf children: oralism.

Oralists believe that the priority for deaf children is for them to access information by using use their 'hearing' and lipreading. Deaf children were given intensive speech therapy to teach them to speak and lip read. Deaf children were forbidden to sign in class[2] and could be punished if caught. I was taught under the oral tradition. I was good at speaking, but I was like a parrot saying words that I did not understand. Deep inside me, I felt that something was missing. It was not until I met Mary Brennan, and joined her research team investigating sign language used by Deaf people in Britain that I eventually discovered my true identity and felt comfortable

---

[1]You can find a useful summary of the Milan Congress at
http://www.bda.org.uk/British_Sign_Language_-
_BSL/British_Sign_Language_History
[2] Even today in the UK, deaf children are not necessary taught by teachers fluent in British Sign Language.

with myself. Sign languages are the natural languages of deaf people. We use signs and facial expressions and gestures in the same way hearing people use the spoken and written word. It was sign language that allowed me to understand and express complex information and access higher education.

My cousins kept in touch with me while I was in boarding school. My closest cousin was Claire, who would send me letters with Snoopy on them. Claire's older brother, Michael, also wrote but, because I couldn't read, I did not understand what was written in them.

When Sister Barbara passed out the letters to the pupils, I would always quickly spot my dad's handwriting. I would open the letter, look at his handwriting, trying to understand the words on the page, and I would sob. Inside my head, I was shouting for my dad, *where are you?* I hid the letters under my pillow in the dormitory to keep my dad close to me. I loved to see those letters, but they also made me feel so lost and alone. I cried myself to sleep at night whenever I received a letter from my dad.

One of those nights, I lay on my bed, gazing through the narrow curtainless window near to my bed. The stars shone brightly in the dark night of the sky. Something switched on in my head: I realised that I recognised those stars! They were the same stars that shone in the sky when I was with my family in Bute. Before I knew it, my mind was back in Bute and I thought of the family holidays, when most mornings I cycled my bike to collect rolls for my mum and dad's breakfast before cycling off to catch fish along the rocky shores. I was sobbing again.

I noticed Sister Barbara walking through the dormitory with her torch. She must have heard the noise when I buried my head as she approached. I didn't want her to see me crying. I held my breath for as long as I could and then burst into tears. I wept so much that night that the pillow and blankets were soaking.

Every day in the class was the same. We put on our headphones and 'listened' and learned to speak. It was exhausting and painful. My eyes stung. My ears ached from the effort. Sometimes we would be asked to write a short story. Everyone would start scribbling but I froze as I stared at the blank page in front of me. I could not do it. I could not write a story. I could write only very short words such as 'Celtic'.

Around me, the other pupils would put their hands up and shout to let the teacher know that they had finished their stories. The teacher would say 'well done' as she waited for the other pupils to finish off their work.

At this point, we had assessments every week at school and the results were posted in the corridor on a Friday. Every Friday was the same; we gathered in the corridor to find out our results. My name was always at the end of the list. I was bottom of the class. I felt humiliated and ashamed because now everybody knew my weakness: I could not read and write.

One day, the head teacher, Sister Barbara, came into the classroom and beckoned me with her finger, indicating that she wanted me to follow her out of the room. I was not sure what was happening but removed my headphones and followed her out of the classroom, along the corridors to the school library. I was terrified because Sister Barbara was very strict. She spoke very clearly so I could lip-read her easily and asked me to read the sentences on the page using my voice.

When I finished, Sister Barbara explained, 'Gerry, you have got a very good voice. Do you understand what it is about?'

I said, 'No.'

'That's fine, Gerry.'

She gave me a wee notebook and asked me to draw a line down the page, dividing it in two. She explained, 'Write down which vocabulary you don't understand and I will write what it means. Or write down which sentences you do not understand.'

When I wrote down my list of words, Sister Barbara said, 'You have very good handwriting, Gerry. Do you know the meaning of those words?'

I said, 'No.'

Unknown to me at that time, Sister Barbara had identified the problem. From that day on, Sister Barbara would sit with me for thirty minutes, five times a week. We would work together, studying vocabulary and sentences. Sister Barbara would explain the meaning of the words, using whatever resources she had available: pictures, diagrams and a dictionary.

After that first day, Sister Barbara did not ask me to read out loud using my voice. I was so relieved because it meant I did not have to worry about how I was pronouncing the words.

I had been taught to 'sound' out the words phonetically, so people could understand what I was saying. But, although I can 'hear' my voice when I wear a hearing aid, I do not hear enough to know if I am pronouncing the words correctly. I needed some else to tell me if my speech was 'correct'. That way I could link the sound to the word. It was a huge pressure: constantly trying to ensure I was pronouncing the words in the 'right way'.

Instead, of reading out loud, Sister Barbara asked me to read a paragraph and then would ask me to explain what the story was about. Then she would explain the paragraph to me to help me work out which parts I had not understood. It was hard work. I was desperate to be able to read, but I just could not understand the words in front of me.

Day after day, month after month, for eighteen months, I sat with Sister Barbara, trying to make sense of the words in front of me. At night, I returned to my dormitory and gazed through the window at the stars. Slowly, through time, the tears began to fade and I would look forward to seeing the stars. Even though they were millions of miles away, they felt close to me. As I lay contemplating the stars, my feelings of hopelessness slipped away as my mind turned to questions about those stars and the skies around them. And then , finally, one day, something changed.

It was bright and the sun was shining directly through the window, lighting up our space in the library. We repeated our daily routine. All of a sudden, Sister Barbara's face lit up with a warm and friendly smile: 'Well done, Gerry. You are getting there. Now read the next paragraph.' It was a different topic but, slowly but surely, I started to pick out the meaning and explain it in my own voice. 'That's correct. Read the next paragraph.' I repeated the exercise and, at last, Sister Barbara said, 'That's good, Gerry. Now choose a book that you would like to read.' I felt very proud of myself, but the books on the shelves were for children aged five or six.

Looking back, I can see that day was the turning point of my life. It was as if a thick grey fog had lifted and I could 'see' the words on the page. I could understand the words and, at last, I could make sense of the world around me. I became hungry for knowledge. I knew that, with this new skill, I could become independent. I would be able to write my own thoughts and opinions, and I would be able to study for a Certificate of Secondary Education (CSE). And, most important of all, I would be able to write letters to my mum and dad.

The Christmas holidays arrived, and I spent the train journey home thinking about my dad's sailing books: stories about Sir Francis Chichester, Robin Knox Johnston and Sir Alec Rose. As I walked towards the house, I could see Patsy at the window waiting for me.

My mind was fixed on those sailing books on the shelf next to the coal fire because I wanted to show my dad that I could read. I opened the first book. The print was small and dense: I could hardly understand a single word on the page. I looked at the book again and then at my dad.

Dad paused and with a gentle face explained, 'This is for an adult. Maybe you will read this book when you grow up. ' I must have been about fifteen years old, but my reading age was much younger, possibly that of a seven-year-old.

I stood back, looking at my dad, with Patsy by my side. I was determined that I wouldn't let myself (or my dad) down. I kept leafing through the books. And then I came across an old newspaper about Sir Francis Chichester. I loved that newspaper.

I skimmed over the words, knowing it would be too difficult for me to read, but it was also full of photographs, diagrams and charts of round the world routing. I used to spend hours looking at them. I searched for a pen and wrote a note along the top of it. It was the first thing I communicated to him in written English: '*One Day I will go like Sir Francis*'.

Chapter 2: 'What is the meaning of "explorer"?' asked Gerry

My life changed the day I began to understand the words in front of me. Not only was I hungry for knowledge, but I had made a secret promise to myself: I would make my mum and dad proud of me to thank them for making my education possible. But progress was painfully slow. I was struggling to fully understand meaning because I had to focus on lipreading and match this to the words on the page. I felt there was something missing. I was not confident that I understood what I was reading. I was still making lots of mistakes in grammar, syntax and punctuation in my written English. But I refused to give up.

I am sure my parents understood how much I was struggling because one evening my dad explained to me that he would be a very, very happy man if I could get just one CSE. I remember looking at him and thinking: *you think I can't do this! Just watch me!*

I spent every minute possible trying to improve my reading. I loved to read books about the sea, the Navy and adventures, but I struggled to understand the meaning of new words. One day I was walking along a school corridor, reading a book about a mountain adventure. There was one word that I really could not grasp the meaning of.

I spotted Paul Fletcher (now Rev Paul Fletcher, Jesuit priest), in the corridor. I knew Paul was very clever so I approached him, pointed to the word and asked him to explain it to me. Even though sign language was strictly forbidden, Paul replied in sign language: with furrowed brows and the shapes of his hands describing searching. I immediately understood the meaning: explorer! Someone who goes on adventures.

I looked to my book to find the other words that I could not understand so I could ask Paul to sign the meaning to me. But when I looked up, Paul had disappeared: he would be punished if he was caught signing. Paul used sign language to explain the meaning of 'explorer' to me because he knew that there would be no point in expecting me to understand via lipreading. That was what was missing in school: sign language! I could easily understand if someone used sign language to explain the meaning to me. From that day on, I would ask other pupils to sign to me to make sure I understood the words in front of me and slowly, but surely, my vocabulary expanded.

Dad received a letter from the head teacher, Sister Barbara. She told him I was making progress and catching up with the other pupils. I knew within myself that I was making progress because I had begun to take part in conversations in the classroom and my schoolwork was improving. I sat my first CSE in 1973: Technical Drawing. I passed and achieved a Grade One.

I had proved to myself that I could pass an exam, but when I compared myself to the older boys in fifth form, I could see that they had passed so many more exams. Some of them had ten CSEs. I looked at my one CSE and thought to myself: *I wonder if I can do that too? Will I ever have ten CSEs for myself?* It didn't take me very long to answer my question: *yes, I will, because I am interested in learning different subjects and I am hungry for knowledge.*

During the mid-winter holiday in November 1973, my dad surprised me by asking me to go with him to look at a boat. He had received a letter from a marine officer about an admiral lifeboat that was built in 1936 and had been converted to a gaff ketch (36ft length by 9ft beam). The boat was berthed at Bowling near Dumbarton. The note explained that she (the boat) was a wooden boat that had just recently completed a voyage around the British Isles and on to Paris. She had a coal stove and four berths, gas cooker, toilet, engine and six different kinds of sail, log and a large black dinghy.

I remember excitedly waiting for my dad to return home from work so we could discuss the boat. The next morning, the weather looked promising so we drove to Bowling to look at her. Bowling Harbour was busy with old yachts and motorboats. My dad had told me that she was called *Faraway*. We hurried along the pier searching for her. The boats in the harbour were so close to each other that it was difficult to see their names. There was no sign of *Faraway*. Dad thought she must have been sold, or moved somewhere else.

As we walked back to the car, Dad met a couple friends. My dad and his pals stopped to chat. I knew they would be a while because Dad took out a cigarette. So, rather than stand about waiting, I decided to keep searching for *Faraway*. The only information I had was that she was an old gaff ketch, so I knew to look for two masts.

I slowly walked along the pier, scanning the boats. And then I noticed a pretty yacht with old canvas in the cockpit. There was smoke coming out of the chimney on coach roof. She had two masts. I checked the stern. The name of the boat was painted in decorative script: *Faraway*

I shouted towards my dad, pointing to the boat. Dad gave me a 'thumbs up' and rushed over. He took one glance at *Faraway* and agreed that we must take a closer look. Dad boarded *Faraway*, knocking on the coach roof for attention.

A very young man climbed out of the cabin. He was unshaven, with hair that reminded me of a plate of tangled spaghetti. His face and clothes were grubby from cleaning the cabin. My dad asked about the boat and, to his delight, was informed that she was still on the market. Without hesitating, Dad decided he was going to buy *Faraway*. She was ours by the next day.

Faraway was old and in need of lots of care and attention. She was sailed to Inverkip marina and lifted to dry dock so we could start work on her. We spent the whole day working on *Faraway*. During the following spring, once the weather had improved and the temperature had risen, we painted the hull. We painted it brilliant white and applied black anti-fouling below the water line. We painted the bilge to make it look clean and polished the old brass round portholes.

Faraway was a beautiful boat with lots of character. Even on the most miserable wet days, the smell of cabin polish and the cosy glow from the coal fire, warmed my heart.

Meanwhile, progress at school was slow. When I look back at my old school jotters, I see that I was still struggling with grammar. At that time, I did not realise that my struggles were not due to my ability but the methods used to teach deaf children; still I understood that sign language was essential to me if I had any chance of reading and writing. And I knew that I had to keep trying at school if I was ever going to be able to sail around the world.

At night, as I lay in my bed in the dormitory after 'lights out', gazing through the window at the twinkling stars, I wondered whether there were aliens living somewhere out there in the dark night sky. Or I would think about the many times I fell asleep watching stars twinkling over Rothesay Bay as I lay next to our Labrador.

Deep inside me, I knew that, one day, I would sail round the world. It would be a long slow process of building up my skills so I had a plan: first, I would need to learn to read and write. Then, I would have to prove to people that I was a skilled yachtsman. I would do this by sailing round the British Isles to develop my sailing skills, then across the Atlantic Ocean, and eventually round the world.

School was tough. Even though I was heart-broken, and ill with home sickness, I have to thank my mum and dad for making that hard decision to move me to a school in England. And Sister Barbara too; without her patience and persistence, I would never have learned to read and write. Sister Barbara spotted that the key to improving education was to link my studies at school to the two subjects that I enjoyed the most: the sea and the weather.

While I was studying a history project about battle ships, Dad suggested that we go to Malta on our summer holidays. He had planned to take me to visit where HMS Sparrow was berthed to help me with my projects. While we were there, he also told me about his uncle who served on HMS Hood, in The Battle of Jutland. My mum explained that her older brother (Kevin) was killed at sea by a German submarine. He was only eighteen when he died.

I had no idea that members of my family had gone to sea to fight in the Great Wars. I began to understand the great sacrifices made by the people who died for us, and asked myself, *what else happened, if I don't know this?*

My Geography project was about the weather and the River Clyde. Dad and I visited the dredger (MV Blythswood) at the River Clyde, near the City of Glasgow. I studied how the tides are influenced by the moon. In my Art class, I was given an A3 sheet of paper and asked to recall my most vivid memory from when I was young. I painted an old wooden rowing boat at low tide alongside the old pier at Kilchattan Bay on the Isle of Bute.

In another Art project, I completed a fine line drawing (white ink on black paper) of HMS Hood. Dad was so proud when I left Boston Spa. I had achieved more than he had dared to hope for. I had ten CSEs: Mathematics, English, Geography, History, Arts, Woodwork, Typing, Technical Drawing, Biology and Physics. But there was still one big challenge: Mathematics.

I failed my Mathematics 'O' Level. I just could not understand what the questions on the examination paper were asking of me. In class, I would lip read the teacher but could not visualise the concepts for myself.

I left school with my ten CSEs and was eager to find a job that was linked to sailing, hopefully in marine engineering. But, very quickly, my ambitions were shattered. Every interview ended in the same way. I was told that they could not give me a job because I was deaf. Nobody at school had warned me that being deaf would be a barrier to my career. I had been taught that being able to speak would help me to succeed in the world.

So, with my hopes of becoming a marine engineer shattered, I decided that I would try further study. I applied to the local college in Glasgow but, once again, I was rejected. The college refused me a place because I was deaf. I was bitterly disappointed.

However, Dad learned about a Sixth Form College for the deaf in England and suggested that I try to apply for a place. After a long train journey to Walter on Thames, Surrey, I was interviewed by the Head of Norfolk House College for the Deaf and offered a place to study for a City and Guilds of London Institute Mechanical Engineering Technician Part One Certificate, A Level Technical Drawing and to repeat my G.C.E 'O' Level Mathematics and Physics.

On the first day at college, the students sat in a horseshoe shape so they could see each other to lip read. I was introduced to the staff and other students. One of the senior staff gave an A4 sheet of paper to each student and asked us to draw a table on it. I was not sure why he wanted us to draw a table but, thinking that it might be something to do with technical drawing, I got out a pencil and ruler to draw a neat rectangle shape for the table.

About ten minutes later, the tutor came round each student to check our drawings. He picked up my drawing, and he didn't need to say anything because his facial expression told me everything I needed to know. He roared with laughter and said to everyone, 'look at this!'

I asked, 'what is wrong with my drawing? I got the first prize across England in a Visual Arts Competition for my skills in free hand drawing, and you are laughing at me?' It was then that I found out that he had meant for us to draw a table so we could plan our timetables. I had drawn a picture of a dining table because I misunderstood the word.

Deaf students at Norfolk House followed the curriculum taught at Brookland College. We cycled to Brookland College and returned to Norfolk House in the afternoon to meet with our tutor. But the tutor had no sign language skills. He would look though the notes I had copied from the board and repeat them over and over again. I channelled my energy into lipreading him and 'listening' to match the sounds in my ears to the words on his mouth, trying to make sure I understood the coursework. It was tiring and frustrating work and I could feel myself thinking, *I can't be bothered with this. This is like the oralism in school.*

I am not a naturally academic person, but I was hungry for knowledge and willing to study and work hard. I enjoyed learning but I also understood that 'spoon feeding' information to me so I could focus on listening and lipreading would not help me in the long run. But I had no choice: I knew I must improve my education if I was to have any chance of a long-term career.

Despite trying, I failed my Mathematics 'O' Level examination again, and again. Determined that I would achieve my 'O' level in Mathematics, I insisted to the House Master that I be allowed to sit the exam for a fourth time at the Christmas exam diet. He roared with laughter at me.

Deep inside, I was sure I had the ability to pass the test. In class, I could easily solve mathematics problems, but I struggled to understand the questions on the exam paper. The next time I met my friends at the student pub, I asked for their support. They used sign language to explain how to tackle the questions and I sat the examination again. I was over the moon when I received the results confirming that, at last, I had passed my Mathematics 'O' Level. This meant I could progress to A Level Mathematics. I could now see a possible future for myself.

Life at Norfolk House was very busy. I still loved sports and joined Surbiton Deaf Football Club, Surrey. I played midfield. For the first time in my life, I met lots of deaf people communicating in sign language. It was not easy at first, because I was brought up to lip-read and was not skilled at using sign language. Despite this, I was fascinated by sign language and could see that these deaf people had a different culture that I had never come across before.

Eventually, I was elected to be captain for Surbiton Football Club. And then something amazing happened. It was a very hot day and the team was playing in a deaf football competition. I met a former pupil from St Vincent's School for the Deaf and Blind in Glasgow. It was Dan Kerr.

He was now playing for Lewisham Deaf Football Club in London. I had not seen Dan for years, but he knew that I had moved to England, and that I played for Surbition, and had been looking out for me. Dan had some fantastic news for me.

St Vincent's football team was competing in the British Deaf Football six-a-side Championships in Surrey. He took me over to meet the St Vincent's Team. I could not believe my eyes as I stood looking at my mates from St

Vincent's School. John Church was standing right in front of me! I had not seen him since our holiday in Bute! 'Where have you been?' asked John. 'You just disappeared and nobody in St Vincent's knows what happened to you.' I was stunned and delighted. I vowed to myself that I would never lose contact with John again. We are still very good friends.

Despite all the studying and football at Norfolk House, I never lost sight of my dream of sailing round the world. I stayed positive and hopeful. I knew, deep inside me, that one day I would do it. Looking back at my diary for 4th August, 1977, I can see I was upset that nobody seemed to take me seriously. Even Dad advised me to stop talking about sailing around the world for fear that people would think I was a 'bighead' and I would end up embarrassed if it did not happen. But I was very, very, serious about sailing around the world and I knew that one day I would do it. It was just so difficult to explain to my parents how important it was to me.

One weekend, I visited my former school at Boston Spa. The teachers were pleased to see me again and asked about Sixth Form College and my plans for the future. I remember Sister Barbara asking, 'What are you going to do when you finish college at Surrey?'

I explained to her that I was not sure, but my ambition was to sail round the British Isles.

Suddenly, she became very nasty and snapped at me: 'What about church? Grow up!'

I did not reply. I looked back at her and silently said to myself, *you just wait and see… you will be surprised.*

But there was one person who listened to me: Aunt Edith. Aunt Edith was my dad's older sister and my favourite aunt. She lived in Largs and we would talk for hours and hours about sailing. Aunt Edith never doubted that it was possible for me to sail around the world and always took time to listen to me. I felt so much better that I could talk to Aunt Edith.

Around that time, I read a book about Clare Frances, the first woman to sail solo across the Atlantic. I told myself: *I want to be the same as Clare Frances; I want to be the first person to achieve something.*

By summer 1977, I was feeling much better about my prospects. I had made the decision that I would return to Glasgow after I finished my exams. But I knew that, whatever happened with my exam results, I would have to find some way to achieve my sailing ambitions.

I had no fear of sailing solo. I was used to being on my own. I was an only child and a deaf child born into a hearing world. I was alone even when I was with my family because communication was so difficult. It is impossible to lip read more than one person at a time, so when my cousins or my parents and aunts and uncles where chatting at the same time, I did not know what they were talking about. It was so difficult to understand their conversations that I was happier when I was on my own.

Even as a young boy, I had ambitions to buy a wee GP14 dinghy and sail around the Isle of Bute on my own. I had everything planned out: I could take out the mast and sleep in the upturned dinghy at night. In the mornings, I would catch a few fish and cook on my small stove for breakfast. But I also knew that people would try to stop me reaching for my sailing ambitions. They would try to stop me because I was deaf and they believed they knew better than me. When I look at my diary from August 1977, I can see that I also understood that I needed a long-term strategy:

I would be better to ignore what other people are saying to me. I am going determine my own my future and sail around the world alone.

I do very often ignore what other people are saying; I feel that it would be foolish to agree with them because it would mean that they are controlling my life. I cannot spend my life depending on other people to make decisions for me about my own life.

I will find it very hard to get sponsorship. I think I will need to start by buying a small day boat, maybe a fast keel yacht, called 'The Flying Fifteen' to keep up my skills and build up from there. Maybe I could borrow Dad's boat so that I can sail much further afield, like sailing around the British Isles.

If I raise money for charity at the same time, people will know about me, bit by bit, and perhaps get sponsorship from firms to buy a yacht. If this happened – my dreams will come true. I am always thinking about sailing to Cape Town, and then sailing around Cape Horn. Cape Horn is the most dangerous sea in the world. Of course, my father will not want me to do this. That is why I need to leave my parents out of this and find a boat on my own. That means my father will not be able to do anything about it.

I passed my exams and returned to Norfolk House in the hope of getting more qualifications. But I was restless. I was struggling to keep up with the hearing students in the class at Brookland College.

The lecturer would tell us to copy his notes from the blackboard. While we were busily copying notes, he explained theory. Hearing students can listen and take notes. Deaf students cannot. This meant we would miss the lecturer's explanations because we were busy copying notes from the board.

The deaf students fell further and further behind the rest of the class and eventually gave up all hope of catching up. The lecturer just ignored us when we sat at the front of the class having conversations in sign language. When I put my hand up to explain to the lecturer that I could not understand something, he just smiled and kept talking. The same would happen when we returned to Norfolk House. I had been appointed as chair of the student council, so I brought this to the attention of the board. But the board were all hearing. How could they understand?

Inside me, I could feel something changing. I was becoming more confused about myself. I thought about how well I had been taught to speak and listen like hearing people, and about how much I loved my social and sports life with my deaf friends: my life in sign language. I was happy when I was with deaf people, but I was a different person at college.

All I did at college was copy from the board. There was no opportunity to think for myself and ask questions. I was becoming more and more frustrated. Through time, I became angry inside and decided that I had no option but to leave college and return to Glasgow.

Dad was shocked by my decision because he knew how important it was to me. After a long discussion with him, he understood that I would not be able to study if I had to rely on lipreading in tutorials, but he suggested I persevere until Christmas term to see if there was any improvement. I agreed that it was a good plan.

My last few months at Norfolk House were a struggle but something fantastic happened that autumn. In November, 1977, I got a letter from my dad to tell me that we were both enrolled in an RYA sailing course in Poole during my half term holiday. I was delighted.

I checked the location of Poole on a map and identified that it was not far across the English Channel to France. I wondered what it would be like sailing in the English Channel. At the same time, I felt a little anxious; I knew I had enough practical experience of sailing, but I would also have to sit a navigation theory test. I didn't want to fail another exam and disappoint myself (and my parents). My parents calmly reassured me that I was not to worry and that everything would work out fine.

Mum and Dad picked me up from Norfolk House at half-term and we all drove to Poole. We arrived late at night at a small flat that my parents had rented for the week. The next morning, Dad and I sat together, studying navigation, learning Morse code and the rules of sailing.

On the following Monday, we set off for the sailing school for our five-day course. I remember thinking to myself *this is much better than being stuck in the classroom studying*. The weather was not kind to us that week. The seas were rough, with wind strengths up to Force 6. But we coped with the challenges the sea presented to us.

The other members of the crew were hearing and enjoyed chatting to each other while we were at sea. It was impossible for me to follow their conversations. Instead, I concentrated my efforts on steering, pulling up sails and practicing my navigation and survival skills, tidying up the boat by folding sails, and arranging the ropes in order.

At end of the week, the course was finished. I was stunned when the yachtmaster said 'congratulations' and handed me a RYA Coastal Skipper Certificate. I had not been told this was a skipper's course. I was over the moon.

Dad also passed his exams. I asked to see his certificate, but his was different. He had been awarded a Yachtmaster Offshore Certificate. I was puzzled because I didn't understand 'offshore'. I asked, 'What does offshore mean?'

Dad explained that offshore sailing meant sailing far out to sea, away from sight of land, and across large distances. I realised that it was what I dreamed of doing. I patted Dad on the back to congratulate him on achieving his certificate and he clicked his heels with delight. As we walked back to our car, I asked if I would be able to train for the Yachtmaster Offshore Certificate in the future.

By Christmas that year, I could see that I was right in my decision to leave Norfolk House. But, although I was in Glasgow, I was alone again. I asked my dad, 'Where do the St Vincent's Deaf people meet?' He told me that he was in charge of a building in Tobago Street, Glasgow – the new building for St Vincent's Centre for the Deaf. I decided to go along and my love of St Vincent's Deaf community was rekindled. I was back home with the friends I made at school, when I was a young child.

I began to really enjoy my life in Glasgow and hoped that one day I would be given the chance to play for St Vincent's football team. St Vincent's had a very strong squad and that meant it would be difficult to get a place on the team. John Starr was the manager at the time and looked very like the legendary Celtic manager Jock Stein. John Church had played with Celtic Boys club but left because of the difficulties in communication. George MacDonald was a former pupil of Donaldson's School for the Deaf in Edinburgh and played for Ross County, but like John, had struggled due to communication barriers.

There were other great players in that team – like Michael Connelly who was a great winger (and looked like Jimmy Johnston). John Davidson and Tom Coyle were skilled footballers too. But I persevered and trained regularly with the squad three times a week in Glasgow Green.

After a while, I got to know everyone and could see that the squad's players were very skilled in their trades, and could easily organise the team and its social events. I was planning to apply to a local college in Glasgow to study Mathematics, Physics, Technical Drawing and Engineering, so I asked my pals which of the local colleges they recommended that I apply to.

I was very confused by their replies. None of them had taken mathematics exams at school. They didn't use the term mathematics but 'sums'. Not only had they never been taught physics, they had never heard of physics. I thought back to those awful days when I first arrived at school in Yorkshire. I realised that if my father had not made the decision to move me to a school in England I would have been in the same position, with no qualifications.

Then, once again, I felt anger deep within me. I was angry because I understood how this had happened. It was oralism. My friends had spent their schooldays learning to lip-read and 'speak' at the expense of their education. Even today, I meet people who have no idea how badly deaf children struggled under the oralist regime. The penalties for being caught signing in school were severe – corporal punishment or worse. I know of deaf people who had their hands tied at school to stop them signing. Families were instructed not to sign with their deaf children. Instead, they were told to take every opportunity to make them speak and lip-read.

At that moment, I made a decision that altered the course of my life. I decided that I would become a teacher and teach deaf children so they could have the same opportunities that my parents had given me. Deaf pupils must be given the same opportunities as other children.

I researched what I needed to do to train to become a school teacher. I would have to apply to Jordanhill College to study a Diploma in Technical Education. This would mean putting my ambition of sailing round the world on hold for a while, but I knew I had to prioritise becoming teacher. There was just one more challenge I needed to overcome before I could apply for teacher training college: I needed more qualifications. I applied to Langside College Glasgow to study for three Highers: Mathematics, Engineering Science and Technical Drawing.

On July 22nd of that year (1978), I had a great surprise. I was in my bedroom passing time, when my Labrador, Cindy, (Patsy's pup) came in, barking to let me know someone was at the door. I was puzzled because we were not expecting visitors. I walked to the door, wondering who it might me. I could not believe my eyes when I opened the door. It was my mate Andrew Taylor from Norfolk House.

He introduced me to the two other men that were standing next to him. They were Mike Aston and Matthew Jackson. Andrew explained to me that (like us) they were also very keen on sailing. I ushered them into the house and introduced them to my dad, explaining that these three men had travelled from England to visit me and enjoyed sailing.

Our Old Gaff Ketch, *Faraway*, was on the market for sale but I asked if we could borrow it. Dad agreed and the three of us set off to sail in the Firth of Clyde. Our plan was to sail from Inverkip to Rothesay and return to Inverkip at night. That evening, there was a heavy mist but the sea was calm, so we enjoyed a few beers as we sailed under the engine back to Inverkip.

The cabin was very damp from the heavy mist so, as soon as we arrived alongside the pontoon, I lit up the stove to clear away the dampness. We quickly fell into a deep sleep. I was awakened by an intense heat on the left side of my face. All I could see was flames next to my sleeping bag, and I could feel vibrations from Mike, Matthew and Andrew frantically rushing around.

The heat against my face became more and more intense as the flames approached. I reached out with my right hand and grabbed the fire extinguisher from the shelf above me but I was struggling with the cords as the flames spread across the whole cabin.

One of the boys managed to escape through the forward hatch. Another scrambled into the cockpit. They had no choice but to leave me behind: they had not been able to wake me in time. They were rushing about trying to find some way to stop the flames. One of them quickly picked up the pee bucket from outside cockpit and threw the contents at the cabin. But unfortunately, instead of dousing the flames, they soaked one of my mates who had rushed out towards the cockpit.

I thought about my dad. He had trusted us to look after his beautiful old gaff ketch. Now it was ablaze. He would be furious and so disappointed in me. But, to my surprise, he did not seem angry. Instead he simply said, 'You have learned your lesson.'

Luckily, the paint and varnish had protected the wood from damage so we were able to restore her and ensure she could be put back on the market for sale. I am not really sure how that fire started, but we suspected that the fire was caused from a spark from the stove igniting a towel that we had we had hung up to dry.

Langside College was great, but it wasn't easy. There were no sign language interpreters[3] at that time. This meant that I had to rely on lipreading the lecturers. None of the lecturers had ever had a deaf student in their class, but they were fantastic and gave me detailed notes. After the class, the lecturers asked me if I understood the notes and gave me follow up with explanations if I did not understand.

On Friday evenings, I joined the other students in my class at the local pub. Looking back, I can't remember how I managed to communicate with them. Most of the time in class, I had to lip read or exchange written notes. We often shared our notes from class with each other. I even joined Langside College football team. Despite enjoying my time at college, I was still planning my first sailing adventure.

My favourite place to study was in the old building of the Mitchell Library in Glasgow City Centre. I spent hours and hours sitting at the old wooden tables. Sometimes I was studying for my Highers but, on other occasions, I was researching navigation of the English Channel.

I also applied to train as an RYA Dinghy Instructor. I trained for this over two years at Blairvadach Sailing Centre, Rhu, where they provide elementary to advanced level dinghy courses, and we participated in races. I had to sit both theory and practical tests to become a qualified RYA instructor. My instructor was a bit concerned about me because he was trying to figure out how I would be able to communicate using sign language while holding the tiller.

---

[3] Sign Language Interpreting is a relatively new profession

Two of my mates from St Vincent's Deaf Football team (John Creane, Goalkeeper and Brian Sweeney, Right Back) bravely volunteered to come sailing with me. Neither of them had ever sailed before. Strong winds of Force 4/5 had been forecast, so it would not be easy sailing for them.

The boat shot out from the shore in the heavy and fast seas. They were a fantastic crew, following every instruction carefully. The weather was so fierce that, at one point, we nearly capsized, but my crew placed their faith in me and remained calm even, though they were anxious.

At the end of the sail, my crew told me they had loved every minute of it. The examiner came over from the dinghy that he had been using to follow my progress and handed me a certificate and said 'Congratulations.' Then he turned to the crew and said, 'Well done.'

My social life had also become very busy by that time. I used the train journey home from visiting friends in England to make sure I kept up to date with my studies. I was selected for St Vincent's Deaf Club football team too. I felt so proud when I pulled the green and white striped football shirt (just like the Celtic jersey) over my head. We were a strong squad and progressed to win the Scottish Deaf Cup, the British Deaf Cup and got as far as the finals of the Europe tournament Cup. Unfortunately, we lost in the final itself and had to console ourselves that we were runners-up.

Around that time, our assistant manager (Joe Devlin) took me aside and explained to me that I must try to improve my sign language skills. I was confused. I struggled to understand lipreading and now I was being told that I had to learn how to communicate with the deaf community. I felt stuck between two worlds. I now felt that I could not communicate with anyone in either of them.

Joe explained my signs were not really sign language and that I was relying on using 'English'. Joe taught me 'real' sign language: hand shapes, facial expressions and the one-handed finger spelling used by the St Vincent's deaf. I fell in love with it. Communication was so much easier with sign language. I didn't have to struggle to watch the lip patterns on people's mouths to work out what they were saying. Lipreading relies heavily on guesswork. Even the best lip readers do not receive full information. They need to use their knowledge of the English language to fill in the missing information.

My life was transformed. At last I could communicate easily and have complex and meaningful conversations. I never looked back. I had such a wonderful time that year. I was no longer isolated and had become part of the St Vincent's deaf community.

Two days before Christmas of 1978, Andrew, Mike and Matthew visited me at my parents' house. By that time, we had become good friends and were chatting about our plans for summer of 1979 over a few pints. Andrew suggested chartering a yacht for the next summer. We carefully worked out the finances and agreed that, between us, we could afford to charter a yacht for sailing in the summer of 1979. By that time, Dad was a Yachtmaster Instructor and had set up his own sailing school '*Faraway II*' on a Westerly Longbow 31ft.

He felt it would be best if Andrew, Mike and Matthew received full training to ensure they had the necessary skills for the sail. He offered us the opportunity to attend sailing school, with Anne Potter instructing us. We spent six days sailing in the Firth of Clyde: departing from Troon, sailing and to Lamlash, in Arran and onwards to Tarbert, Gareloch via Colintraive, and Blairvadach. We finished with an overnight passage from Campbeltown, around Ailsa Craig and back to Troon. We covered many nautical miles in just six days and celebrated our achievement with a bottle of champagne.

I had agreed to meet Mike, Matthew and Andrew at Lymington for our sail. Buoyed up by our success in the Firth of Clyde, I decided to sail to England rather than take the train. I applied to join the crew on the Ocean Youth Club ketch Taikoo, on a passage from Inverkip, Wemyss Bay, Firth of Clyde and then via the Irish Sea and the Scilly Isles, then onwards to Plymouth.

I met Andrew, Mike, Matthew, Richard Ellis (along with some hearing crew) the next day at Lymington. It was my first experience as a skipper. We sailed for seven days, covering Cherbourg, Alderney, Jersey, Guernsey, Yarmouth and then returning to Lymington.

Afterwards, I reflected on our experiences during the sail. I decided that I had to do this again. I could see that my skills in sailing were improving and that not only did I have a very good crew, but it was very easy for us to communicate with each other using sign language. I set myself another challenge for the following year: I would sail in the Bay of Biscay. The Bay of Biscay is famous for its difficult sailing conditions, so I knew that this would be a real test of my ability.

Everything seemed to be going well that summer. I had applied to teacher training college earlier in the year and received a conditional offer of a place, subject to achieving my Highers, an interview and the compulsory medical checks that all teachers need to pass to register with the General Teaching Council of Scotland (GTCS).

I passed my three Highers and was called to an interview at Jordanhill College. My dad accompanied me to interpret (again because there were no sign language interpreters). I was delighted when the chair of the interview panel told me that I was accepted on the course as long as I passed the medical.

I pushed open the old wooden doors of the medical room and saw the doctor at the other side of the dull room, head down, busy writing a note. I was sure she did not know I was there so walked towards her, but she immediately held up her hand like a police officer halting traffic.

She looked up at me and pointed her finger towards the left. I asked her, 'What do you want me to do?' She impatiently pointed her finger left so I walked towards the corner of the room. As I approached the corner, I turned around and saw her circling her finger to indicate that I should face the corner. I could not understand why she wanted me to do this, but I turned round and faced the wall. Then, before I had time to think, she handed me a brown envelope and asked me to take it back to the panel.

My dad was sitting outside the room waiting for me. He was surprised to see me so quickly. I told him that the doctor had not done the medical but he just said, 'Oh well, that's good. Let's go.'

My dad and I returned to the interview room. The panel were busy chatting and welcomed us back. I handed the brown envelope to the chair of the panel and took my seat. The chair continued chatting as he opened then envelope but, as he read the paper, I watched his face fall and he was silent.

He turned to the panel members on either side of him and whispered. It was impossible to know what he was saying because he shielded his mouth with his hand. Then the chair of the panel spoke to my dad.

I could not follow what they were saying to each other, but I could see that Dad was livid. Dad threw his half-finished cigarette on the floor and sat forward in his seat. The chair of the panel had informed my dad that I was refused entry to teacher training. I failed the medical because of my inability to hear. I was heart-broken. Not once had anybody told me that deaf people were not allowed to teach. The GTCS standards in those days required teachers to be able to hear over a certain distance.

At the same time as I was upset and deeply disappointed, I was furious. I could not stop thinking of all those deaf pupils sitting in classes being taught to lip-read and speak and told to copy from the blackboard. What about their education? How would they develop skills such as problem solving, critical thinking skills or have the opportunity to ask questions and think about the world around them? I could not sit back and do nothing, knowing that many deaf pupils were leaving school, unaware of the realities of the worlds they would be joining, or the skills they needed to be able to succeed.

I told myself that I would fight this decision, no matter how hard and difficult the battle, and promised myself that I would be a teacher one day. But I knew I needed to strengthen my position to allow me to apply to teacher training college again. I decided I would try to find some way to work in education with deaf pupils and began writing regularly to the education department, asking if I could work as an instructor in a school for the deaf.

I don't know how many times I wrote to the Education Department asking to be allowed to work at St Vincent's School for the Deaf in Glasgow. Every time I wrote to the Education Department, they refused my request. And then, one day, while I was sitting in the living room with Dad, Cindy's ears pricked up because the telephone was ringing.

Dad left the room to answer the call. He returned to the living room with a puzzled look of his face: 'What have you been doing? That was 129 Bath Street. The deputy director of education wants to speak to you tomorrow morning.' My heart sank. I hadn't told my dad about all the letters I had written to the Education Department.

I arrived the next morning and waited in the corridor to be called into the meeting. The deputy director sat behind an enormous wooden desk covered in paper work. I nervously took my seat, expecting to be instructed to stop annoying him with my constant requests for work in a deaf school.

Instead, the deputy director handed me an application form and offered me a job: Temporary Instructor at St Vincent's School for the Deaf. I was to start full-time from Monday 18th August 1980.

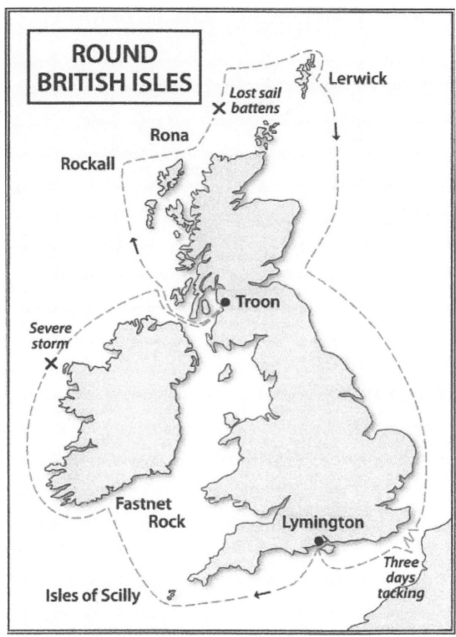

Map of the British Isles with Navigation Route

Chapter 3: Robin Knox Johnston Opens the Door

On Saturday afternoons, after playing football at Glasgow Green (the public football pitches near the Gorbals area of Glasgow), the members of St Vincent's Football Team would either head home or pop into a local pub in Bridgeton for a few pints with pies, before going on to St Vincent's Deaf Club, in Tobago Street, for a social evening. One afternoon, instead of joining the others, I decided to visit the Kelvin Hughes shop on the corner of St Vincent's Street and Holland Street in Glasgow City Centre. Kelvin Hughes is famous for their maritime navigation equipment. I was keen to have a look at their nautical charts.

I bought a nautical chart of the British Isles and a book called the *Reeds Yacht Master Series, Coastal Navigation* (by T.J. Williams). I planned to use these to study more on latitude, longitude, nautical miles, chart projections, dead reckoning and estimated positions. I was particularly interested in reading the chapter 'The Coastal Passage'. I pinned the chart on my bedroom wall when I arrived home to allow me to study the seabed, location of light houses etc.

I was committed in my own thinking to being adventurous, but I knew that Dad was not keen on my idea about sailing around the British Isles, so I began to spend more and more time in the Mitchell Library to study and prepare myself for the challenge. My dad and I were very close, but at that time, I didn't have the words I needed to be able to explain to him just how important this was to me.

My mum felt that I should focus on getting a job and developing a career. I agreed with her, but part of me felt that I was accepting what other people said to make them happy. I knew that I had to achieve this goal for myself, no matter what other people thought of my ideas. At that time, I did not realise that Dad was really worried about the prospect of me sailing around the British Isles, but it was not long before he made his concerns clear to me.

We had been invited to share an evening meal with Trish and Alan (long-time friends of the family). Everyone sat around the table chatting to each other. Alan was sitting near me and asked about my plans for my future. Using my voice, I replied, 'I am planning to sail around the British Isles.'

Dad placed his knife and fork by his plate, looked straight at me and firmly said, 'You are not going.' Everyone stopped talking.

I challenged him. 'What do you mean, I am not going?'

Dad's face was very stern. 'You are not going, no questions. That is the end of the matter.'

All the guests sitting at the dinner table looked down at their plates to avoid making eye contact with either Dad or me. I was fuming. Inside, I asked myself, *Why are people always telling me what I can and cannot do? Why do they believe they should make decisions about my life just because I can't hear?* I knew I had the skills to sail round the British Isles.

Trish had worked very hard to cook our lovely meal, but I had spent the whole evening politely sitting at the table unable to follow their conversations. And, once again, I was being told what to do. I could feel myself thinking: *Is this what the rest of my life will be like? Sitting on my own amongst other people while they chat to each other, having interesting discussions? A life of gazing at peoples' faces, unable to keep up with their conversations?* No! This time I had had enough. I could not do it any longer.

I stood up and, with my voice, politely said, 'Excuse me, I have to go.'

I looked straight into my dad's eyes. I could no longer pretend that I was happy. I picked up my jacket and walked out. As I walked home, I asked myself, *why do people always expect me to make them happy by sitting politely, even when I don't know what they are saying?*

I had been trained to use a hearing aid and to 'listen and speak', but I was totally lost in the hearing world. It was impossible for me to understand what was being said unless someone had a very clear lip pattern and spoke directly to me. But I never felt isolated or alone when I was amongst deaf people. I went straight to bed as soon as I arrived home to get some sleep before my football match with St Vincent's the next morning.

Meanwhile, Dad's sailing school, *Faraway II*, was very successful and was in its second year of business. We made a great team: Dad taught theory and I demonstrated the practical skills.

One evening, after a day of sailing, we berthed in Troon marina. There was a boat show on and a huge marquee had been set up. Dad was teaching theory so I slipped out of the boat, over to the boat show, and ordered a pint of Guinness at the bar. I stood on my own with my pint.

To my surprise, Robin Knox Johnston walked up the bar, stood next to me, and nodded to me. I have admired Robin Knox Johnston for as long as I can remember. Robin Knox Johnston's yacht, Suhaili (a tiny ketch), was berthed in Troon. It crossed my mind that perhaps he could give me some advice about sailing around Great Britain. But I needed some Dutch courage before I could speak to him, so I ordered another pint of Guinness.

Dad had mentioned that Robin was preparing to sail to America so I wrote a wee note and passed it to him: 'I wish you all the best of luck sailing to America. I wish it was me.'

Robin read the note and replied to me by writing, 'What do you mean I wish it was me?'

I scribbled my reply: 'I want to sail round Great Britain but can't get insurance.' We spent the night drinking and passing notes to each other. At the end of the night, Robin asked me to go to his office the following morning.

I woke very early the following morning. It was my responsibility to cook breakfast for the four members of the crew. The crew noticed something different about my manner.

Dad asked, 'What are looking so cheery about?'

I told him, 'I have a meeting with Robin Knox Johnston in his office at 09.00. It will only take a few minutes.'

Dad frowned; he was not happy with me. 'We have to leave soon after breakfast.'

I served the breakfasts as quickly as I could, and rushed to Robin Knox Johnston's office. Robin was seated behind his desk, talking on the telephone. He beckoned me to come in and sit down. He kept talking on the telephone and was writing notes at the same time.

Eventually, he put the phone down. He handed me a note and said, 'Use my name for your insurance. Go sail round Great Britain. Good luck.'

I was stunned. 'Really?'

'Yes,' he replied. 'Let me know how you get on.'

I folded the note, put it into my pocket and rushed back to join my dad and the crew. I must have looked delighted because Dad immediately asked, 'What are you looking so happy about?'

I replied, 'I am a going to sail round Great Britain. Robin Knox Johnston is going to support me with the insurance.'

Dad flipped and he threw his cigarette into the air. I said nothing. I smiled to myself as I pulled on my gear and prepared myself for a day of teaching the crew.

Now that the insurance had been sorted, the next challenge was to find a suitable boat for the sail. I enquired about the possibility of chartering an OOD 34 (Offshore One Design 34) from Robin Knox Johnston in Troon, but it just was too expensive. I tried everything I could to raise the funds but there was no way I could afford it.

Not long after that, I received a letter from Matthew Jackson. Matthew was to be my crew on the sail, but his letter told me that he would not be able to join me sailing round the British Isles: Matthew, like me, is profoundly deaf and a sign language user. He was educated in England and attended college in Birmingham. He had a background in engineering and mechanics. He would not be joining me after all because his parents refused to let him go. My plans had been scuppered.

One day during late November, Dad and I drove to Troon to clear *Faraway II*, before she was lifted into dry dock in preparation for the winter months. Dad and I walked along the pontoon. All of a sudden, Dad asked, 'Do you still want to sail round the British Isles?'

I stopped in my tracks and looked him. I was puzzled. Neither of us had mentioned my plans since the morning of my meeting with Robin Knox Johnston. Why was he suddenly asking about it now? 'Yes,' I replied, 'but I have to find money to cover the costs.'

Dad looked at me. I could see he was thinking carefully. After a slight pause, he said, 'We will have a good talk tonight when we get home.'

The hours seemed to drag that evening as I waited in my bedroom with my dog, Cindy. I paced the floor, trying to figure what Dad was going to say to me. At last, after what seemed like hours and hours, Dad came into my bedroom. He stood, smoking his cigarette, and looked at the chart on my wall. We talked about my plans. He explained that sailing round the British Isles was very difficult and Robin Knox Johnston himself believed that sailing round the British Isles was more difficult than sailing around the world because of the varying sea and weather conditions, and the thousands of fishing boats and naval boats in the seas around Britain. I could see that he was trying to avoid being negative, or saying to me that I could not do it.

I calmly interrupted him. I had planned to explain to Dad that this had been my ambition for years and years and that I was confident in my ability, but before I realised what was happening, years of frustration and upset came tumbling out. 'All my life you have made decisions because you think you know what is best for me. I have faced barriers all my life because I am deaf and, even now, you expect me to let other people decide what is best for me.

'I struggled at school because I was forced to rely on lipreading. I had been promised at school that being able to speak would help me get a good job and then I was refused work because I am deaf. I tried to improve my education by going to sixth form college but, again, I struggled because of being forced to rely on lipreading and 'listening'. I was offered a place in teacher training college, but then refused entry because I am deaf.

'Even with relatives and family friends, I am expected to lip read and please everyone, but I can't. I've tried, but I feel as if I look stupid. But, when I go to the Deaf Club, I feel like I am alive and part of the world. I can discuss my ideas with deaf people and we can argue our points of view. I can't do this at home. I am not allowed to make my own decisions. You and Mum decide what is best for me. I feel like a dog on a lead.

'For years and years, I have had this ambition to sail round the British Isles and now Robin Knox Johnston has given me the green light and is prepared to support me because he sees me as a sailor. He's doesn't think being deaf is a problem. He didn't even ask me about it. But you have given me a hard time over this. What I am supposed to do?'

Dad sat quietly listening to me. I could see that I had hurt him. I loved and admired my father, and it upset me that I had hurt him so deeply, but I could not stop the words coming out of my mouth. I had to find some way to explain to him how I was feeling inside.

Dad paused, took a cigarette out of its packet and calmly lit it. He inhaled deeply and then exhaled a large puff of smoke. 'OK,' he gestured in sign language. 'Let's get started on the paperwork and see what we can do.'

Cindy followed Dad and me down the stairs and into the living room. Dad took out his A4 notebook. It was a dark and damp November evening. The light from the street lamp outside our house filled the room and Cindy lay at my feet in front of the coal fire. We sat there for hours. I watched my dad fill out the page with calculations and costings. My heart sank. I could not afford the cost of the voyage. There was no way I could save enough from my monthly salary to cover the costs. My mind was racing, trying to think of ways to raise funds. Perhaps I could find sponsorship to cover the costs of chartering Robin Knox Johnston's OOD34?

Then, to my surprise, just as he was finishing up his paperwork, Dad asked: 'How would you feel about borrowing *Faraway II* next year in July? It would be much cheaper than chartering the OOD 34. She might not be as fast, but she is solid.'

I was speechless. I didn't know what to say. All I could manage was, 'You mean that?'

Dad and I shook hands to confirm the deal and hugged each other. Cindy jumped up, barking angrily. She was very protective of me so didn't like anyone getting too close. Mum rushed into the living room holding a dish towel in her hand. Cindy was barking so loud that she thought that something terrible must have happened to one of us and was a bit puzzled to see us laughing and chatting together.

Dad and I chatted late into the night about the plans for my circumnavigation. Not long after that evening, I received a letter from Matthew. He had decided (against his parents' wishes) that he would be joining me.

After years of planning and preparation, my dream was coming true. This was the biggest challenge I had faced in my life so far, but I knew I could do it. To this day, I thank Robin Knox Johnston for putting me on his company insurance. He made it possible.

Now that I had Dad's support and Matthew as my crew, it was time to start a serious plan of action. We made checklists of everything we needed – food supplies, clothes, and equipment – but it was going to be very, very expensive. We tried sending letters to ask for sponsorship but had no luck. Thankfully, we did receive offers of help and support in kind.

We planned to depart from Troon harbour on Sunday 5th July, 1981. On the night before our departure, went to a pub at Troon harbour. It was the pub used by local fishermen. The walls were covered in photos of sailing boats, battleships, naval memorabilia, and there was an old wooden oar above the bar.

The barman and owner of the pub (Bill) lived upstairs. Like me, he loved sailing. He had a yacht berthed in Troon and was also a member of the Troon

RNLI crew. I was a regular face in that pub, because I loved the atmosphere. When Bill saw me, he automatically knew what pint to pull for me.

Matthew and I were chatting to each other in sign language. Bill watched our animated discussion but was unable to follow it. He knew of our plans and, with a big smirk on his face, said, 'You are going to sail round the British Isles?'

'Yes!' I replied. 'We are going tomorrow. You want to bet?' I took at £10 note out of my pocket (a lot of money in 1981), showed it to Bill and said, 'I bet you this £10 that I will sail round the British Isles and arrive safely back here in Troon.'

'OK,' laughed Bill. 'Hand it over.'

A few of the fishermen in the pub applauded in approval as Bill took the £10 note from me and pinned it next to the whisky and spirit bottles behind the bar. Matthew and I returned to the boat for a good night's sleep before heading off the next day.

On Sunday 5th July 1981 a few of our family assembled along Troon pier to wish us 'good luck' and wave us off. Matthew and I left Troon under engine on Sunday 5th July 1981 at 09.25. It had been pouring with rain and there was a gale warning in place for strong southwest winds.

Faraway II was sailing beautifully in the high waves under second reef and No.2 jib. Unfortunately, we developed engine trouble as we sailed south of Arran. We had no choice but to return to Troon. Sailing rules state that no sails should be used as you approach a marina, but our engine was not working. This meant our only option was to sail into Troon using the No.2 jib.

Faraway II was heading downwind and was sailing very fast. Matthew stood by – ready to jump. I let go of the jib as soon as we entered the marina. *Faraway II* slowed down, turned very quickly in a half circle and safely berthed at the pontoon.

The repairs to the engine were completed by the Monday, but there were warnings of more gales. We were forced to delay our start. Early on Tuesday morning, I noticed the barometer had risen, so switched on the engine, and we slipped unnoticed from Troon at 08.15.

The strong southwest wind made it uncomfortably wet sailing to the Mull of Kintyre. My aim was to sail towards the Mull of Kintrye Lighthouse and then out towards the Atlantic so I could circumnavigate all of the British Isles (not just the mainland). By 18.45 the Mull Light was on our starboard side, and visibility had improved considerably. We were soon able to alter course, drop the mainsail and run under No.2 jib alone for more comfort.

To the west the sunset was spectacular, but to the south the sky was black and made the white horse waves look even more pale and ferocious. We prepared for our first night at sea and, as per our routine, we placed white flares and a strong torch in the cockpit and donned safety harnesses.

Barra Head was starboard by 17.45 on 8th July, and our next sighting would be St Kilda some seventy miles distant. At midnight, we still had sufficient light in the cockpit to communicate in sign language without difficulty. It was not long before I could see that Matthew and I made a great team. I had been nervous before our voyage as my mind raced, thinking about what might happen at sea. Now all my anxieties had completely disappeared. I was relaxed and comfortable and felt at home. I knew I could cope with whatever challenges the weather would bring us.

Very early in the morning of 9th July, we spotted St Kilda. We had never seen such a sinister, lonely, dark and desolate place. I noticed an error in the compass bearing but I was not sure if, perhaps, this was due to the strong magnetic field near St Kilda. We were both glad when the eerie islands were behind us and we were able to enjoy a delicious meal of pasta. Matthew also used this time to carry out some running repairs to his oilskins.

We had also successfully completed our first night sail at sea. Before we left, we developed a system of alerting each other to danger while one of us was on watch and the other was sleeping. It was a visual alert system. If I was on watch and Matthew was asleep inside, I could flip a switch and a flashing light would wake Matthew. This meant we did not have to rely on shouting or banging on the cabin to create vibrations to wake each other.

At long last, we were making positive progress, but we lost some sail battens en route because of the gales. After a thorough search, we concluded that our spare battens had been left neatly stowed at home. It was then that we decided we must call at Shetland to replace the lost battens (and hopefully buy some spares as well). So much for our hopes of a non-stop circumnavigation!

Much of the time was spent checking and re-checking my tidal calculations as our last sighting had been Rona some three days earlier and on Sunday 12th I was very relieved to catch sight of Shetland ahead. A brief alteration of course gave more sea room to clear Muckle Flugga off northern Shetland.

By 14.30, a long swell was coming from the northeast making it more difficult for Matthew to cook the tomato soup we had planned for lunch. I still have a laugh with Matthew about the tomato soup, telling him that I lost count of the number of times that it splashed everywhere on the boat between Troon and Shetland.

Shetland looked bleak in the dull conditions of wind and rain. After clearing the Out Skerries light, we altered course to bring us close to Bressay and, by 06.00 on Monday 13th July, we were alongside at Lerwick, now six days out of Troon.

There was little life ashore at that time in the morning, but we met the local postman on his bicycle. He gave us a cheery smile. Matthew and I explained that we are both deaf, asking him to notify the coastguard of our safe arrival. The postman cycled off and Matthew and I returned to the boat to cook our breakfast.

Before long, I felt we were losing light inside the boat. The tide was ebbing so *Faraway II* was dropping her level as the waters receded, but that did not explain the lack of light. I looked out of the hatch to see if I could work out what was causing the light to fade. There was a large crowd of people on shore, chatting to each other, and pointing to *Faraway II*. News of the two deaf yachtsmen had travelled quickly across the island and the locals had come to have a look for themselves.

Matthew and I had a wonderful time on Shetland. Everyone was so kind and welcoming. We met the local teacher of the deaf and were invited by a deaf couple to stay at their home on a farm. They gave us feast of homemade bread, scones and jam and showed us around the island by car, explaining the history of Shetland. The deaf man was a sheep farmer and entertained us with stories about the different 'characters' in his flock, telling us, 'That one over there? She is a real pest. That one is wild!'

Like many islanders, he had more than one job. As well as farming, he was also a postman and a grave digger. He told us that one day he had been busy digging a grave. As he dug deeper and deeper into the ground, a heavy and blustery shower of rain descended, so he sheltered in the grave from the wind, waiting for the rain to pass. He fell fast asleep. He woke when the rain stopped. Unknown to him, two women were laying flowers at the next grave; he didn't hear their voices. He popped his head out of the ground to have a look around before continuing his work. The two women screamed with terror. They must have thought someone had come back to life and was about to take a stroll around the graveyard! I still laugh when I think of that story.

Matthew and I were also made very welcome by the members of Lerwick Boat Club and exchanged visits with the crews of Dutch and Irish visiting yachts. *Faraway II* was photographed and reporters from the *Shetland Times* also interviewed us about our cruise.

We departed from Lerwick on Thursday 16th July. Progress was slow because of poor visibility and we covered only fifty-eight miles in twenty-six hours. Dawn was welcome on Tuesday 21st, but the early morning sky indicated the approach of bad weather.

> Gerry's log:
> *The wind, which had been SW3/4 throughout the night, giving us a good close-hauled 5/6 knots, died complete by 11.30 and we succumbed to the temptation of four hours of engine as we had no intention of delaying our stay in this over-crowded, unpleasant area, with trawlers, Merchant ships, RN ships and even low flying aircraft appearing. We were coming to the Flamborough Head when traffic started to build up and tides gaining strength.*

The entire night was spent tacking and, at 09.10, we had rounded the East Goodwin Light ship, by which time I believe the wind to have reached Force 7. Cooking was out of the question. Neither of us could leave cockpit, except to have access to the chart table.

I also had to keep my hands covered with either towels or socks. Both of my hands were covered in burst blisters and it was become increasingly painful to touch anything made of metal, such as dividers, which I had to use frequently.

We entered the Dover Strait, on 22nd July. We had been able to forecast the weather reasonably accurately for a least a few hours ahead but, without access to the Shipping Forecast, we had no information about of the pattern or duration of the weather. The barometer was dropping quickly and reached 1012.5, indicating that that bad weather was on its way. I was reluctant to run for shelter but decided it was our best option.

Sodden clothing was strewn over the cockpit. I stayed on watch throughout the night. I managed to heat up some soup; it seemed like a banquet after the Mars bars that had been our sole food for almost three days. By 06.20,

St Catherine's Pt was starboard, visibility was improving by the minute and I altered course towards the Needles.

We edged *Faraway II* into a berth at Lymington White Haven marina on Friday 24th July. *Faraway II* deserved a good rest. Matthew and I were also ready to catch up on lost sleep. We reported our arrival at the marina office and asked the manager to notify the coastguard of our safe arrival and to telephone my parents.

Matthew and I were swamped with kindness from the staff at the White Haven marina. *Faraway II* was given a prime berth free of charge and the staff saw to our every need by making and receiving telephone calls for us. It was comforting to slide into a sleeping bag that night knowing that we could look forward to a full night of uninterrupted sleep.

The next morning, we were visited by a reporter from the *Lymington Times*. He wanted our account of why we had undertaken this cruise, how we had fared without shipping forecast and other audible navigation aids that are available in small boats. Then he saw my hands. They were a mess of blisters. He closed his notebook, put it in his pocket and told me he was taking me to the local hospital. There the doctors informed me that my hands would only heal if I kept them dry. They tried to discourage me from continuing the voyage but reluctantly provided me with a supply of surgical gloves and ointments. I think they probably understood that it was impossible for me to remain in Lymington indefinitely.

Matthew and I received a message from Mike Aston and Andrew Taylor (via the marine noticeboard) that they would meet us at the King's Head pub at 20.00. We headed over to the pub to treat ourselves to an evening meal, catch up with Mike and Andrew, and share our news. We were also visited by the crew of Eclipse (Admiral's Cup contestant who came second at the Fastnet race in 1979). They were interested in the simplicity of our navigation equipment, which consisted of a barometer, a clock, echo sounder, compasses, dividers, sailing directions and charts. We understood why they were so interested in our basic navigation equipment when we accepted their invitation on board Eclipse. We had never seen anything like it: rows of instrumentation and electronic equipment and a chart table that seemed to take up half the cabin. They were carrying twenty-four sail bags; we had six.

I was anxious to know what the weather had in store for us so Matthew and I visited the local TV shop and I asked if I could borrow a remote control to use the Ceefax service on one of the TVs. I immediately looked up page 107: The Shipping Forecast. The forecast was light winds for the entire south coast.

We cast off from our berth at 19.30 on Monday 27th July, with what little wind there was coming from the west, and we motored briefly to clear the Needles. Through the night leading to 1st August, the Fastnet Rock, Mizzen Head and Bull Rock all gave us good positive position lines and the NE4 wind a series of easy courses.

My plan was to maintain a course that would take us well offshore and gradually ease round to the north-east, towards the coast of Northern Ireland until we caught sight of the Mull of Kintyre, and then sailed home to Troon. It seemed quite straightforward. As I did my usual checks, I caught a glimpse of an enormous tail thrashing about the water about 200 yards from the starboard side of *Faraway II* and a shark's fin disappearing into the sea.

I estimated that we might be some sixty miles or so west of Slyne Head (Slyne Head is one hour north of the Aran Islands off Galway Bay). Bad weather was approaching fast. Matthew and I stowed everything moveable below, returned to deck, doubled the lashing on the mainsail, checked the life raft lashing, looked again at the straining No.2 jib and the ever-mounting seas creaming up from the stern. We were travelling much too fast, and given the conditions, I decided that the only option was to run before the wind and sea.

The question niggling at the back of my mind was: how long would the gales last? I checked the barometer again. I had only ten or so hours of sea room before I was on lee shore. There was only one sensible course of action available to us: batten down the hatches and take shelter until the barometer rose or the cold front passed. We dropped the mainsail and secured it.

By 19.30, the hatches were closed and the washboards locked, meaning that Matthew and I were hermetically sealed below. The movement below was unbelievable. Matthew and I were each seated on a bunk and wedged in as far as possible. But this did not stop us being catapulted from security by churning swells of the furious sea.

There was very little conversation between us because we needed both hands to brace ourselves. We were left with our private thoughts. Vibrations shook through the length of *Faraway II's* hull. I tried to imagine what the gale sounded like as I felt the pressure from the storm in my ears. Every minute on the bulkhead clock dragged past. I decided not to look at it again.

My mind was full of questions: *How long will this storm last? Are there any weak spots on the hull? Will the temporary mainsheet hold out or will we find ourselves trying to cope with a thrashing boom in these awful conditions?* I had to satisfy my curiosity about the storm raging outside.

I slid the hatch partially open to have a look at the sea. It was useless. The torch could not penetrate the thick blackness and I could hardly breathe against the force of the wind. I slammed the hatch back in to place. Even in those few seconds, water had come on board and was swirling over the cabin sole. There was absolutely nothing Matthew or I could do. I glanced at the clock (in spite of my intentions): only fifteen minutes had passed, but it felt like two hours. *What do we do next?*

It was impossible to keep a lookout. My sole concern was whether there was any shipping in the area. I knew I had to stop my mind from racing. I sat on the bunk with both feet braced hard on the top of the table. Matthew sat opposite. Our eyes seldom met. *This is ridiculous*, I told myself, so I suggested that we should place the bunk back rests on the sole and try to sleep.

Soaking oilskins, safety harnesses and lifejackets made a change from the traditional sleeping attire. I glanced at the panic bag to check it was still in place. I examined the washboards hoping that they would stand up to the battering being hurled at them every few seconds. Little squirts of sea water appeared at the joints and found refuge in the comparative peace of *Faraway's* cabin.

Thoughts of gratitude passed through my mind as I tried to sleep; we had a double quantity of flares and smoke floats, both on board and in the panic bag, thanks to Painswessex Ltd. They had generously answered our request for assistance. Thanks also to Electronic Marine Ltd for the local emergency distress radio beacon that we carried and had been kindly loaned to us.

Next thing I knew, I was awakened from a deep sleep. The violent rolling and tossing had stopped. *Faraway II* was completely still. I checked the clock: six hours had passed. For a moment, I wondered if I was still alive. Or, perhaps *Farway II* had hit a rock and it would be matter of time before the tides returned and would sink us.

I slowly and carefully stood up, wiped the thick condensation from the porthole and peered through it. It was a sunrise. I tapped Matthew to wake him up and we climbed through the hatch. It was almost impossible to take in the scene. It was cold but the sea was so calm that it gleamed like a mirror. The cockpit was glimmering after being scoured by the crashing waves that had battered *Faraway II* through the night. It was a new day and we were alive and safe. I checked the sails and riggings. Everything was in place. But we had no idea where we were. I had to work on my instincts, so I set a course: head east knowing that it was our best chance of meeting land. We ate our evening meal at about 21.00: mince, savoury rice, corned beef and fruit pudding. It was a real hash up of whatever came tumbling out of the locker first, but to us, it felt like a Christmas dinner. *Faraway ll* had guarded us well, and now our confidence in her knew no limits.

Shortly after midnight, we saw the lights of a ship. Within two hours, four more ships passed to starboard. We knew that we had to have been getting near 'somewhere'. Wherever we were heading, we would arrive quickly; as the S/W wind was gusting, our speed was about 8/9 knots, the depth reduced to 150 metres and the sea was becoming confused, with heights varying between ten and fifteen feet.

We stayed on the same course all morning until sighting land at 13.50. We reckoned that we had to have been northwest of Ireland. Matthew and I looked at the contours of the distant hills and compared them with the charts in front of us: nothing matched up. We pulled out the charts for the Scottish coast, and gradually, as we approached land, fragments of information came together and we concluded that we must be approaching the Scottish Islands.

By 21.15, we sighted Dubh Artach Lighthouse, confirming that we were in the North Atlantic Ocean northwards of the Isle of Islay. We had been carried roughly 270 miles by the power of the storm.

The wind remained SW, about Force 5/6, until about 06.00 on 5th August and then it politely died away as we started to round the Mull of Kintyre. We were nearly home and could afford to become reckless with fuel. We motored between the Mull and Sanda.

As I stood the helm of *Faraway II*, heading towards Arran, I took time to enjoy the view on all sides. To my left, the golden and green hills behind the Mull of Kintyre lighthouse signalled that I was nearly home in the Firth of Clyde. I had loved every minute of my voyage with Matthew.

We were sailing under the engine so I had time to think and reflect on our voyage: *Why is it that I am always relaxed and confident in my abilities when I am at sea?* I was totally lost in a world that demanded that I listen and speak. And yet here I was, about to complete my circumnavigation of the British Isles with my deaf mate Matthew. We navigated our course using just basic equipment – a chart, compass, divider, barometer and clock – and predicted the weather by observing the clouds, the sea and the changes in the wind.

Before long, the familiar shapes of Pladda and Arran came into view. Matthew and I enjoyed our last meal of the cruise, washing it down with a bottle of wine that we had saved especially for the occasion.

We arrived at Troon marina 17.45 on Wednesday 5th August, but there was no welcome party. Matthew and I were exhausted but exhilarated by the events of the past month. We headed towards the marina office to inform them of our safe arrival and to ask if they could make a few phone calls to our families.

At that time, I was not aware that the marina were about to contact the RNLI and Navy to search for us because *Faraway II* had not been sighted for two days. Dad, however, was confident we were still alive and insisted that they wait a few more days before taking action.

The man on duty was sitting back on his chair, feet on the desk, nodding off to sleep, and was jolted awake by the noise of Matthew and I plodding into the office. He couldn't believe his eyes. He lifted the phone receiver out of its cradle but he was so shocked by the sight of Matthew and me in our oilskins that he dropped the phone. Every time he tried to catch it, he fumbled and the curled cable became more and more entangled in itself. Finally, he managed to get hold of the receiver and dialled a number to let the authorities know that we were safely ashore. Then he called my dad and he told me that my parents were on their way to meet me.

'Tell them to meet us in the pub,' I replied.

The pub was bustling with people that evening. Bill was busy behind the bar but looked up as Matthew and I trampled towards the bar. 'You've done it?' he exclaimed.

'Yes,' I answered, 'and I am here for my £10. Hand it back.' Bill paused, smiled, then shouted, 'Free drinks for everyone! On the house!' Shortly afterwards, my parents and a few other members of our family arrived and joined the party. What a fantastic night!

In total, our voyage around the British Isles lasted twenty-nine days and covered 2,169 miles. We spent twenty-three days at sea, three days at Lerwick and three days in Lymington. I was proud of Matthew and honoured that he had agreed to join me as my crew. We had focussed on our goal, risked the elements, believed in our abilities, and were now the first totally deaf skipper and crew to circumnavigate the British Isles.

I was especially thankful to my dad because he made a decision that changed me as a person. He had taken the time to listen, placed his faith in my ability and trusted me to take care of *Faraway II*. I felt like a new man. I had a new-found confidence within myself. I believed in my own ability and had proven that I didn't need someone to 'hold my hand' because I was deaf. I knew in my heart that I was ready for the next stage of my journey: sailing across the Atlantic Ocean.

Chapter 4: I Began to see Myself for who I was

After Matthew and I completed our circumnavigation of the British Isles, I began to spend more and more time reflecting upon my life. I loved my family. My parents were so good to me; they focussed all their love and attention on me and had given me a wonderful life. My aunts, uncles and cousins were always there. But something was missing.

I never really felt a part of the family. I felt as if I was watching from the sidelines. I could only speak to one person at a time because I had to rely on lipreading. It was impossible to join in conversations. I struggled to articulate words and worried that my cousins would not understand me so I restricted my conversations to very simple subjects. I could see from their faces that it was difficult for them as well. I cannot criticise my family for this. I loved my family and I have many happy memories of my childhood. My family did what they had been advised was best for me.

Life with sign language users was so different. I did not have to concentrate my energy on picking out meaning and making sure others could understand me. My mind was alive, full of questions, and I could feel my understanding of the world around me develop as we challenged each other and explored our ideas and opinions. The Deaf Club became my second family and my home.

The committee gave me a very warm welcome after sailing round the British Isles and invited me to give a talk about my adventures with Matthew and *Faraway II*. I was also invited to give a lecture to the Scottish Deaf workshop.

After meeting my friends at the Deaf Club and giving my lecture, I wondered whether the pupils at school might be interested in my voyage with Matthew and *Faraway II*. I thought back to my own school days. We were taught history, poetry and about famous people, but they were all hearing. I recalled how, at school, I believed that you must to be able to hear and speak to be able to succeed in the world and realised that we had never been taught about famous deaf people, such as deaf scholars, businessmen and craftsmen.

I had a short (ten minute) 8mm cine film that had been filmed during our voyage and thought that, perhaps, I could show this to the pupils. I wanted to give them the opportunity to ask questions and discuss the film in sign language. I hoped that by seeing that deaf people (just like them) have adventures, it might boost their self-confidence and belief in their abilities.

I was really pleased when the head teacher gave me permission to show the film, but I felt a bit uncomfortable. The pupils were keen to watch it but the teachers showed no sign of interest. I set up the projector in the classroom and showed the film. It was only short but the pupils applauded loudly and stood on their feet, waving their hands and demanding to see more and asking lots of questions.

It was so good to see them excitedly signing to each other and asking questions. I hoped that I had given them an opportunity to see for themselves that being deaf should not deter them from achieving their ambitions. But I also had a strange feeling that something was amiss. There was an uneasy atmosphere in the room and I began to wonder if I had done something wrong. I could see from the body language of the other staff that they were not happy. They stood at the back of the class with their arms folded and whispered to each other.

A few months later I was summoned to the head teacher's office. I was informed that the teachers had made a formal complaint to the E.I.S. (Teachers' Union) about me. The complaint was that I was teaching deaf pupils. I was advised that my role was a 'recreational instructor' and, as such, I should not assume the role of a teacher. I couldn't understand what was going on: I hadn't been teaching pupils. But then it dawned on me that the teachers must have been angry with me because I could easily communicate with the pupils using sign language. The teachers did not have fluent sign language so sometimes pupils asked me to clarify what the teacher had said. Sometimes I would demonstrate technical drawing but I was not teaching. Nobody had ever mentioned to me that I was doing anything wrong, but now the head teacher was telling me that it was in my best interests to look for another job.

I was deeply wounded by the teachers but continued to work in the school because I loved the job. One day, a man named Martin Colville from Research Project of British Sign Language, Edinburgh University visited the school to educate hearing staff about sign language. I learned sign language at St Vincent's Deaf Club. The members of St Vincent's Deaf Club were former pupils of St Vincent's School for the Deaf in Tollcross, Glasgow – a Roman Catholic school[4].

---

[4] Like mainstream schools at that time, schools for deaf children in the west of Scotland were segregated by religion.

I could see that Martin, unlike the teachers, was fluent in sign language. My mind was full of questions: *how could this hearing person be so skilled in sign language?* None of the hearing people I knew could sign like this. Martin's sign language flowed so easily – it was beautiful. I had to admit to myself that his finger spelling was much better than mine!

After that day, I noticed the staff who had attended the training signing 'cake' and 'football'. I was puzzled because they were not the same signs that were used by the deaf people I knew in Glasgow. I kept ruminating about this: *why did he use those signs and not the signs that we used at St Vincent's[5]?*

I decided that I would ask my pals about this when I went over to St Vincent's for football training. I spoke to several deaf people who told me that this was sign language used by Protestants![6] I decided to ask Martin about this the next time I saw him at school. It was then that Martin explained that the signs he used were part of a national sign language called British Sign Language (BSL). I didn't know what he was talking about. I had never seen this term: 'British Sign Language'. So next time I was at the Deaf Club[7], I asked around trying to get clarification: 'what is BSL?' Nobody knew anything about it. Looking back, I can see myself in the Deaf Club, pint of lager in one hand and signing with the other: 'I am going to campaign against this! Why should a hearing person be teaching people to sign? Why are the deaf people not teaching sign language? Why has the deaf community not been told about this? Who are these hearing people that are running our lives? And,' I added, 'deaf people are not even allowed to teach deaf pupils because of the regulations of the General Teaching Council of Scotland (GTCS).'

By that time, I was a regular member of St Vincent's, but I did not know of any deaf person in Glasgow who held a professional job. I didn't know if there were deaf professionals elsewhere in Scotland, but then I thought – how would I know? I knew about the national deaf organisation, called the British Deaf Association (BDA). And then it struck me! Of course! I had met deaf people from all over the British Isles while playing football. But

---

[5] At that time, I did not know that sign languages have regional variations in the same way spoken languages have regional accents.

[6] At that time in Glasgow, there were still deep sectarian divides in parts of Glasgow. 'Catholic' and 'protestant' signs evolved in different ways as a result of religious segregation, in both the school system, and social life. The St Vincent's signs have a strong link to Irish Sign Language.

[7] Before the invention of email and instant messaging, Skype and 'FaceTime' deaf people had to attend deaf clubs if they wanted to keep up to date with news.

still I did not know of any deaf people who had professional jobs. I decided that I would speak to Martin when he next visited our school.

When Martin arrived, I challenged him, telling him that the signs he used were not those of our deaf community and that he should have respect for our language. To my surprise, Martin agreed with me and handed me a poster. It was an advert for a job as a research associate for the British Sign Language Research Project (BSL) at Moray House College of Education. Martin suggested that I should think about applying for the post.

It took me a wee while to decide to apply for the job. I knew it was going to be a huge challenge. It had never, ever, crossed my mind that I could work in a university. One Saturday morning, when Dad and I were driving to the sailing school in Troon, I asked my dad, 'What is research?' To be honest, I was not sure I really understood what Martin was talking about. I explained to Dad that there was a research team, at the University of Edinburgh, who were researching sign language. I asked my dad how people could research sign language.

He replied, 'Honestly? I don't know. But I think someone has discovered the language; the way we communicate.' While we were at sea that morning, I looked deep into the waves, trying to work out what my next move should be. I had so many questions: *what is this research project about? What are they doing with the deaf? Are they trying to educate us? Are they trying to find a way for the deaf to be able to improve their sign language skills instead of oralism?* I really could not understand what this research project could be about and, the more I thought about it, the more questions I had.

Then I thought about my friends at the Deaf Club. I knew they were intelligent. They were skilled at running the Deaf Club, and organising events and meetings, but not one single person had any qualifications from school. I realised that these were skills that the deaf community had taught each other. They had not learned these skills at school and I understood how this had happened.

Their school days had been dedicated to learning to lip read and using hearing aids to try to use their residual hearing to 'listen'. Education in schools for the deaf consisted of copying from the blackboard. We would race each other to be first to finish copying the notes. It was as if the schools believed that 'fixing' deafness was more important than education. That is why my parents decided to move me to a school in England.

My mind went back to the research project and I knew right there and then that I would never accept deaf people being used as 'guinea pigs' in any research project. The only way to solve this would be to find out more about this research project and apply for the job. But then I asked myself, *what about my ambition of sailing across the Atlantic Ocean?* I knew that I would probably have to fund myself so I needed to earn wages and save as hard as I could to build up my funds. So, after our day's sailing, I told my dad that I would apply for the job at Moray House and see what happened.

I was shocked when a letter arrived inviting me to an interview at Moray House. I was very nervous as I sat on the train from Glasgow Queen Station to Waverly Station in Edinburgh. I walked along the beautiful streets of Edinburgh, searching for the university buildings and wondering what I would be asked, and still not sure how people could research sign language. I was also worrying about how I would communicate with the interview panel because my dad would not be there to help. Eventually, I found the building and, to my surprise, was greeted by Martin Colville (I did not know he was on the interview panel).

I couldn't believe my eyes – the interview panel were all using sign language! Martin introduced me to a tall woman with white hair and explained that she was the lead researcher in the team. Her name was Mary Brennan and her research specialism was linguistics. I politely said 'hello' but inside my head I was thinking 'Shit! What is linguistics?'

I spent a couple of hours at the University that morning because there were several candidates to be interviewed. Mary Brennan was hearing and not fluent in sign language at that time, because she had only recently started learning the language. During the group discussion with other candidates, Mary asked me about my views on the education of deaf children. I explained that I believed that finger spelling was essential because it was the key to helping deaf children understand written English and, from there, learning to read and write.

The panel fell silent and I could feel the atmosphere change. Martin's head tilted and he raised his finger to his mouth; I knew instinctively that he was wondering if I was a suitable person for the job.

Mary told me that she did not agree with me. I was not happy, so I told Mary, 'I am deaf. You are not. I have experienced years of struggling to read and write under oralism.' I was upset and angry. These hearing people in front of me had no idea what it was like to be a deaf child trying to survive in a hearing world. I was not going to miss the opportunity to challenge them. The interview did not go well. Mary and I started to argue and we failed to reach any agreement.

The next morning, Dad and I were sitting at the table eating breakfast. My Labrador dog, Cindy, was in her usual position: sitting behind me, drooling, waiting for me to pass her a wee bit of sausage and toast. I can still see my dad lifting his knife to cut the top off his boiled eggs as he asked, 'How was the interview?'

I explained what had happened, and Dad's face fell. I could not hear his voice, but I could see he was very angry with me. I looked at Cindy and her ears dropped, low and flat against her head, and her face was so sad, as if she felt sorry for me.

My mum must have heard my dad's voice because she came in from the kitchen, telling us to stop arguing and that I should campaign for what I believed was right for deaf people. You can imagine how shocked I was when a letter arrived from the University informing me that I had been successful in the interview and that I was expected to start work in July. I stood frozen, staring at the letter, and totally bewildered. I could not understand it at all. I did not know anything about how to research BSL, I argued with the lead researcher during the interview and didn't even get the chance to ask what the job would involve.

The panic and sleepless nights set in soon after I accepted the job. I tossed and turned every night, worrying about whether I had made the right decision. Deep inside, I was worried about my literacy skills. I knew I was not good at reading and writing so how would I be able to write the research reports they mentioned in the interview? I was so anxious that I decided that I had made a big mistake and told Dad that I planned to write to the University to explain that I had changed my mind.

Dad and I sat down together and talked things through. My dad explained, 'Gerry, there is no turning back for you now. You know that the school will not support you if you continue to encourage the pupils to ask you for explanations and you use sign language. The Teachers of the Deaf will complain to Bath Street and to the Union. You know you sat all your examinations so you could to enter teacher training, but you failed the medical because you are deaf. Deaf people are not allowed to teach deaf pupils. It will be years and years before deaf people are allowed to teach. Your only option is to take the job and see what happens from there.'

I went to the Deaf Club that night, but I was in a terrible mood and very quiet. I was deeply troubled, worried about my future and how I was going to ensure deaf people had the right to an education. At that time, I did not realise that I was searching for my own identity and belief in myself as a deaf person. And I did not realise that the answers to my questions were already there – deep inside me.

The first day of my job at the University arrived. I polished my shoes and put on my grey pinstriped suit. I had bought myself a new briefcase for my new job but I only had some A4 paper and a pencil inside it. I boarded the train to Edinburgh Waverley station and sat watching the commuters around me reading their broadsheet newspapers. Most of them were reading *The Glasgow Herald.*

I arrived at the room in the University. There was a notice on the door 'BSL Research' and I paused as my hand touched the door handle. I closed my eyes, took a deep breath and told myself, *if this doesn't work and I don't have the ability to do this, then I will leave and go back to sea.*

I opened the door and could not believe my eyes. There was Martin in the middle of the room, with a dirty coffee mug, sunglasses on his head and wearing cut-off jeans. Mary Brennan was there too. She was eating an apple and also had a dirty coffee mug in her hand. I was so embarrassed in my smart business suit, looking as if I was ready to attend a formal meeting. I wanted the ground to open up and swallow me. I could feel my legs trembling as Mary and Martin introduced to the team and showed me to my desk, a wobbly old oak desk that was falling apart.

From that very first day in the BSL Research Project I began to ask more and more questions of myself. The more I studied and learned about sign language, and the more I discussed sign language with Mary and Martin and understood the linguistic features of sign language, the more comfortable and confident I became within myself.

Through time, I realised that sign language (the language that came naturally to me and my deaf friends) was a real language. I understood that that term 'BSL' referred to visual-gestural language used by many deaf people in Britain as their native language. It was the language that allowed me to make sense of the world, to learn and communicate. For years, I was confused and struggled to make sense of the world and now I understood why: I was forced by oralism to learn to 'listen' and 'speak' and denied access to my innate language in its own right. No wonder I had struggled for all those years trying to understand who I was.

My confusion and inner conflict was the product of oralism: trying to shape me and fix me to be able to hear and speak so I could fit into a hearing world. I had been taught that sign language was wrong and had no value. I was taught that I needed to speak and listen if I wanted to succeed in the world. We were told that Deaf Clubs were places for people who failed to learn to speak and listen. I could, at last, see the cause of my confusion: I was torn between two worlds. And, now I had discovered my true identity: I am Deaf[8]. I am part of the deaf community, a community with a rich linguistic and cultural heritage. I was proud to be deaf and to be a sign language user.

When I went to the Deaf Club, I would watch in wonder as the members chatted in sign language. It was as if I was seeing the beautiful St Vincent's variations of BSL for the first time. I was awestruck. My confidence and belief in myself strengthened as my knowledge and understanding of BSL developed.

Mary Brennan changed my life in a way I could never have anticipated. In 1975, she published a paper in the American Annals of the Deaf: *'Can Deaf Children Acquire Language: An Evaluation of Linguistic Principles in Deaf Education.* I still have a copy of that paper. Mary argued that deaf children had the same ability to acquire language as hearing children but the natural language of deaf people is sign language.

Through years of detailed research, she identified that sign language is a 'real' language with complex linguistic structures (in the same way spoken languages have complex linguistic structures). Mary believed and argued that sign language was the key to language acquisition, the education of deaf children and for developing their literacy skills. She bravely fought against the harsh views of oralism and stood up for, and insisted in involving, the deaf community in her work[9]. Mary and I became close

---

[8] I use 'Deaf' to indicate that the Deaf community is a recognised cultural and linguistic minority. I realised this while attending a course organised by Paddy Ladd about Deaf Cultural Issues. Dr Ladd is the author of 'Understanding Deaf Culture: In Search of Deafhood' which is widely regarded as a key text for anyone working with the Deaf community.

[9] The legacy of Dr Mary Brennen's commitment to the deaf community and the role of sign language is alive today. Along with the British Deaf Association (BDA) Dr Brennan liaised with Dr Winnie Ewing (Member of Scottish Parliament) to put a motion about BSL on the agenda of the Scottish Parliament. On 16th February 2000, members of the Scottish Parliament discussed 'the natural first language of deaf people in this country' (Scottish Parliament Report, volume 14, No.11). This debate and the subsequent of work of the Cross Party Group led to the British Sign Language (Scotland) Act 2015.

colleagues and, through time, understood that during that first argument we were both arguing for the same thing but from different perspectives.

To this very day, I thank my dad for having faith in my ability and insisting that I joined the BSL Research Project. Mary Brennan was my mentor and my teacher. She encouraged me to travel to attend research conferences. It was an amazing experience to travel to European conferences and meet people from all over the world (all who understood and researched sign languages). Thanks to Mary Brennan and the BSL Research Project, I was transformed into a completely different person. I was still passionate about sailing but I had also identified something I must do before I could embark on another sailing adventure: I had to ensure that deaf children were allowed their human right to education and being part of society.

Chapter 5: How are you Deaf?

I really enjoyed working with Mary Brennan. I was happy and content within myself in a way that I had never experienced before but I also began to reflect upon my own experiences of school. I asked myself why it had been decided that deaf children should be expected to access education by listening and speaking. I could see that, if I had access to lessons taught in BSL at school, I would not have struggled to learn.

Mary encouraged me to travel to meet deaf and hearing sign language users, attend lectures and conferences. Not only did I learn about the richness and complexity of BSL, but I also learned about Deaf history, Deaf culture and Deaf issues. And I learned about Alexander Graham Bell, the Milan Convention of 1880 and the universal ban on the use of sign language in schools. Deaf teachers and deaf professionals lost their jobs, school curricula designed by deaf professionals were discarded and books written by deaf authors were destroyed. Sign language was strictly forbidden in school and at home. Instead, Deaf children would be trained to listen and speak. And I began to ask myself *why was I never taught about this*?

I looked back at my school days. Our history lessons were about the hearing world: we learned hearing poems and read books about hearing people. We had no deaf role models. We were not taught about famous deaf scholars, deaf businessmen and deaf sports people. Most of the time, 'listening' and 'speaking' was more important to our teachers than our education. And even when we learned to speak, we were denied the opportunity to contribute to society because we lacked education.

Mary Brennan identified that British Sign Language is a rich and complex language and advocated that deaf children are inherently linguistically capable. She believed that access to sign language at an early stage in life was the key to success for deaf children because it allowed deaf children to access to world around them. And thanks to Mary, my world had opened up and I never looked back.

Mary was very keen that I should develop my understanding of linguistics to allow me to do more advanced work in the study of sign language. But if I was honest with myself, I could not see myself remaining at the University for the long term. I loved linguistics, but I also love mathematics and still wanted to become a teacher. My heart told me that becoming a teacher had to be my priority. I now had the knowledge and proof I needed that teaching using BSL would improve their educational opportunities. I wanted to teach deaf children in Glasgow, give them the opportunity to learn and obtain the qualifications they needed to get good jobs.

Like most university projects, our jobs at the Moray House depended on continued funding. The time came when I had to look for a new job so I applied for a role as a communications officer at Glasgow and West of Scotland Society for the Deaf. It was not an easy decision because, in those days, like many places in the west of Scotland, sectarianism was a very powerful force. There was conflict between the catholic and protestant communities in Glasgow. Children attended separate schools and it was not unusual to be refused a job because of your religious background. This was true in the deaf community too.

The interview was very difficult. If I got the job, it meant it would be the first time a Roman Catholic would be appointed to work in West Regent Street Deaf Club, Glasgow. I knew that one of the interview panel had very strong religious convictions (and also very strong views about Roman Catholics). I had also visited West Regent Street Deaf Club before the interview and been told by one of the members that it would be impossible for me to get the job because West Regent Street club was for 'Protestants only'.

On the train back to Edinburgh, I mulled things over and wondered if I had made the right decision in applying for the job. I thought about my treasured green and white jersey for St Vincent's football club and some of the matches we had played against Glasgow Deaf Athletic Football Club. These matches were our equivalent of the famous 'Old Firm' (Celtic versus Rangers) matches in Glasgow.

My worst fears were confirmed the next time I arrived at St Vincent's Deaf Club. The chairman of the club approached me and discretely asked me to leave the club. At the same time, he pleaded with me not to work at West Regent Street. I was bitterly disappointed, but I left without making any protest because I knew there was no point staying and fighting with them. Then things went from bad to worse.

Nobody at West Regent Street would speak to me. I was totally alone and no longer welcome in the Glasgow Deaf community. Looking back, I can see that this happened because we were taught to be prejudiced, and I now know it was just the same in the hearing community. I am so glad that things have changed and you can see deaf people from different cultures and backgrounds mixing together every day.

The isolation continued for at least eight months. I could sense it eating me up as a feeling of darkness grew within me. A deep dark depression developed within me as I searched for people who would like to learn more about sign language. It seemed nobody wanted to learn.

One night, I suggested to my girlfriend Kay (we married in 1985) that we go to the cinema to see a film called *Quest for Fire*[10]. It was a film about three prehistoric 'ape-men' exploring the world, learning how to survive and protecting themselves from their enemies and predators. It was so interesting to watch them progress and learn from each other and identify their tribes. I thought, *this is just like the deaf community! We are struggling to find our identity in the hearing world.* It was as if a light had switched on in my head.

I returned to work with my head held high and announced that I would run a sign language school for both hearing and deaf people. The school would be called 'Quest for a Language'. It would be called this to reflect the years of struggling with lipreading and 'listening' without any thought to our own natural language. I could now clearly see what Dr Mary Brennan had taught me: there were so many deaf people in Glasgow who did not see the richness and beauty of their own language. If they could see this for themselves, then they too could share in the treasure that had been given to me by Mary Brennan; an understanding of myself (and pride in our language). Just like the prehistoric ape-man, we had been searching for our language, culture and community to protect ourselves. Deaf clubs gave us the opportunity to meet up with each other, communicate using our own language and to teach each other new skills.

Quest for Language became very popular around Strathclyde. As a result of this, Glasgow and West of Scotland Society Board of Directors unanimously agreed that I be promoted to the post of Director of Quest for a Language. The promotion brought new challenges. We wanted to set up formal qualifications in sign language that would be nationally recognised. The starting point for this was to negotiate with ScotVec[11] to set up a certificate in sign language.

Meanwhile, I was also studying for my degree in Mathematics via the Open University. The first two years of my University studies were the most difficult. I had study books and transcripts of the TV programmes,

---

[10] http://www.imdb.com/title/tt0082484/
[11] ScotVec later became the Scottish Qualifications Authority (SQA)

but summer schools or study days were a struggle because, once again, I had to rely on lipreading.

One day, I noticed that a student on one of my sign language courses was wearing a red Open University sweatshirt. It was Margo Currie. Margo told me that she was studying for a science degree and was in the year above me. Margo wasn't a qualified interpreter, but she was a great student and very enthusiastic about BSL. So, I asked Margo if she would sign for me. I knew it was a lot to ask, but I was confident in her skills and knew she would do a good job. What a difference Margo made!

With BSL, I had full access to the information. I could go to summer schools, enjoy lectures, and ask questions and also join in discussions with other students. Margo and I worked very closely together, agreeing BSL for mathematics. Although Margo wasn't an interpreter, it was my first experience of accessing education in BSL. I couldn't believe the difference it made – I never looked back. To this day, I don't know whether I would have achieved my degree without access to the course via BSL. Margo went on to become a well-known interpreter and also a highly respected trainer and teacher in BSL via her company SLIC (Sign Language Information Centre). I have met so many people who have been taught by Margo. They always say the same thing: how good a teacher she was, full of enthusiasm and fun, but also firm and fair when it was needed. To this day, I thank Margo for all her hard work with me.

It was very, very, tough combining University studies, family life, working full time, voluntary teaching two nights per week and a full day on a Saturday once per month. But I have such happy memories from that time too. Our daughter Nicola was born in November 1989 and Ashley was born in August 1992. Nicola and Ashley are both hearing and bilingual.

Nicola was such an energetic wee girl. She loved to run about and play with the Vistel phone and piano. But she always made sure she had good eye contact with me. Once, while I was sitting watching TV, I did not hear the pram rocking. Nicola was hungry. She threw her bottle to get my attention. It landed right beside me!

My dad's family is full of very talented musicians. All of my grandparents had died by the time I was born, but Dad told me that my grandmother was a music teacher. Dad inherited her love of music. He decided he would teach Nicola to play the piano. I will never forget my dad telling me about Nicola sitting beside him on the piano stool in her pretty wee dress listening carefully as he explained what to do. The next thing he knew, Nicola was hammering the piano keys like monster. The sound was so loud that the thick stone walls of the living room vibrated. Dad could not believe that his beautiful wee granddaughter could make such an awful noise. I am sure he must have thought that Kay and I had brought back the wrong baby from the hospital.

Our younger daughter Ashley was so different. She had blue eyes, just like my aunt Edith, and was a very quiet baby. She would sleep quietly in her pram, hardly moving (unlike Nicola who would throw her blankets all over the place). Ashley was so quiet and still that, sometimes, I could not settle to watch TV. My eyes would dart back and forth towards Ashley while she lay sleeping. She slept so peacefully that hardly a hair on her head would move. I often jumped out of my chair and put my hand on her chest just to check that she was still breathing. What a sense of relief when I felt her heart gently thumping under my hand.

As time passed, my mind turned back to becoming a school teacher and I began to contemplate my next move in my campaign to become a teacher. First, I would complete my degree in Mathematics. Then I would need to find a way to tackle GTCS regulations than prevented deaf people from teaching. I sat my final university examinations in late 1990. The results were due to arrive in December.

I spent the weeks after my exams secretly praying for good results. I didn't want to let myself (or my family) down. One particularly dark morning in December, I was lying in my bed. To be honest, I had a hangover after our staff Christmas party the night before. Nicola was just about the height of the bed and I lay smiling to myself as I watched her having fun scampering around the room.

Kay appeared at the bedroom door with a large brown envelope. I knew what it was. It was from the Open University. I held my breath, knowing there were only two possibilities: I had passed my exams and achieved my degree, or I faced resit examinations. I didn't know if I would be able face Christmas if it was bad news.

I said to Kay, 'best if you open the letter.' Meanwhile, Nicola was still happily skipping about the bed, oblivious to what was going on. I watched Kay carefully open the letter, not sure if I really wanted to know what it said. I kept thinking, what *am I going to do if I have failed my exams? I don't know if I can do this again.* Kay seemed to take forever as she read the letter, studying every word from top to bottom of the page. Suddenly, the letter was flying through the air, passing Nicola's head. Kay leapt onto the bed, hugged me, and told me 'you have passed!'

Six years of studying had paid off. Eleven years after I was refused entry to teacher training, I now had the qualification I need to allow me to challenge the GTCS and reapply to be admitted to teacher training.

Nicola stood watching us talking in fast and excited sign language.

My first thought was, *I need to tell my dad.* In those days, we used a Vistel phone to communicate and had to type messages to each other. My dad was very ill at that time and was under doctor's orders to stay in bed. Mum answered the phone, and shouted the news up to my dad in his bed. Dad leapt out of bed and drove over to our house with a big bottle of champagne to celebrate. My mum was furious with him for breaking the doctor's orders. But I understood how my dad felt – he remembered all those years ago when he was so worried about my education and asked me if I could try to get just one CSE. It made me so happy to see my dad so proud that morning. I was delighted that, at last, my mum and dad could see that they had made the right decision all those years ago.

In January 1991, I decided that it was time to return to St Vincent's and ask to meet the head teacher. I wanted to take the next step towards becoming a qualified teacher. I don't think I was expecting the meeting to go well because I was surprised when I was offered a position as a graduate instructor. This meant it would be possible for me to teach mathematics along with the professional teacher. I was thrilled.

I thought back to Milan, 1880 and the worldwide ban on sign language in schools. I was delighted that at last deaf pupils would get the chance to learn in their own language without having to strain their eyes to follow the teacher's lip pattern and to work out what the teacher was saying or worrying about how their voices sounded.

By this time, Dad was very seriously ill. He had suffered three heart attacks, and now had been diagnosed with a brain tumour. It was a terrible time for the family. Dad had been complaining to his GP about headaches for about ten years without getting anywhere. Eventually, he decided that he had had enough and paid to have tests done privately. That was when he was diagnosed with a brain tumour.

He had surgery. I can still see him lying in his bed in intensive care with tubes all over him. He woke up to the sound of my mum's voice and saw that he clenched her hand so he knew she was there. I am sure Dad knew that I was there with him in intensive care, holding his hand, sitting quietly, in tears, hoping that he would pull through and survive.

Glasgow does not have severe winters but in January 1993 terrible blizzards covered the city in a thick blanket of snow. My dad was due to retire on 23rd January. On 10th January, I called him in the evening via the Vistel phone and joked with him that he would need to get his false teeth and bus pass ready for retirement. We laughed and joked as he said that instead of going to work in his business every day by car he would take his 'pieces'[12] and a *Daily Record* on bus trips using his bus pass.

The next day, January 11th at about eleven in the morning, the snow started to fall. The pupils became more and more excited as the blizzard continued and a thick blanket on snow covered the ground. Then, out of nowhere, I felt very strange. I didn't know what it was, but I knew I had to contact Kay.

I asked the teacher if I could leave the room for a few minutes. I rushed downstairs and picked up the Vistel phone to call Kay. There was no answer, I just knew something was terribly wrong. I decided to try calling my mum. But again, there was no answer. I returned to the class.

The blizzards continued throughout the day. After lunch, while I was teaching, I looked through the window into the thick flakes of snow swirling around in the blizzard outside the classroom. I knew that something was wrong with my dad.

The head teacher came in and said, 'Gerry, your mum has just called.'

Immediately, I replied, 'Is it my dad?'

The head teacher paused and smiled and said, 'No, she wants you to go over to her house after school.'

Finally, the school bell rang and I hurried out to get to my car to drive from Tollcross to my parents' house on Blairbeth Road. There were no tyre marks anywhere and the snow was so deep that it was impossible to make a distinction between the pavement and the road. I thought to myself, *Ah, that's what it must be. My parents don't want to risk driving over to my house to drop off Nicola. That is why they have asked me to come to their house. I bet Dad and Nicola are playing in the snow and have built a snowman.*

It took a long time to navigate Blairbeth Road but I eventually I arrived at my parents' house. I pressed the doorbell. The door opened. Nicola usually

---

[12] A 'piece' is local Glasgow dialect for 'sandwich'

rushed past my mum to welcome me, but she was not there. Mum was in tears. Without asking, my worst fear had been confirmed. Mum gently beckoned me into the house and I felt my heart break as she explained to me that my dad had died just along the road. One of our neighbours had been walking along the road and found my dad lying covered in the snow.

My father's funeral was arranged: requiem mass at nearby Christ the King Church, Kings Park, Glasgow and then on to the Linn Crematorium. The church and crematorium were packed with both deaf and hearing people who had travelled from across Britain to pay their respects to my dad. Unlike most funerals, it was not close family members who carried Dad's coffin in his final journey, it was members of both the Catholic and Protestant Deaf communities. Any differences based on religious beliefs had been set aside.

I stood watching my dad's coffin. It felt unreal. Only a few days before we had been joking and chatting on the Vistel and my dad was telling me how wonderful it was to have this technology so that we could communicate without having to drive to each other's house. And here I was, just a few days later, looking at his coffin.

Then the priest said the prayer that is said just before the coffin is committed and taken down. I don't know what happened, but the only way I can describe it is that I felt that my brain went into meltdown. Thoughts flooded through my mind like the rapids in a river splashing and plunging over rocks. Someone behind me grabbed my shoulders and held me still. They had realised I was about to stand up and grab my father's coffin. I lost all control of my emotions as the tears streamed down my face. Everyone looked at me in shock. They had never seen me like this before. Usually, I am very stoic and do not show my emotions. But somewhere amongst the turmoil inside me, I received a message. A very clear voice said, *go to see your lawyer.*

For days and weeks after the funeral, I wondered about that voice, but I didn't tell anyone about it. Every day I asked myself, *why do I need to go to see a lawyer? I don't understand why I need to see a lawyer.* I was at school, working with deaf pupils and, to everyone else, Gerry was back to normal. But I was still fighting inside… fighting to be accepted into a teacher-training course.

One day at school, one of the staff asked how I was getting on with my campaign to be accepted into teacher training college. Just as I began to update them on my progress, another member of staff burst out laughing,

'Oh Gerry! You will be an old man with a walking stick before you can get the GTCS to change their rules to allow you to be a teacher.'

I froze as I watched the staff laugh at me. I was not prepared to be mocked like this. I understood the value of sign language for deaf pupils in the classroom because I had personal experience of oralism. And then, to make matters worse, not long after that, someone from the deaf community said the same. They told me I was wasting my time fighting the GTCS because I would never win.

But then I would look at our bilingual daughters, whom I loved so much: two wee girls happily using both sign language and spoken English. They would play away with their hearing friends and family, and use sign language with their mum and dad and deaf friends of the family.

I remember one afternoon in particular. I was sitting working at the kitchen table. Nicola was playing with her friends in the back garden and running in and out of the kitchen. Suddenly, she burst in and asked in sign language, 'Their mum and dad no sign language, why? They not deaf. How you deaf?'[13] That same night, I watched my Nicola and Ashley chatting away to each other, busying themselves listening to music, watching their favourite TV programme (*The Singing Kettle*) and reading their books. Suddenly, I knew why I had to see a lawyer. Deaf children need to have the same variety and opportunities as hearing children if they are ever going to be able to be able to reach their full potential. Deaf children spend school lives isolated in their classrooms, trying to figure out what they can hear and lip read what they can pick up from the teacher. I realised that this was not just about education. This was about basic human rights. Deaf children must be given access to the same opportunities as hearing children.

I had one very close ally at St Vincent's School: Bridget Hill. Bridget had retired after being a primary school teacher for thirty years. She came to St Vincent's to do voluntary work and had no experience in deaf education. I was asked to work with Bridget to support her to teach English to deaf pupils. I was very sceptical. But Bridget was an excellent teacher and, despite having no sign language, quickly established a rapport with the pupils.

She developed a great way to engage with the pupils and encourage them to be enthusiastic about learning English: encouraging the deaf pupils to

---

[13] I have kept the original written BSL structure here because it shows that Nicola was fluent in BSL.

tell stories. The pupils signed their stories in BSL. I translated these to English and Bridget wrote the English onto the board. I can still see the faces of the pupils light up we explained that those words on the board were 'their stories'. The stories they had signed in BSL. They were amazed! They loved it and they loved Bridget.

Bridget and I made a good team and I learned a lot from working with her. One day she told me that she thought I should be a teacher. I explained that I had applied to teacher training college and been rejected because of the GTCS regulation that deaf people are not allowed to teach. Bridget could not understand how being deaf should prevent someone from becoming a teacher – especially of deaf pupils. From that day on, she was an incredible support to me.

I made an appointment to see my lawyer. I took along my folder full of legal letters, minutes of meetings, and handed it over to him saying, 'You are my last chance. If I don't make a breakthrough now, I will call it a day.' I gave him my fax number in case he might want to contact me (on those days we didn't have email or mobile phones for SMS messages).

A few days later, the fax machine started running and there was a message from my lawyer asking me to go to his office. I was not really sure what to expect but I was not optimistic. I went into his office and saw him sitting there with all my thick files of paperwork. He looked up at me and said, 'This is barbaric! This is like Hitler to the deaf community. We must do something to stop the GTCS to stop ignoring you. I will challenge the GTCS at the European Court of Human Rights.'

So, with grateful thanks to my lawyer, Peter B. Watson, in September 1994, I joined the PGCE course at St Andrews College, Glasgow, to train as a secondary school teacher in mathematics. It was almost eighteen years since I had first applied to teacher training college and one year since my dad had died. At the end of the course, like everyone else, I was anxious for my grades.

On the day of the results, all the students waited patiently at the noticeboard. Eventually, one of the lecturers appeared and pinned the results up on the wall. I looked at the papers and my heart sank. I couldn't see my name. Then someone patted my shoulder and pointed to the list on the other side of the wall. And there it was: my name.

At last, I was a qualified teacher and could now start my two years probationary service to allow full registration with the GTCS. It was a bright sunny afternoon. As I walked through the campus, I gazed up towards the bright white cumulus clouds that dotted the azure sky. I knew my dad was watching me. I smiled back at him with tears in my eyes.

Just after that, there was an enormous surprise party for me at my local pub, the Beechwood. Kay and her friends had organised it and invited one of the lecturers from the course – Valerie Friel, our lecturer on Professional Studies. Valerie told me that she had never seen so many deaf people in one place. Everyone was laughing and dancing. But they were not just celebrating my results. They were celebrating something much more significant: it was the first time since the Milan Convention in 1880 that a native BSL user was accepted into the teaching profession in Scotland.

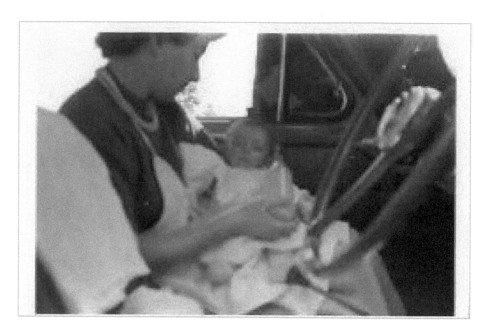

Me and Mum. I was a really tiny baby and very ill for the first few years of my life.

HMS Sparrow (1947). My Dad's battleship

Me and Dad on Ballymoney beach, Ireland, 1960.

Sailing with Dad. I must be about four years old, but already trying to take control of the tiller

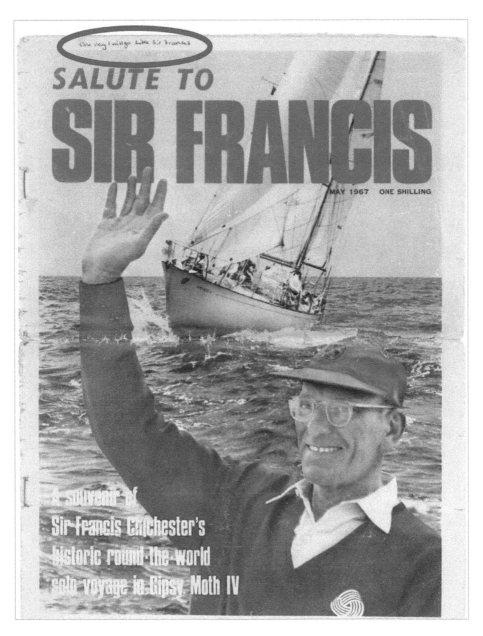

My first scribbled note to my dad '*One day I will go like Sir Francis*'. He kept this for the rest of his life.

Faraway (left to right: Andrew Taylor, me, Mike Aston)

My crew in 1980 (left to right): Mike Aston, Richard Ellis, Andrew Taylor, Matthew Jackson and me at the Clyde Cruising Club in 1980 receiving the Ferrier Seamanship Awards. We sailed through a terrible storm in the Bay of Biscay in July 1980.

Matthew and I sailing towards St Kilda during our circumnavigation of the British Isles

Visiting the Croft House Museum in Shetland.

Faraway II berthed in Lymington

Our Wedding Day, 7th September 1985

Kay and I at a family party with Mum and Dad.

Graduation Day. The Open University Graduations were held at the University of Edinburgh. My dad told Kay 'I am so proud of Gerry. This is the best day of my life.'

Graduating from St Andrews's Teacher Training College. Professor Bart McGettrick (Principal) is handing me my parchment.

Kay and I with Ashley (left) and Nicola (right) at the surprise party to celebrate my qualifying as a teacher.

So, after years and years of campaigning, I was now a probationary teacher. But late in the summer of 1996, I received terrible news. Sandy Cunningham (the adviser for Special Educational Needs) informed me that there was consultation in progress about the possible closure of St Vincent's School for the Deaf. I set up a group to campaign against the closure. We organised meetings in the Deaf Club and invited the deaf community and representatives of the Education Department. I made myself very unpopular with the people who wanted to close our school.

One day, while I busy teaching, I was given a message to attend an urgent meeting with the director of education in John Street, Glasgow. I was sure I was going to be sacked. I asked my colleagues in the Deaf Education Group to come with me for moral support and to witness the meeting. I was white-faced and sick with nerves as I waited to be called into the meeting.

A councillor sat at a long dark table. Before I got the chance to speak (there was no interpreter), Ken Corsa, the Director of Education, entered the room and sat across from me. I was certain I was about to be dismissed so was shocked when he said, 'Thank you, Gerry. We have learned a lot from the Glasgow Deaf community,' and shook my hand. The Education Department and the City Councillors had listened to the deaf community and decided against closing St Vincent's.

I learned so much whilst working at St Vincent's. I had the opportunity to develop new materials and adjust them to meet the differing needs of the pupils. Every pupil is different, so I tailored individual plans to support them in achieving their personal goals. I was learning so much from this work that I felt it was important to expand my knowledge more formally. I applied for, and gained, a Postgraduate Certificate in Special Educational Needs in 1998 and then a Post Graduate Diploma in Deaf Education in 2000 (both from the University of Edinburgh). But even though I really enjoyed my work and the two courses, I was ready for a new challenge. There was a rumour going around that Donaldson's School for the Deaf in Edinburgh was planning to create a new post in Deaf Studies. It would be the first post of its kind in Scotland. In 2000, I decided to apply for the job: Senior Teacher of Deaf Studies. I was successful and appointed to the post.

At that time, Donaldson's College was located within the looming Victorian Gothic-style building, close to Haymarket Station in Edinburgh. It had many old unused rooms that lacked even the most basic decoration. However, this worked to my advantage because I was allocated four rooms to allow me to set the new department – the Department of Deaf Studies. I used one room for sign language classes for staff and parents and set aside another room for administration and a new book and video library. The pupils were divided between two classrooms.

The head teacher at the time (Janet Allen) had a strong belief that it was important to give deaf pupils the opportunity for education in Deaf Studies. This would allow them to research and ask questions about the deaf world, improve their confidence in themselves, and be given the chance to stand up and tell others about their views. It was my job to take the lead on this. Nothing like this had ever been done before so it meant setting up a completely new curriculum.

The strategy for this new 5-14 National Curriculum also involved working in collaboration with the Deaf Studies Working Party at Moray House College of Education (University of Edinburgh), to develop new sign language classes for staff and relevant professionals. We organised a conference to present our ideas and receive feedback. The conference was well received and everyone was keen to see the ideas we presented on that day progress into action.

An important part of the curriculum was to bring deaf and hearing parents together and foster a positive sense of individual and group identity among deaf pupils. This would be reinforced by teaching about the various historical and social influences on the lives of deaf people and include acknowledgement of different forms of linguistic expression. We also felt that it would help young deaf people in developing their own perspectives on the political and policy issues that directly affected their lives and their lives after school.

As a result of the close collaboration with Moray House, Mary Brennan suggested that we work together to organise a one-day seminar in which older deaf people could tell the pupils about their experiences of education, and employment and living through the Second World War.

The Deaf Studies curriculum was still in draft form, but I believed it would be beneficial for pupils if we invited members of the local deaf community to meet the pupils. This would give the pupils an opportunity to learn from the lives of local deaf people rather than focus solely on famous deaf people. It would also help the pupils to understand the role of sign language in deaf history and deaf culture. So, in November 2000 we held the seminar 'Orating Deaf Lives'.

The pupils were both fascinated and horrified by what they learned from the older deaf adults. They were very keen to ask the presenters about the obstacles they had faced during their lives. The pupils not only enjoyed themselves, they relished learning from the local deaf community. I also invited Doug Alker from the Federation of Deaf People. The children loved it – especially when he ordered the teachers out of the room, telling them 'I didn't come here to speak to teachers, I came here to speak to you!' As the pupils met and learned from Deaf role models, I could see their confidence grow and they became motivated to learn for themselves.

It was the first time the Scottish Education system had witnessed a Deaf Studies curriculum delivered from nursery to secondary levels. The curriculum covered four main areas:
- Deaf People in Society
- Deaf People in the Past
- Deaf Arts and Media
- Deaf People's language and communication

The Deaf Studies Department created a communication policy that sign language must be used at all times in school. The reason for this policy was simple: to ensure that deaf children were not excluded from the everyday life of the school. Prior to this, most staff used spoken English when they were not in the class (this was the same for most schools). This meant pupils were completely excluded from conversations. I wanted deaf children to have the same experiences as hearing children; to feel included and part of the school and benefit from incidental learning that comes with everyday conversations. My own experiences had taught me that it was essential that staff sign at all times in the presence of deaf pupils. This would help develop the language skills of both the pupils and the staff.

In November 2001, I was promoted to Assistant Head of Donaldson's College for the Deaf. This role was combined with my position as Head of the Deaf Studies Department and allowed me to further develop my vision for Deaf Studies and an expansion in staff.

While working at Donaldson's, I realised that while the deaf pupils there were happy and content, they had no contact with deaf children in mainstream schools in Scotland. I was also aware that some deaf children in mainstream schools have no contact with the deaf community. They lived their lives entirely in the hearing world.

Communication can be a real struggle for deaf children in mainstream schools. I thought there must be a way to give the pupils in Donaldson's, and deaf pupils in mainstream schools, the opportunity to meet up with each other. We set up a sports day and invited deaf pupils from mainstream school across the central belt of Scotland. Over 180 pupils attended from across the Central Belt of Scotland. The event was very successful, even though the deaf pupils were a mixture of those who communicated via lipreading and sign language. The highlight of the day for the pupils was when Craig Levein (Manager of Hearts Football Club and Scotland at that time) presented the trophies.

Life was very busy at Donaldson's but in 2003 I became very unwell. Eventually, one day, I had no choice but to go the Accident and Emergency Department of my local hospital – I was having severe pains in my chest.

Chapter 6: Holy Island, Arran

I arrived at Accident and Emergency and was immediately sent for tests. The medical team attached me to an ECG machine to monitor my heart. Nurses and doctors popped in and out of the room to read the ECG results. After about five to six hours of monitoring, I was told that my heart was fine and that the pain was in my chest wall. I was sent home with a note to give to my GP.

After my visit to Accident and Emergency, I was sent for heart and lung function tests. The results showed that there were no problems. But my health continued to deteriorate. And then, my life seemed to stop. My mind and body were completely numb. I felt nothing and I could not think. Even the food in my mouth had no taste. I had been diagnosed with ME and SAD some years before, but this was something completely different.

I made another appointment with my GP and we had a long discussion. He asked me question and after question: 'was I having difficulty at work?', 'were there problems at home?' No, I wasn't experiencing any problems. My GP ordered complete rest and forbade me to go to work. Looking back, I now know that I was experiencing severe depression and that I have experienced depression through most of my life. My mum had mentioned that there were a few people on my father's side of the family who had been diagnosed with depression, but it was many years later (when I was reading one of Uncle's Gerry's books) that I found out that several members of the family had experienced very severe depression. In fact, two of my aunts had committed suicide.

It was approaching the school holidays, so Kay and I decided to take the girls to spend the holidays in Arran to our wee one-bedroom caravan at Lamlash. The caravan had a lovely view of Holy Island. As the school holidays drew to an end, Kay and the girls took the ferry to the mainland, although I stayed on Arran. I needed time and space to myself. That evening, I sat on the couch looking out across the Firth of Clyde thinking about how I would use my time. For some reason (I don't know why) I decided that the next day, if the weather was good, I would catch the wee ferry to Holy Island.

Holy Island is a tiny island in the Firth of Clyde and located off the eastern coast of Arran. It has an ancient spiritual heritage. There is a hill on it called Marilyn of Mullach Mor and you can reach the summit via a steep footpath. The spiritual significance of the island continues today. It is owned by the Samye Ling Buddhist Community. They bought the island and established the Centre for World Peace and Health on the north of island[14]. From the very moment I thought of visiting Holy Island, something deep in my gut told me that I must climb to the top of the hill at sunrise and spend the day there until sunset. I could not understand why I felt I was being told I must do this but, at the same time, I felt happier knowing that I had something to look forward to. I went to bed but decided to leave the curtains open so I could be ready to catch the sunrise in the morning.

I awoke at sunrise the next morning and looked eastwards out of the caravan window towards Holy Island. It was low tide and the sea was calm, with dark patches of seaweed gently floating in the soft morning light. Beyond Holy Island, a gentle mist hung over the Firth of Clyde. I filled my flask, made some sandwiches, stuck a couple of Mars bars in my pocket and made my way to Lamlash pier.

As I stood waiting for the boat to Holy Island (a tiny boat with only six seats), the smell of the sea reminded me of my boyhood days and our family holidays in Bute. When the ferry arrived at Holy Island, I followed the footpath to the summit of Mullach Mor. I inhaled deeply, filling my lungs with the air of the Firth of Clyde. I sat at the summit, enjoying the fresh wind rising from the southwest. I sat there all day watching the Firth of Clyde – the motion of the sea, the sailing boats and ferries, and the seagulls gliding through the air on the thermal currents. I gazed along the distant shoreline of mainland Scotland, picking out and identifying each of the towns and islands. I could identify them all – the southern tip of Bute, the Cumbraes, the towns of Ardrossan and Troon. I looked at the cairn next to me and wondered how many people had climbed this wee mountain and placed a stone on this cairn to let others know someone had been there before them. There must have been thousands of visitors over the years.

As I looked out to sea, my eyes filled with tears and I wept. My mind was in turmoil: *what has happened to you Gerry? Where have you gone? What happened to all those dreams and ambitions you had to sail across the Atlantic and round the world?* I knew there was only one person who could help me answer those questions: my dad. I desperately needed to speak to my dad.

I remember looking across the sea and skies with tears streaming down my face and asking, 'Where are you, Dad?' And then, before I had time to

---

[14] http://www.holyisland.org

think, I was experiencing flashbacks. I was transported back in time to my first vivid memory. I was just a small boy and Dad had taken me to Skelmorlie Golf Club, near Wemyss Bay, which was just across the Clyde and slightly north from where I was sitting. My late grandfather (Dad's father) was a member. I stood quietly with my mum and my aunt Edith as Dad approached the first tee. Dad prepared for his first swing, determined to make the ball fly from the tee far into the distance. But the ball didn't fly off into the distance. It plopped onto the ground just in front of the tee. I thought it was hilarious. I laughed so hard that I fell to the ground pointing at my dad's 'hopeless' golf swing. Dad was furious! Without saying a word, he lifted me up, put me in the car, and drove home.

Then another story popped into my mind. It was a story about my uncle Gerry (my dad's older brother). My grandfather was playing to win in a golf competition. A big crowd had gathered to watch him play. I think my uncle Gerry must have been about seven years old at the time. He was waiting for his dad to arrive at the 18th green. As my grandfather's ball shot over the green, Uncle Gerry ran out through the crowd, picked up the ball and ran off. I laughed out loud at the thought of my uncle, who later became a well-known Jesuit priest, getting into trouble for being so naughty.

As I looked down at the sea, watching the ferries transporting people and goods between the mainland and the islands, and the sails of the yachts, I thought back to my adventures in our beautiful old wooden boat 'Faraway' with the three crazy men: Mike Aston, Matthew Jackson and Andrew Taylor. I could smell the rich varnish on the side of the coach roof, and could feel the warmth from the wee stove that was so useful for preventing dampness. And then I was seeing the fire! I laughed out loud thinking about one of my mates being drenched with the contents of the pee bucket. More and more wonderful memories came back to me. My eyes filled with tears again. But this time they were not tears of despair, they were tears of laughter.

The sea had calmed me by reminding me of the many wonderful times I had with family and friends. A spark of hope ignited somewhere deep inside me. I realised that, somewhere amongst those years of struggling and campaigning, I had lost myself.

The following morning, I felt like a different person. I was Gerry again. As I looked at the mirror while shaving, I asked myself how I would feel if when I was aged sixty looking into the mirror and had not at least tried to achieve my sailing ambitions. I knew it would bitterly regret it. I had hope once again and set myself a new challenge: to sail solo across the Atlantic Ocean.

I returned to Glasgow with no doubt in my mind that I must return to the sea. But I had to think of Kay and our daughters. My family knew how much I loved sailing, and of my childhood ambition to sail round the world, but they were also acutely aware how dangerous sailing could be. I would need to discuss my plans with Kay before taking the next step. And, although I had unlocked the key to my recovery, I was still very unwell. I decided it was best to wait a while, give myself time to recover, and think everything through before taking the next step.

I loved my job at Donaldson's. My ambition was to see Donaldson's become a flagship in deaf education that would prepare deaf pupils for whatever they wanted to achieve after school (career, college or university). I applied for the post of Deputy Head of School and made it to the short-list. It was a tough interview and, unfortunately, I wasn't successful. I understood that, but when I asked for feedback it became clear there was a glass ceiling for Deaf teachers: I would never be a Head Teacher.

I was proud of my work at Donaldson's. The senior management team had made big changes in the school and I was sure that the school would continue to improve. Like all jobs, there were stresses and conflicts. I was spending hours and hours travelling everyday back and forth to Edinburgh. But I also knew that there would be no opportunities for me to progress in my career if I stayed at Donaldson's. I spoke to Kay and told her that I had decided to resign and look for a job in Glasgow. Kay accepted my decision but was also worried about my prospects of finding a new job.

Early one morning in May 2003, I entered the head teacher's office and handed over my letter of resignation to Janet Allen. It was so hard to do because she had placed so much trust in me and had supported me. But she also knew I was frustrated and troubled. Janet asked why I wanted to resign. I could only reply, 'I have thought carefully about this and it has been a very difficult decision.' My letter of resignation was rejected.

I reluctantly returned to school, knowing that I had no alternative. Kay and I had a mortgage to pay, a family to look after, and I would need to save up to finance my sailing. There must have been rumours circulating that I was looking for a new job because I started to receive offers of work. One of these offers was from the head teacher of St Vincent's who invited me to return to the school and offered me a position teaching Science. I didn't need to think twice.

I returned to St Vincent's in August 2003. It was lovely to see the faces of the pupils when I walked back into the classroom. They were delighted to be using BSL all the time but also very keen to return to winning football trophies! It took me a while to settle back into classroom teaching after being assistant head teacher at Donaldson's, but I was happy because I knew I had made the right decision. My family and friends were also delighted that I was able to spend more time at home and in Glasgow.

Mary Brennan contacted me a few months after I returned to St Vincent's. Mary wanted to discuss the possibility of developing a pilot project that would involve creating a BSL glossary for mathematics. I agreed to volunteer my time because I knew from my own experiences, and from my observations of deaf pupils in the class, that developing BSL for the mathematics curriculum was essential.

On 29th November, I received news that there was a Nicholson 26 for sale at Inverkip marina, and also another boat that might be suitable on sale at Largs marina. I tried to contact Largs via Type Talk. At that time, Type Talk was the only way for a deaf person to (independently) make a phone call to a hearing person. Type Talk is relay system. The deaf person types a message to an operator who then relays this message to a hearing person on the other end of the line (and vice versa). I tried calling the broker based at Largs marina via Type Talk but the person who answered the phone hung up. I was desperate to know if the yacht was still on the market. I redialled. But again, the person hung up as soon as they answered. I tried again but this time the Type Talk operator relayed the message 'oh no, not you again' and the put the receiver down.

I was furious. I could not understand why this was happening and I was not accepting that behaviour! I picked up my car keys, quickly said cheerio to Kay and jumped in to my car. I drove though the driving rain past Glasgow airport and along the narrow hilly roads towards Largs. It was raining so heavily that it was difficult to see beyond the windscreen.

As I approached the Ayrshire countryside, I noticed that the fuel gauge was showing red. It was about to run out of petrol. I realised that I did not have enough fuel to get to Largs. But I was too far from any petrol station to turn back. I dropped my speed to save fuel. I was in trouble.

I had been so angry when I left the house that I forgot pick up my wallet and mobile phone. I had very little cash in my pocket. I reached my right hand into the pocket on the door, hoping I might find a few coins in there. As one hand searched around for coins, I could feel the steering wheel vibrating as windscreen wipers thumped against the glass, struggling to cope with the rain. I could feel the rain hammering on to the roof of the car. I peered through the water streaming down the windscreen. Visibility was so poor that I could only just make out the outline of the hills on either side of me. I thought, *this is what it will be like when you are in the Atlantic Ocean, all by yourself in the heavy rain and ocean swell.* Thankfully, I found a few pounds coins and I breathed a deep sigh of relief knowing that I could get some fuel in Largs.

I drove past the graveyard where my dad and my favourite Aunt (Edith) lay at rest. I smiled as I thought back to the time that she lived with us for a few years. Every morning, I would nip into her room, trying to communicate with her in sign language. But Aunt Edith could not sign and struggled to understand me. One morning, I was trying to explain something to her so I drew a picture on a piece of white paper to ask her 'can you get me a horse for my back garden?' Aunt Edith's blue eyes opened wide as she explained in gestures, 'oh no! It would not be fair to the horse. It is too small a garden!'

I dropped into neutral to save fuel as I drove down Haylie Brae (the steep winding road that leads into Largs). I knew there was a garage nearby. I realised just how lucky I had been as the car came to a halt.

I made my way to the marina. I was still angry but I was determined to find out exactly why they refused to accept my call. I opened that door of yacht broker's shop and walked straight to the desk. Around me, people were searching the tiny photos on the wall, looking at the details of the boats.

The broker looked up at me in shock. 'It, was you?'

I was furious and replied, 'Yes! It was !'

The broker wrote a note to me explaining that they had been receiving lots of nuisance calls, that they thought the Type Talk call was a nuisance caller. We both calmed down and he asked me what type of yacht I was looking for. I explained I was looking for a Contessa 26. A Contessa 26 is very similar to a folkboat but made of fibreglass. The broker looked though his files and explained that the boat was in Tighnabruaich. That was too far away for me to get to that day so I drove home. I had been away so long that it was dark by the time I got home.

I spent the long dark winter months planning my strategy for sailing across the Atlantic Ocean. I had to think through every possible expense:

insurance, fuel, food, equipment etc. On 10th January 2004, I woke very early to catch the 04.30 flight to London. I was visiting the London Boat Show. I could hardly believe my eyes when I saw all the expensive yachts. They were beautiful but very expensive. I realised that with my budget, I would be lucky if I could afford just one of the dinghies on show. I met up my friend Simeon, his wife Denise and their son Zac. All the boats on show fascinated us but they were too expensive, so I used my time there to find out more about insurance needed for a transatlantic sail.

I could not believe what I was told. The insurance company told me that a folkboat was far too small, I must have a yacht with a minimum value of £50,000 and, because I am deaf, I must have at least one hearing person in the crew. I decided to make enquiries with another insurance a company. Straight away, I could see they doubted that I had either the skills or the ability to sail. They wrote me a note: *'three people on board, one who has transatlantic experience, 2 who have good offshore experience. Also, we do not cover the US side only the crossing.'* Deaf people are very good at reading body language and facial expressions. I am sure they were thinking 'this deaf man is talking out the back of his head'. My heart sank. I realised that I had another barrier to overcome. I decided to call it a day and go for a few pints with my friends. Perhaps, we could think of a way to tackle this new obstacle. As I sat on the plane home to Glasgow that evening, my mind worked overtime trying to figure out what to do.

The next day I awoke to heavy rain and gale force winds. Nicola asked, 'what we are we doing today?'

I thought, *why not drive to Troon and watch the fierce waves coming in from the Atlantic Ocean.* I knew that the family would enjoy the trip and it would cheer me up because I love the smell of the sea. The wind at Troon was so strong that it rocked the car from side to side and was whipped up sea spray as the waves crashed against the shore.

We were all snugly wrapped up in our winter clothes, but the wind was so strong that I struggled to hold open the car door to let the girls out. Ashley was so tiny and light that the powerful gusts almost lifted her off her feet. She grasped my hand tightly, as her cap flew right off her head and her hair blew around her face. Nicola watched the waves crashing over the rocks, and the flocks of seagulls circling above the sea. Kay stayed in the car. She knew that she would be soaked. Nicola, Ashley and I returned to the car feeling exhilarated by the feel of the wind and sea spray blowing hard against our faces.

For some reason, I took a notion to visit Troon marina. I hadn't been there since 1982. It had completely changed, so you can imagine my surprise when one of the people working on the reception desk remembered me. We shook hands and caught up on news.

I looked around at the boats and noticed there was a folkboat for sale. She was lovely! But although I felt quite excited, I knew I had to sort out the insurance before I could decide to buy a boat. We finished our day out in Troon with a visit to an Italian café: ice cream for the girls, tea and scones for Kay and me. On the way home, I mulled over a possible Plan C: *Chartered yacht?*

For weeks and months, I could not get the thought of sailing across the Atlantic out of my mind. I sat in my wee study room in the attic, dividing my time between studying for my Master's Degree, preparing letters asking for sponsorship for the Deaf Golf World Cup in Sweden (I was delighted to have been asked to play in the Scotland team) and thinking through my options for my next sailing challenge.

It didn't matter where I was, or what I was doing, I could not stop thinking about sailing. I remember one morning in May (it must have been about 04.00), standing in my kitchen and looking out into our back garden. The mind was awash with thoughts: *what about a folkboat, about twenty-six feet long? Or should I try the 5-Oceans race that is organised by Sir Robin Knox Johnston, but then I would need to think about the cost of chartering a yacht and then insurance on top of that!* My mind felt like the inside of a washing machine with thoughts tumbling about inside it. And, on top of that, I was about to start training for the fifth World Deaf Golf Championships in Sweden in July.

Not long after that morning, I received an email from Mark Turner (Mark is well known in yacht racing and worked with Ellen McArthur) explaining that it would cost approximately £50,000 to charter a yacht for three months plus and additional £5,000 to £17,000 for insurance. *No chance! Kay will ask for a divorce!* I had to find another way. I had not sailed for over twenty years so I also had to polish up my sailing skills.

Later, in May of that year, we had a family holiday in Arran. One day, I took Nicola out sailing in a wooden GP 14 dinghy while Ashley and Kay went shopping in Brodick. We sailed from Lamlash pier out into Lamlash Bay. Nicola was enjoying herself as we sailed gently around the bay, her confidence growing minute by minute.

I could see Nicola was ready to sail further out to sea so I thought she might enjoy a wee sail around Holy Island. My plan was to sail south, pass the lighthouse on Holy Island on the south coast and then veer towards the northeast coast and then turn back towards a Lamlash Bay.

We were about 400 to 500 yards from the shore, sailing fast under full sails. It was great fun. Suddenly, a strong gust of wind blew downwards from the peak of Mullach Mor piling the waves against out wee dinghy. The wind caught Nicola and threw her to the opposite end off the boat from me and then capsized the dinghy. As soon as we hit the water my first thought was of Nicola. *Where is she? Is she OK?* I swam quickly in search of her hoping she was OK.

I was so proud when I saw her bobbing about with her lifejacket on and coping well with the sea. I think that must have been Nicola's first experience of swimming in the Firth of Clyde. We quickly up-righted the dinghy, climbed on board, and started bailing out the water.

While I was busy, Nicola spotted a passing RNLI boat and shouted for help. I explained to her that we didn't need the RNLI, all we had to do was bail out the water and we could sail the dinghy back to Lamlash.

Meanwhile, Kay and Ashley were wondering what had happened to us. I had a wee mobile phone in my pocket to keep in contact with Kay via text message, but it had filled up with water during the capsize, meaning Kay and Ashley had lost contact with us. They had lots of questions for Nicola and me when we returned to shore soaking wet!

Then on 1st June, things took a sudden change. I looked up Royal Western Yacht Club of England 'Original Singlehanded Transatlantic Race' – 'OSTAR 2005'. I looked through the race notice and thought to myself *why not?* and sent an email to the administration:

> *Hi*
> *Could u let me know if you would accept a Deaf Skipper entering this race next year as I am profoundly deaf but have sailed for many years. Could you let me know before I apply? Thks. Gerry.*

I received a reply from the administrator at 17.28 on 6th June:

> *have passed your email to our race director who will contact you direct. Best of luck.*

I was up in the attic. It was very hot and humid. I tried to stay calm and replied 'many thanks' and waited for news. Then, at 18.49, an email popped into my mail box: it was from OSTAR 2005. I hadn't expected them to get back to me so quickly. I felt nervous as I looked out of the Velux window. I told myself that if they say 'sorry, no' I would understand. I inhaled deeply and opened the email, trying to stay calm as I carefully read each line:

Hi Gerry
We would be delighted to have you as a competitor in the race, but we will have to ensure that you can comply with the requirement of the NOR (Notice of Race), particularly the section on communication (providing you have Iridium system I would not envisage a problem).
Regards,
Chris Arscott

Race Director STAR 2005.

My hand punched the air as I shouted, 'Yes! Yes! Yes!' The challenge was on – I had nine months to find a boat and prepare for the race. But, first of all, I had to tell Kay.

Chapter 7: Road to the Transatlantic Race

I printed the email from Chris Arscott and rushed downstairs. Kay was standing at the kitchen sink. I handed over the sheet of paper and watched as she carefully read it. She looked at me and then read it again. 'You mean you are going?'

I asked, 'What do you think?'

Kay thought things over and over. 'I can't believe it is time. I remember you saying to me almost nineteen years ago that one day you would go. Time has flown passed so quickly.' Kay fully understood the dangers of a transatlantic crossing, but she insisted I should try OSTAR 2005. We both agreed that it would be better to speak to our daughters before making the final decision.

I knew that, if I succeeded in becoming the first deaf person to sail solo across the Atlantic Ocean, l would be one step closer to following my ambitions and solo circumnavigating the globe like Sir Francis Chichester. I picked up my copy of *Deep Sea Sailing* by Erroll Bruce and looked at the second page: 'To Gerry from Dad – Christmas 1979'. I wondered if my dad was watching and knew that I was getting closer to achieving my dream.

I thought about the transatlantic chart pinned on my bedroom wall, with potential routes plotted on it, and sneaking off to the Mitchell Library to study the ocean currents and weather forecast. Dad had made his views very clear to me: I did not have money to go on sailing adventures and I had to learn to be independent. I had to have an education and a job and be able to look after myself. As I looked down at the book, I couldn't help wondering if Dad knew what I was planning.

Meanwhile, I was still working on the BSL glossary for mathematics. But we received dreadful news – Mary was diagnosed with breast cancer. Although, she refused to give in to the illness and kept working, deep down I felt heart-broken.

One December night, after working in Edinburgh on the glossary, I decided to take the coach rather than the train home to Glasgow. As I got off the bus, I spotted a drunken man leaning against a lamppost. He seemed very content as he staggered while trying to steady himself. I could see that he was a heavy drinker – one of those men who had been drinking all their life.

As I watched him, I wondered what it would be like to be him. I thought about the times I went out boozing with my deaf mates and we would forget our troubles for a while. But as I watched this happy, unshaven man, I knew that he did not spend much of his life sober and that part of his life was missing. I knew that if I did not take on the challenge of sailing across the Atlantic, that man could easily be me. I silently wished him well and decided to walk down to George Square.

George Square is beautiful in the winter. I watched Christmas lights twinkle in the darkness and the people (young and old) having fun skating on the ice rink. I looked over at the Glasgow City Chambers standing proud on the east side of the Square, bathed in the soft lights that illuminate many of Glasgow's historic buildings. Glasgow is my home and, as I looked around, I felt proud of my city and to be able to call myself a Glaswegian. I popped into the newsagent on the way to Central Station and bought myself a copy of *Yachting Monthly* in the hope that I might find some information on a boat that might suit me.

I had one last thing to do before I started my search for a boat: discuss OSTAR with Nicola and Ashley. Kay informed Nicola and Ashley that their dad would like to hold a family meeting. Nicola and Ashley are very talkative and constantly chat to each other. I realised that they must have been expecting very bad news because they were sitting at the kitchen table in complete silence. Their faces looked very serious.

I explained that I still had my dreams and ambitions, and that I needed to return to the sea. I asked if they would agree to me sailing across the Atlantic. Immediately, Nicola jumped right out of her chair and said, 'For God's sake! Yes, you can go! I have been hearing about your dreams about sailing since I was small. Yes Dad, of course you can go!'

Ashley was very quiet. I could see she was thinking very seriously and very carefully. I thought perhaps she was scared to say 'No' in case she hurt my feelings. But slowly she signed 'yes' using her hand in a 'Y' hand shape (the St Vincent's sign for 'yes').

I looked at Kay and asked what she thought. 'Yes,' she replied. 'You best go get it done.' With my family behind me, I felt my strength and determination growing. I had no doubts. I knew I could do it.

I immediately looked up the OSTAR 2005 Notice of Race, carefully checking their rules for eligibility. The race was open to cruising and racing boats between thirty and fifty feet long. I needed to find the right yacht to match the entry requirements and had about nine months to prepare for the race. I had to meet all the eligibility criteria.

The race notice said that it was the skipper's responsibility to judge whether he or she was physically psychologically and medically fit. It was also my responsibility to ensure that the boat was of an appropriate design and construction and adequately maintained, and equipped with safety equipment that would meet the conditions that may be encountered during the race. As well as having a suitable boat, I also had to obtain the RYA certificate in Sea Survival and First Aid, with a qualifying date of 1st May 2005, as well as evidence of a qualifying cruise that had to be no less than 500 miles. The qualifying cruise would have to be logged and the charts and extracts of the log would need to be checked and dated by the harbour authorities. I knew that it would be ideal to have a sign language interpreter to help with communication during my preparations but there was no way on my limited budget that I could afford to pay for interpreters.

The school summer break came around again and, in July 2004, we set off to Arran. I bought a copy of *Yachting Life* on the way to Arran and spotted two boats for sale that might be suitable for a transatlantic crossing. One yacht was a Sigma 38, based in Inverkip, Wemyss Bay. The other was a J-35 in Belfast. I decided that I would visit Inverkip after we returned from our holiday in Arran.

On 14th July, Kay and I drove to Inverkip to look at the Sigma 38. She was a very good yacht, but I was not sure about her. I knew there was a Rodger OOD34 (Offshore One Design) on the market. She was called *Red Alert*, and was berthed in Largs. I don't know why but something in my gut was telling me that I should look at this boat, so Kay and I drove to the marina.

I asked the broker for the keys and walked to the pontoon where she was berthed. She was not there! So, I returned to the broker and explained that the Rodger OOD 34 was missing. I thought he was going to have a heart attack when he exclaimed, 'What?' The owner had taken the boat out sailing and had not told him. I was bitterly disappointed but I knew I should have contacted the marina before going. I handed over my email address and asked the broker to email me when the boat was available for me to look over.

By that time, the Scotland Team were preparing for the Fifth World Deaf Golf Championship (26th to 30th July) in Stockholm, Sweden. I practiced for the tournament in Arran and also at my local club (Cathkin Braes Golf Club). Just as I was heading to meet my team-mates at Prestwick airport, I received an email from the broker in Largs, saying the Rodger OOD 34 would arrive in Largs on until 25th July. I replied to let him know that I would be out of the country until 30th July.

I have to admit that my golf was not up to its usual standard during the competition. The team captain was very worried by my poor scores. During the second round, Scotland was heading for third place and the captain asked us to stay steady, keep our nerve, and we would return good scores. In the third round, we were in the same position but closing in on the USA (who were in first place), and England (who were in second place). Our captain warned us against any late-night drinking because we had to stay steady and focussed for the final.

After the end of the fourth and final round, we waited anxiously for the results: first place, USA; second place, England. When the third place was announced we looked at each other, confused by the Swedish Sign Language. The president switched to International Sign and announced that Scotland had won third place in the World Deaf Golf Championships. We jumped with joy, knowing it was the first time Scotland had achieved third place in a World Championship since the competition was established at Forest of Arden, Coventry in 1995.

That same day I received a fax at the hotel in Sweden. It was Kay: the Rodger OOD 34 *Red Alert* had arrived in Largs and would be ready for us to see when I arrived home. *Thank goodness*, I thought to myself. You see, while I was playing golf in Sweden, I could not fully concentrate on my game. I could not stop thinking about that boat!

On 31st July, Kay and I arrived in Largs to meet the owner of the Rodger OOD34. I was amazed when I saw him using gestures. He explained to us that his son was deaf. I don't know why I was surprised, but I felt very comfortable knowing the owner was aware of what it is like to be deaf. It was good to be able to relax and discuss everything I needed to know before deciding to buy the boat.

By September, all the insurance and legal documentation was in place and I was the new owner of *Red Alert*. I was really pleased. Red Alert was originally called Redcoat and owned by the British Army Sailing Association, based in the south of England. She was later bought by Stuart MacDonald. Stuart renamed her *Red Alert* and she had been based at

Largs, Scotland. Stuart raced Red Alert extensively in the Clyde, Scotland, competing in many Scottish Series and also the Cork Week. Stuart had also raced her single-handedly across the Atlantic in the 2000 OSTAR. And now Red Alert belonged to Gerry Hughes.

Not long afterwards, I received a letter from the Royal Western Yacht Club of England, Singlehanded Transatlantic Race 2005:

Thank you very much for your entry form and the deposit for the Singlehanded Transatlantic Race 2005, and a big welcome from the Commodore and Member of the Royal Western Yacht Club.

I know that the preparation for the race is a long and exacting business and if there is anything we can do to help, please do not hesitate to contact us,
Good luck in your preparations.

CR Arscott, Race Director.

After reading it, I felt like a different person. I thought back to my previous sailing adventures: sailing in the Bay of Biscay in 1980 with Richard Ellis, Peter Hickman, Geoffrey Adams and the three crazy men sailing round the British Isles with Matthew in 1981; sailing to the Faroes in 1982 with Erelend Tulloch. It had been roughly twenty years since I had done any real sailing.

I sold my East Germany Folkboat (25ft) when Nicola was one year old to commit my time to my family and to campaign for better deaf education. In those days, I used the same technology as my dad: barometer, clock, pencil, rubber, divider and slide ruler with chart. Nothing else. There were no electronic aids. Now the sailing world had completely changed and there was so much new technology. I didn't know where to start or what equipment to trust. But I told myself, *just get on with it. This is the challenge you have set yourself. You will just need to build up your skills again from scratch.*

There are very strict criteria for entry to OSTAR and lots of paperwork, including insurance, evidence of the successfully completed qualifying cruise, sea survival and first aid certificates. By October 2004, I had created my plan of action to prepare for OSTAR 2005. I started by examining sails and equipment at Troon marina, noting down what needed done and what equipment would need to be replaced.

In November, I set up a committee (of both deaf and hearing individuals) to help with fund raising. One question that kept coming up was what I would call my new boat? Would she still be called Red Alert? I explained to the team that my previous yacht (from my dad) was called *Faraway II* so I thought perhaps I would call this new boat *Faraway III*.

I paused slightly as the committee made eye contact with me. To my surprise they suggested I should call the boat *Quest II*. I asked, 'Why?'

One of the committee (Elizabeth Lafferty) replied, 'You taught us to become BSL tutors when we were students at Quest for a Language.' That was twenty years ago. So, *Quest II* was born, and I declared that *Quest II* would be sailed by the first deaf skipper to ever sail across the Atlantic.

In November, I started sailing with *Quest II* to get to know and understand her. In the December of that year, the weather was poor with lots of gales, so I took her out and tested her around the Firth of Clyde, as well as studying nutritional requirements for the sail and the rules for the race. My log from that sail on 2nd Dec states: '*I feel as if the countdown to OSTAR has started: 5 months, 26 days, 21hours, 55mins, 43 seconds!*' But I was also beginning to get anxious about how quickly time was passing. The weather was foggy, damp and miserable and I was losing sleep over the lack of sponsorship. Then I was forced to make a visit to our local hospital (the Victoria Infirmary).

Quest II and I had been sailing in Force 6/7 winds because I wanted to test her resilience in heavy seas. At one point, the waves threw me and I collided with a large winch. It was agony! It was so painful that I could barely walk. The sea was strong and churning black and there were strong low squalls. I knew it was foolish to take any chances. I sailed back to Troon as fast as I could before I got any worse. When I arrived home, my GP sent me for X-rays. The X-rays showed a tiny hairline crack on my pelvis.

In January, I did a major refit of the equipment on Red Alert with the help from David Wayt and David Wayt Jr. – both Davids are British Sign Language users and David Snr is an expert on fibreglass. I also checked the mast and riggings and completed the Ocean Safety checks. In February, *Quest II* went back to sea and I added new technology such as radar, GPS and a satellite phone. The final phase of my preparation was studying the Atlantic Crossing and Newfoundland.

The deadline for submitting completed paperwork to OSTAR was 1st of March and I was required to submit: a) passport size of skipper, b) information about the skipper and boat for the racing programme, c) completed entry form. In April, I took *Quest II* out for our qualifying cruise to test the navigation equipment, self-steering. Thanks to BSLIS (British Sign Language Interpreting Services, a local sign language interpreting agency who sponsored me), I also had my certificate of Sea Survivals and First Aid. Helen Dunipace and Janice Murdoch interpreted free of charge (and even got in the swimming pool to interpret for the sea survival training).

One of the entrance criteria for OSTAR is that you must sail 500 nautical miles, non-stop, offshore and in one direction. I decided to sail to Rockall and back. I set off on 3rd April. The forecast for Rockall West was Gale 8 to Storm 10. It was a disaster! Everything seemed to go wrong: winches jammed, the sails needed repair, the self-steering rudder broke, and I lost the para anchor due to chafing. But, as I sailed home, I realised that I was still polishing up skills.

I arrived back in Troon on 15th April, satisfied in the knowledge that *Quest ll* handled well in heavy seas. However, I had learned during the sail that I would need to alter the sails and make sure the mast and the riggings were secure. All I had to do now was have my log signed by the Troon manager so I could send it off to Royal Western Yacht Club (RWYC) with my charts as evidence that I had completed the qualifying sail.

Not long after that, I received a letter from the RWYC of England signed R. R. Lictherce to inform me that they were satisfied with my qualifying cruise. The next stage would be the journey to the Plymouth Queen Anne Ferry Battery for the race.

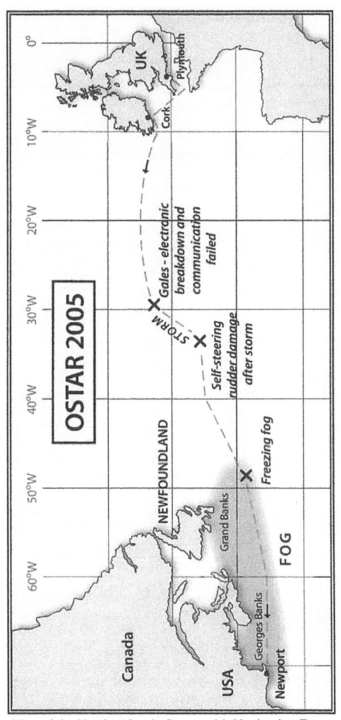

Map of the North Atlantic Ocean with Navigation Route

Chapter 8: Me and the Oil Lamp

My preparations for the race were going well. I had four weeks to go before leaving Troon and sailing to Plymouth for the start of the race on 29th May. But on 27th April, I encountered yet another problem. The race director emailed all participants to say that everyone must submit their visas (for America) to the race officials in Plymouth by 26th May. This was to ensure that all paperwork was completed before 29th May. It was impossible for me to apply for a visa in Scotland. The only dates available for an appointment at the Embassy were 26th May in Belfast or 31st May in London. There was no chance of the American Embassy issuing an emergency visa.

My heart sank. I knew that if I failed to get the visa in time, the whole project would collapse. All the work, and planning would be for nothing and my dream would vanish. I was furious with myself. All these years I had dreamt of sailing across the Atlantic and the only thing that stood in my way was a piece of paper!

That day, I approached John Dunipace (a sign language interpreter at BSLIS) and asked if he could make a few phone calls. He was astonished when he found out the difficulties I was experiencing so he and his wife Helen both decided to back me up in my attempts to get through to the Embassy.

On 28th April, John sent a very formal email to the US Embassy in London. He explained that he was writing on behalf of Gerry Hughes, who would be participating in the Original Single-Handed Transatlantic Ocean Race. He asked if there was any way to speed up the process. The Embassy replied to say they could not issue an emergency appointment but John persisted, asking them to reconsider.

By 12th May, my brother-in-law, Liam Sheridan (who was also helping with our enquiries at the Embassy), had contacted our Local Councillor Bill Timoney. Bill gave us his backing. I received a text message from John: 'Do not give up – there is a chance!'

I didn't know whether to believe him, or whether he was just saying that to make me feel better. But then I received wonderful news. Liam emailed me to tell me that Tom Harris (our local MP) had been in touch with the US Embassy and secured an appointment for me the Embassy in London on 25th May 2005 at 09.00.

I was in the classroom when the email came through. My eyes filled with tears as I shouted out. The other teachers rushed into the room to find out what was wrong. I was holding a paper copy of the email in my hand. I looked up and just said 'VISA! VISA!' None of them knew what I was talking about.

On 17th May at 21.00, *Quest II* sailed past the south of Arran, heading towards Plymouth. Weather permitting, we would arrive at the Queen Anne Battery, Plymouth by 24th May. We arrived at Queen Anne Battery, Plymouth 04.30 on 23rd May 2005 and toasted the sun rising in the east. The next day, I travelled to the American Embassy in London by train and stayed at the house of our deaf friend, Linda Richards.

Linda is a BSL/English sign language interpreter and translator who regularly works in TV. This meant I could complete all the paper work using BSL because Linda could work between languages. I submitted the paperwork and prayed that I would get the visa on that day. We were advised to wait at a nearby hotel.

Linda's eyes darted to her phone every time it rang to check the name of the caller. She immediately cancelled the call if it was not the Embassy number to ensure that she would not miss the call about my visa. A motorbike courier arrived. The courier handed my passport to me. I instructed the courier to wait while I leafed through it to check that the visa was there.

At last!

I rushed to catch the next train back to Plymouth. As the train ploughed through the countryside, I sat gazing out of the window, thinking about what lay ahead of me. It would not be long until I was sailing in the Atlantic Ocean and I knew, deep in my gut, that I was ready for the challenge.

I awoke on 26th May clutching my visa and passport in my hand. I walked into the main race fleet assembly room. The atmosphere was suddenly very still as all eyes turned in my direction. The bearing officers and skippers stopped what they were doing and stood silently, their eyes following me as I walked into the room. I looked round at them, put my hand into my back pocket and lifted out my passport, waving it as high as could reach. The crowd burst into applause and fellow skippers patted my back saying, 'Well done, Gerry!'

It was 28th May 2005 and the day before the race. All my final checklists were complete and the iridium satellite phoned was connected for communication. Everyone was busy preparing for the start of the race. We (including the volunteers that were helping me) had been on our feet all day: running back and forth, loading food and fuel supplies onto *Quest II*, and attending lectures and briefing meetings with the race organisers.

The *Yachting Monthly* team and TV cameraman were going around each boat, interviewing and filming each skipper and their volunteers. But when they arrived at *Quest II* they turned their heads in the opposite direction and moved on the next boat. I was used to this type of behaviour, but I still felt shocked. The volunteers helping could not believe what happened and were lost for words. But it is a typical everyday experience for a deaf person in a hearing world.

On 29th May 2005 (Race Day) Kay, Nicola and Ashley and I joined the other skippers in the Royal Western Yacht Club House for our farewell breakfast. Kay and I chatted in sign language, but Nicola and Ashley were quiet. I wondered if they were anxious about what might happen over the next few weeks. After our 'Final Breakfast', the skippers prepared to cast off from the Queen Anne Battery marina and all the boats were in the Plymouth Sound by 11.00. There were boats everywhere; so many people had turned out to make this day possible.

I made my way to the starting point knowing that HRH Prince Philip, the Duke of Edinburgh was on the Royal Navy vessel watching at our fleet. I sailed past the press boat and spotted Helen Dunipace on it. Kay, Nicola, Ashley, and my small team of volunteers were on a viewing boat. I felt awful saying goodbye to my family.

I kept my eyes on the racing flags, waiting for the race to start but, at the same time, I had to watch out for the nearby yachts. I could see that Nicola and Ashley were crying as they waved. I felt a huge lump in my throat as I looked at their faces.

Before I knew what was happening, a French yacht was approaching *Quest II* at speed. I had no time to think. The yacht was about to collide with me and would have knocked off my self-steering. I pulled the tiller and turned *Quest II* – narrowly escaping a collision by about 5 cm.

The French yacht crashed into another instead. The two yachts were tangled together. I could see that the skipper was yelling – both his hands in the air as he rushed to the stern to inspect the damage. A few minutes later a puff of smoke told me that Van Howells (the only surviving competitor from the Atlantic crossing in 1960) had fired the starting gun from on board his folkboat, *Patricia*.

I got off to a good start, but it was not long before the wind reduced. This slowed me down because of the extra weight on board *Quest II* (mostly food and supplies). The first day of sailing was very slow. The sea was so calm that the glass-like surface glistened in the sunshine.

By 20.00 *Quest II* was surrounded by heavy mist and fog. It was difficult to see more than one or two miles. I switched on the navigation lights and used the foghorn to warn others about my position. As I sailed past the Scilly Isles, a warning light indicated that the satellite navigation had no power and must be shut down. I couldn't understand how the battery could be running low so soon after leaving Plymouth.

I rushed to switch on the engine to recharge the battery. But the battery was too low to even start the engine running. I tried again but there was no way to get the engine started. I decided that there must be a problem with the alternator. This was really serious – I needed power for the navigation equipment and to communicate by email to inform people of my position, and for safety.

I had no option but to sail to the nearest marina for repairs. I checked my chart and decided to sail to Cork Harbour. It would add around a hundred miles to my journey, but without essential repairs, I would have to retire from the race.

I arrived in Crosshaven, Cork, at around 05.30 on 1st June 2005. It was raining heavily. I was stuck at the front gate, which required a security number to open. Luckily, someone was walking past and gave me the security number to let me open the gate. There was nobody in the marina office so I decided to go to the Royal Cork Yacht Club (RCYC) in Crosshaven[15]. I needed to find someone who understood yachting and could help me to communicate with equipment suppliers.

It took hours and hours to identify and sort the problems with the battery and alternator. I was so relieved when I found out that John Dunipace had already been in contact with them and informed them of the problems I was experiencing. I decided to check the connection wires from my battery and alternator before buying new parts. I was shocked to find that the twenty-two wires (eleven each side) were rusty and damaged. There was

---

[15] Royal Cork Yacht Club is the oldest yacht club in the world (established 1720).

only one option available to me if I wanted to get back to sea: replace all the electrical wires.

I disconnected the plug connections and then reconnected them. As I was doing this, I couldn't help thinking to myself, *I have only just started the race. The other boats will be headed out across the Atlantic and I am losing time as soon already. My dream is fading before I have even started.*

The engine compartment in an OOD 34 is very small. I had just enough room to manoeuvre my hands and wrists. I gingerly cut the wires one by one. Sweat dripped down my face and my glasses steamed up in the cramped conditions. I worked on the engine for four hours. At one point (around 14.00), I realised that three differently coloured wires were disconnected and I didn't know where and on which side of the connection they belonged.

'Oh, *F@$#S#F#!'

I went to a motorboat in the marina to examine its motor and electrical connections. They looked similar so I drew a diagram of its electrical layout. After finishing the job, all that was left to do was press the starter button and pray.

At last! The engine was running. I watched the battery charge to 13.8 volts. *That's good enough*, I thought to myself. Now I can turn my attention to the self-steering to check everything was in order.

I thanked Richie Allen (the sailing secretary at RCYC) for helping me with communications and signed the yacht club visitor's book. He gave me a pint of Beamish Irish Stout and the club's chef gave me a delicious chicken sandwich to help me on my way. I had planned to have a hot shower but I was running out of time if I was to catch up with the other boats. Richie was standing outside the clubhouse as I sailed out of Crosshaven marina. I saluted him to thank RCYC for giving me time to sort out the engine and the self-steering. All I had to do now was catch up with my competitors.

The seas of the Atlantic Ocean were rough sailing. The challenges of the weather and heavy sea did not worry me – I was enjoying it. On 2nd June the water pump blew a fuse. Then on 3rd June I woke at 03.30 and noticed that the GPS navigation chart was blank. My heart raced as I checked all navigation equipment. There was no sign of it working. I tried to switch on the engine. It was dead.

I switched to a second battery and let out a huge sigh of relief as the engine started. But my troubles were not over – something was wrong with the mast. The mast was moving around and shaking too much as *Quest II* bounced over the waves. It was not safe to continue sailing. I had no option but to slow down and adjust the riggings in the rough conditions of the North Atlantic Ocean.

I was puzzled. *What was happening?* I had adjusted the mast and riggings after my qualifying sail to Rockall to ensure that they could withstand heavy seas and strong winds. I also checked them again before leaving Plymouth, but now I was in the North Atlantic, trying to find a way to strengthen the mast or risk being dismasted and being forced to retire from the race. Thankfully, I was able to tune the riggings and reduce the shaking at the top of the mast and make good progress.

By 7th June, my cruising speed was exceptional. I was making good progress towards my next target position. But at 06.40 on 8th June a thick fog arrived. Visibility was reduced to around fifty metres. The wind speed dropped to 0.5knts and I had to pull up the asymmetric sail to get more speed. It didn't work.

I was left twiddling my thumbs. There was nothing else I could do. I put the kettle on to have a coffee while I was waiting for the wind to arrive. The fog cleared at around 09.15, but the sea was calm and there was no wind. I had another 200 miles to go before changing course. I decided to make the most of my time and treat myself to another coffee, some Weetabix (chunky fruit bar strawberry) and a Mars bar for breakfast. It was very tasty!

On 9th June, the engine began cutting out after five minutes running. Without an engine, I had no way to build power in the battery. I checked the oil levels, looking for signs of leakage, then I checked the engine, wondering if there were any loose parts. Next, I checked the bilge to see if there were any leaks. Everything was fine. I couldn't understand it; the power in the batteries was still getting lower and lower.

I had no choice but to email Mark McQueen. Mark is deaf and an engineer and had completed the checks on the engine before the race started. I couldn't get hold of Mark – he was busy at college. It was now an emergency. Helen Dunipace emailed: 'keep up your spirit'. My reply was brief: 'I am f*****g trying!!'

I had to do everything possible to save power. I emailed Kay:

'right now, I am ok.

I try save battery so I can go Newport I will email u every 4 days ok I love u. bye Gerry xxx

p.s. tell Nic and Ashley not to worry I will be ok. Love them too. Xxxx

I turned off the main power switch to conserve what little power was left in the batteries. My spirits plummeted. I was in the middle of the Atlantic Ocean with no power. This meant I had no access to GPS information and no navigation lights. Other boats and ships would be unable to see me in the dark (or in fog). Nobody would know I was there unless they could see me on their radar by picking up the signal from the radar reflector on the mast.

I began to wonder if I should contact the coastguard, but I managed to clear my head and focus on the task in front of me: deciding my route. I had two options: head towards south of Grand Banks of Newfoundland, Canada or head further south to Latitude 43N. Both routes were potentially risky. I wanted to stay away from the fog and icebergs on the Grand Banks, but if I headed south I needed to stay as close as possible to the same latitude as Newport (Latitude 41.2N).

I carefully considered both options. Without electronic navigation aids, I had no access to iceberg reports. That meant I was dependent on good visibility because l had to be able to see at all times. What if there was fog? If I headed south, I would need to be able to ensure that I had avoided sailing into the Gulf Stream. The Gulf Stream has fast currents. If *Quest II* got caught in the Gulf Stream, she could be carried eastwards (backwards) for miles and miles. I reckoned that *Quest II* was positioned at Lat 53N. My safest option was to head south to Lat 42N (which would keep me near to Newport) and keep lookout for any changes in the colour of the water (indicating the Gulf Stream).

Two days later (on 11th June), the lights on the battery indicated that the power had increased slightly. My first thought was of Kay. I typed a brief email:

'I am afraid the boat is not doing well. She is now failing to charge up the batteries, all down to the problem with engine. I am asking if you would consider me returning back home to Troon and forget racing to NEWPORT USA.'

I also emailed RWYC to let them know of my difficulties and sent it just before the battery went flat. I connected a cable between the laptop and the satellite mobile, clenched my laptop in one hand and used the other to brace myself against the rough sea. It felt like forever as I waited for a signal to let me know whether the message had been sent or received. It was pitch black outside.

Suddenly, *Quest II* shook violently as she was hit by a huge wave from one side. The mainsheets from the boom whipped against my left wrist. The satellite mobile shot out of my hand and landed on the other side of the deck. The disconnected cable flew up and hit me on my forehead. The sea was ferocious. Waves washed over the deck. All I could see was the broken mobile floating slowly away in the sea water washing across the deck.

I threw my laptop onto the seat and dived outside and stretched my left arm as far as I could, trying to catch hold of the phone. I fell. My ribs smashed against the big stainless-steel winches. The pain was excruciating. I grasped the two pieces of my phone and tried to turn and raise my body. It was too painful.

Slowly but surely, I crawled across the deck against the waves and fierce wind and managed to get down below. I ran my hand over my rib cage gently, pressing to find out if I had broken any bones. I suspected at least three broken ribs.

I looked at the mobile phone in my hand. It was dead. The case of my satellite phone had split in two and the antenna was damaged. I gave myself a few minutes to gather my thoughts.

Despite the storm, *Quest II* was on course and making good progress. I decided it was best to focus my energy on trying to repair the satellite mobile. I tried switching it on: no signal. I sat back inside the boat as *Quest II* bounced over the waves and switched off my head torch to save the battery. It was pitch black again.

I decided to call it a day and try to get some sleep. As I dozed off to sleep in the corner of the bulkhead, there was just enough light from the oil lamp for me to see there was water rising from below.

I slept for a couple of hours. When I awoke, my ribs were so painful that it was difficult to breathe. I was freezing cold and shivering. The pain in my ribs was so severe that I could not move. I knew I had to find a way to get moving soon. *Quest II* was moving much faster. The wind was rising and I had to bail out water from below before it got worse. I rested for a few more hours and then managed to raise my body by tying a rope to the ceiling pole and using is to haul myself up. I tried switching on the satellite mobile: nothing. I lit my oil lamp, took some painkillers, and carefully eased myself back into the corner of the bulkhead again.

The weather deteriorated over the course of the next day and the winds increased to Gale Force. The huge waves pushed against *Quest II*. At one point, when I was at the cockpit reefing sails, *Quest II* was knocked down flat by rogue waves from the north. I grabbed hold of the stanchion and managed to climb onto the starboard hull. I braced and waited for the mast to come up but quickly realised that I had lost one of the winch handles and a life jacket had inflated.

After a few minutes (it felt much longer than this), *Quest II* righted herself. I climbed back into the cockpit and took the helm. By 15th June, I had been at sea for just over two weeks. The waves were still high and powerful but the wind had decreased. I spent most of the afternoon trying to reassemble the satellite phone. Finally, I managed to fix the broken phone and connect it to the satellite mobile connection. It was working! I emailed Chris Arscott at RWYC to update him my progress:

'Quest ll, *reported position lat 47 43N and long 03 35W, difficult to call u as batteries now very very low, am still heading for Newport, need someone to tow me when we enter harbour.*'

At last I received a reply from Kay (four days after I had emailed her):

'*Yes, see u at Newport.*'

I felt my spirits lift – Kay, Nicola and Ashley would be waiting for me at Newport. My focus returned and I knew I would arrive at Newport regardless of what lay ahead of me.

Then the light, dim from the screen on my laptop, began to fade and the screen went blank. The battery was completely flat. I calculated my position: I was 2,150 miles from Newport and I had no power. Without power, I had no way of communicating with RWYC or with Kay. I had no access to electronic navigation equipment and no navigation lights. I was completely on my own in the Northern Atlantic Ocean. My only source of light and heat was my oil lamp. But I was confident that I could do it.

My dad taught me to sail using traditional navigational equipment: charts, dividers, parallel ruler, pencil and eraser. Just like my childhood days on the River Clyde and the west coast of Scotland, I would use dead reckoning from a previously determined positioning. Dad's barometer, observing the skies and the clouds, would provide my weather reports.

I slept well for two hours, knowing that I was ready for the challenge ahead. When I awoke, I turned my attention to getting the engine running. I sat near the corner bulkhead (wrapped in my heavy ocean oilskins), peering into the engine compartment and trying to figure out what I should do first.

I replaced the fuel filter. Then I pulled the inlet and outlet tubes to drain the fuel. As I looked at the inlet tube, I spotted that there were two different colours in the tubes: there was water in the tube! I was really puzzled. *How could water get into the inlet tube? Everything had been checked while I was in Plymouth...* I drained the fuel and bled the fuel injection in the hope that it would solve the problem. I tried the switch again, but the batteries were far too low to turn the engine.

My only option was to leave it and allow a couple of days for the batteries to recharge. The old car engines, they could be started by turning *Faraway I* (a gaff ketch) and *Faraway II* (a westerly longbow) had old-fashioned engines. Just like vintage cars, you could start the engine by turning a handle, but modern engines relied on the battery. I tried to stay positive. *Quest ll* and I had worked well together. We would get through this.

My ribs were still very painful. I felt sick with pain after pulling jib sheets. *Quest II* was sailing windward very hard and bouncing against the powerful waves. Intense pain reverberated through my body with every bounce. My clothes were soaking wet and sticking to my body. It was essential to change into dry clothing to prevent my body chilling. I went down below and braced my feet against the base of one of the seats to steady myself against the motion of the waves. I raised my arms to change into a dry T-shirt but the pain was excruciating. Slowly but surely, I gingerly managed to change my clothes and make myself more comfortable against the cold. My ribs were covered in black and purple bruises.

On 18th June, I was joined by a pod of dolphins. They swam along either side of *Quest II*. I relaxed for the first time and smiled as I watched them playfully leaping into the air and splashing into the sea. They were such good company. And they seemed to be enjoying my company too as they escorted *Quest II* across the Atlantic.

By 20th June, I had been at sea for three weeks. Visibility deteriorated and freezing fog began to form. I was injured, had no electronic aids and no navigation lights. I slowed *Quest II*. I estimated that I was about 800 nautical miles from Newport in the Grand Banks of Newfoundland because there were lots of American fishing trawlers around. I was tempted to sail along the same latitude (42N). If I did this, *Quest II* and I would meet the seas south of Nova Scotia, Canada. This would give me the opportunity (hopefully) to catch sight of land, get my bearings and plot my exact position. From there, I could plot my course to the finish line. However, if I did that, I risked sailing near Sable Island. The seas around Sable Island are famous for their dangerous sailing conditions. It was too risky.

On 21st June, I began to feel strange. There was heavy fog and no wind. *Quest II* was drifting, carried by the Ocean currents. I felt uncomfortable inside and something seemed to be amiss with *Quest II*. I couldn't communicate with her. The strange feeling continued until 23rd June when, at last, *Quest II* seemed content and we were sailing as a team again. That evening, a beautiful yacht came past. It was *PINDAR*! (Open 60, a well-known racing yacht) as we waved. I noted *PINDAR's* position in my log: Lat 42N, Long 56W.

The intermittent fog and lack of wind lasted for eight days. I was becoming increasingly frustrated.

Gerry's log, 29th June, 2015:

'Fog, no wind
I want to scream: Come on wind! Get me the wind! Still fog.'

Thankfully, the wind began to pick up but the freezing fog was getting worse. I could feel the fog sticking to my face. Everything was cold and damp and I could barely see the mast. The dolphins were still with me. We had gotten to know each other and become friends. I was approaching George Bank, but I was exhausted and struggling to keep my eyes open. I prayed to God and asked him to give me the strength to keep going. I was approaching one of the busiest shipping lanes in the world and there was no way I would be able to see other crafts in the thick freezing fog. The fog continued to close in, getting thicker and thicker. I had to be prepared for an emergency, so I gathered up my grab bag and flares and kept them with me at all times.

Quest II was still drifting. I was approaching Nantucket shoals, near Cape Cod. Nantucket shoals are famous for their dangerous sailing conditions because of the shallow waters and strong currents. There are lots of shipwrecks there. I also had to avoid Vineyard Sound because it was a busy shipping lane. My aim was to sail south of George's Bank, south of the Nantucket Shoals, and then head to Rhode Island Sound.

On 1st July, the dolphins came to visit me, as usual. It had become our daily routine. As I looked at one of my pals, we made eye contact. I knew that the dolphin understood me: we were friends. I was expecting the dolphin to laugh and splash and play in the sea, but instead it rolled onto its side and showed me its belly and swam away. I was puzzled; none of the dolphins had done this before, what could it mean? That was the last time I saw the dolphins. But soon afterwards, as *Quest II* sailed carefully through the fog, I spotted the first sign of life – an American fishing trawler on the portside.

I shouted, asking where Newport was, but all I could see was the captain on the bridge demanding with a phone hand shape that I pick up the phone. I shouted, 'I am deaf', and wrote on the back of my chart 'Where Newport?'

The boat ignored me and she sailed away through the fog. I was devastated and hoped that I had not sailed to Canada by mistake. But my gut told me that I must be heading in the right direction. Despite the fog, I had been able to follow one bright star and knew that I was heading towards Newport.

Then on 2nd July, after roughly a month at sea, the motions of *Quest II* changed and I could smell land. I knew there was sand close by. The fog was still heavy and sticking to my face. It was impossible to see anything from the cockpit. Something was troubling me. *Quest II* was sailing very fast (roughly 6-7 knots) in the strong breeze but there was something odd about the surface of the sea – it was flat.

There should have been ripples on the surface of the sea from the wind blowing above it. Something was definitely wrong and I knew I had to figure what was happening as quickly as I could. I looked down into the water for clues: seaweed or floating items that might give me an idea of what was nearby. The sea was muddy. It was impossible to work anything out.

I wondered if there was any possibility that the battery had recharged. I knew that if the battery was successfully recharging and I switched it off too soon, that I risked depleting the power. I had no choice. It was essential to get some information. The four small lights on the battery monitor came on. The bottom half of a series of four lights was visible. I picked up my pencil and watched the instrument display screen in the hope that I would get a reading. The numbers became visible. I scribbled down the numbers as quickly as I could: Lat 41 20 24N and Long 70 38 39W. A few seconds later, the fourth, third and the second light on the monitor flickered and then the battery cut out. I hurriedly plotted the position on the chart. I froze.

Quest II was heading at high speed straight towards Martha's Vineyard. I had no time to think. *Quest II* would hit the beach in less than a few minutes. I rushed up to the cockpit, grabbed the tiller and altered my course 180°. I stayed on course towards the east for few hours before going down below to check my position again. As I checked the chart, I could not believe my eyes. I had been within a few feet of the beach at Martha's Vineyard! I breathed a heavy sigh of relief as I thought of my narrow escape – especially as Martha's Vineyard was famous for its deaf community many years ago.

I studied my charts and plotted my route. My plan was to head south of Martha's Vineyard onwards to Newport, Rhode Island, but I had no way of knowing where I was. The fog was still thick and freezing and visibility was so poor I could barely see the length of *Quest II*. I prayed for the fog to lift. Only then would I be able to see lighthouses that would allow me to get my bearings, plot my position and navigate my route.

I decided to stay on the helm. I couldn't see a thing but I could smell fuel. And then, through a huge patch of grey fog, I could see the outline of a large ship travelling from right to left. It must have been a huge cargo ship or oil tanker. Later that afternoon, I spotted a powerboat to the left. It was flying at high speed across the sea and carrying the American flag. I shouted and pressed the foghorn to attract their attention. But this time, instead of showing my chart, I raised my Saltire flag to show them that I was from Scotland.

The man of the boat clapped with congratulations and nodding his head. He was about to speed off when I waved, 'No, no, no! Come back.' So he cruised nearby me, asking me what I wanted. I held my chart high: 'Where Newport?' He gestured to me, indicating the direction with his hand. I was heading straight towards Newport! I thought I must have been imagining things so asked again. He checked his phoned and showed me that I was only one to two miles from the finish line. I couldn't believe. I made it!

I looked at my bottle of whisky but thought, *I best not...* The Brenton Reef near Newport has lots of rocks. I had no engine power so I had to focus on carefully negotiating my way towards Newport. But I could see the beautiful colours of mountain tops peeping through the low-lying bank of fog. The fog did not lift until I reached Brenton Lighthouse.

I altered course to the finish line at Castle Hill Lighthouse then sailed onwards into Newport Yacht Club. A Dutch yachtsman (Leon Bart) spotted me entering the marina and came in his dinghy to tow me to the pontoon. The Rear Commodore (Norman P. Bailey Sr.) came out and shook my hand saying, 'Well done.' He told me that Chris Arscott had just left for the airport, and would be disappointed that he missed me. Then he handed me an envelope. I looked down. It was Kay's handwriting! There was no stamp on the envelope so I knew she must be close by.

'Where is she?'

Norman paused before replying, 'She is here. I will text her.'

It was getting dark as the evening approached. I had been waiting on board *Quest II* for Kay but decided I needed a short walk. As I made my way towards Newport Yacht Club, I looked for a moment. It was Kay, Nicola and Ashley. I couldn't believe my eyes. We ran to each other and hugged closely.

I yelled as I jumped backwards in pain. I was so pleased to see Kay and the girls that I had forgotten my broken ribs. The pain was excruciating. And then Kay asked, 'Do you know about Mary Brennan?'

'No, but she is busy working with the BSL Mathematics Glossary,' I replied.

It was then that Kay told me Mary had passed away. My eyes filled with tears of sadness. Mary had given the deaf community its most precious gift: recognition of our language and culture. And now she was gone. I asked when Mary had passed. Mary died on 23rd June. I returned to *Quest II* and looked at my log book.
23rd June 18.25:

'Something bothers me, 21, 22, and 23rd. My body feels strange and my ear is red. I wonder what it is this. I hope my family is ok.'

Unknown to me, the race organisers did not expect me to arrive at Newport. They knew I had no power, and without communication, had been unable to establish my position. It was not until *Pindar* spotted me on

29th June that they knew I was still alive. Newport Yacht Club sent a message out to the world via email:

'GERRY HUGHES ARRIVES IN NEWPORT
Gerry Hughes crossed the finishing line off Castle Hill, Newport at 11.30hrs (16.30hrs GMT) local time on Saturday morning and is now safely moored up at the Newport Yacht Club.'

I was sure I must have been the last boat in the race to arrive at Newport. But I was wrong. After thirty-four days, four hours and fifteen minutes at sea, I was in 16th place out of the forty-two boats in the Corinthian Race. I was given the 'Spirit of Corinthian' award for OSTAR 2005. I was delighted because the OSTAR skippers vote to decide who receives this award.

Dinner with my family on the eve of departure day, OSTAR 2005.

My living quarters during OSTAR 2005.

Damage to self-steering safety tube during the storm.

Welcome calm after the storm. It didn't last long

Pindar. Pindar (an Open 60) reported my position to the coastguard.

Quest II is becalmed for eight days near Newfoundland.

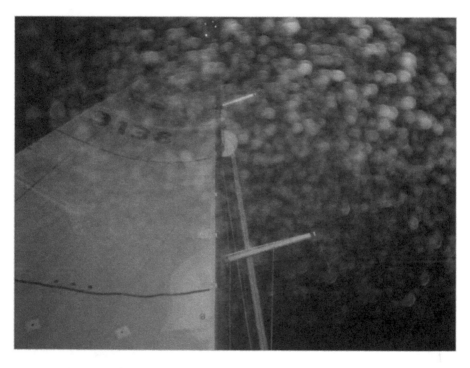

Freezing fog in the North Atlantic Ocean

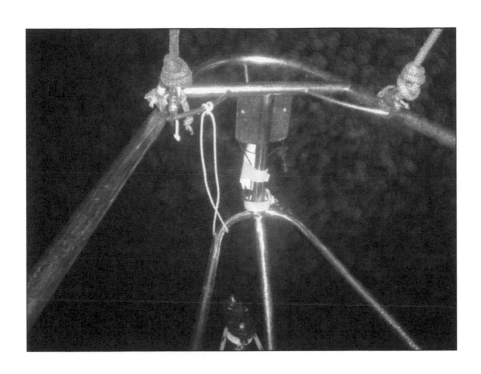

My makeshift navigation light made from a battery-operated torch. Essential
equipment for navigating through a shipping lane in the fog.

Heading towards the shipping lanes near Newport Rhode island

Me and the oil lamp.

Quest II resting at Newport Yacht Club, Rhode Island, USA.

Chapter 9: Beneteau 42s7? No Chance!

As I prepared myself to return to school after the summer holiday and OSTAR, I wondered whether any of the pupils had been following my web updates while I was crossing the Atlantic. I really hoped that they had been able to follow them but my webpage was not ideal for deaf pupils because it was based on written English. I knew that, ideally, I should have uploaded videos in BSL so they would have direct access to the information, but I didn't have the budget to do this. I felt that this would have been a better way to provide the pupils with the opportunity to see that a deaf person (just like them) was achieving their dreams, and that being deaf didn't mean that they lacked the skills and abilities to have ambitions of their own.

When I arrived at school, I was delighted to learn that the supply teacher who had covered my class had been covering my voyage. She had collected information and printed out drawings and diagrams to explain my OSTAR voyage to the pupils. As usual, the staff and pupils were called to the first school assembly of the year. Everyone gathered in the assembly hall at school to exchange news about what happened over the summer holidays.

The staff stood along the back of the hall in a big banana-shaped curve. The head teacher invited the staff, one by one, to tell the pupils about their summer break. I watched as the children 'listened' to the stories, waiting for my turn, looking forward to telling them about OSTAR. But, for some reason, I was missed out and the teacher next to me started to tell their story about the summer holidays. I was puzzled. I looked around and watched as all the other staff were given an opportunity to tell the pupils about their summer holidays. It was difficult to follow what they were saying because they were talking. The head teacher signed as the teachers spoke, but I could see that there was missing information. Then, out of the blue, while one of the teachers was talking, a pupil stood up and signed:

'Gerry sailed far, far away to America. I saw it!'

The head teacher snapped at the pupil: 'Sit down and don't be rude.' I watched the pupils folded their hands together and sat in silence. As the end of assembly approached, I realised that I was not going to be invited by the head teacher to tell my story to the pupils. I looked around at the other staff. They dropped their heads to avoid eye contact with me. I was deeply hurt. I felt that I had been humiliated in front of the staff and pupils.

Why were these deaf children not allowed to see the real story of an adventure of a deaf person just like them?

I felt myself being transported back to my own days at school when sign language was banned and I was struggling to lip-read. I was angry but I bit my lip and said nothing. Once I had calmed down, I asked another member of staff: 'Did the head teacher forget to ask me?' He replied: 'Best just stay calm and say nothing.'

But I couldn't stay calm. Inside, I was confused and in turmoil. What was the head teacher trying to tell me by ignoring me like that? Was I invisible to the other teachers in the school? My colleagues in the school were gifted and intelligent but they did not see education of deaf pupils in the same way as me. Just like them, I had attended teacher training college, spent hours and hours studying and learning about teaching and professional practice. I was applauded when I gave my presentation in Professional Studies, stating that having deaf teachers working in education should be a source of pride to the teaching profession and deaf people, because it was a sign that we were breaking down the barriers.

My own experiences had taught me the importance having the confidence to ask questions, learn about the world and access information without worrying about struggling to understand what I was being told. My parents moved me to a boarding school in England to give me the chance of an education. When I returned to Glasgow I was appalled that none of my mates had ever sat formal examinations. I thought about the pupils in our school and realised that, despite my efforts, nothing had really changed. We were still failing our deaf pupils. I felt tortured inside, asking myself the same questions over and over again: *Why is this still happening? When will this stop? When will someone see what is happening to our deaf children? A deaf pupil is a person not a child that needs to be 'fixed'. Deaf children should be encouraged to strive to reach their full potential in education. Hearing children have two-way communication at all times in school; why can't deaf children have the same? There are children who are hard of hearing and for whom 'listening' and lipreading works in the classroom. But what about the deaf children who are native sign language users? Why are they still expected to sit in the classroom with a radio aid straining to listen and lip-read? When will our deaf children get the opportunity to develop their ability in critical thinking and problem solving? What is happening here?* Eventually, I began to doubt whether I had any meaningful role in the school.

A few months later, the BBC broadcast an episode of *See Hear* (the main magazine programme for deaf viewers) featuring my experiences in

OSTAR 2005. I made a video recording of the programme and asked the head teacher whether it might be possible to show the video at school. I thought it might be interesting for the pupils to see it because it was about a teacher in their school. We could use it to have discussions with pupils to encourage them to think about their own ambitions and how they might achieve them. I hoped that it might help towards their personal and social development. I was gutted when I was told that the pupils could watch ten minutes per week and no more than that.

The more I thought about our pupils, the more sceptical I became. I wanted people to listen to deaf people and value their opinions and experiences. I invested my time in researching as much as I could into the education of deaf children. The more I investigated, the more evident it became to me that deaf pupils are labelled as having Special Educational Needs. And while it was true that some of our pupils had learning disabilities or other challenges that had to be considered in the class, many of our pupils were bright and eager to learn. They just happened to be deaf. They did not have Special Educational Needs. They needed access to education in British Sign Language. But, I knew that nobody was listening to me.

I applied for a Master's Degree to train become a chartered teacher in the hope that this might add authority to my arguments about the education of deaf pupils. I felt heart-broken as I watched what was happening around me – so many bright young people failed by the education system.

I remember one day, in particular. We were called to the assembly hall. Crisps and drinks were handed out to everyone and there was a big cake ready. This meant we knew to expect good news and that the school had something to celebrate. By that time, the Scottish Qualifications Authority (SQA) allowed examination questions to be delivered in BSL and pupils could sign their answer to camera or (write their answer, if that suited them). One of my pupils had passed a formal science examination by accessing her exam in BSL. This pupil was the very first person in her family to pass a formal examination by using BSL and her mum had been thrilled when the news arrived about her success. I was really pleased because I thought this must be to celebrate the good news of our pupil's success. She was a role model for others in the school and had inspired other pupils with her success – they were aiming to sit and pass their exams as well. The head teacher announced the reason for the celebration: one of the teachers passing their basic BSL qualification[16]. I was shocked. I looked across at the pupil who was looking confused and bewildered. I wondered what she was thinking to herself; was she wondering whether

---

[16] This level of BSL is the equivalent of having the fluency of a five-year-old.

the school felt that a teacher passing a basic sign language qualification was considered more important than the success of the pupils?

I discretely asked, 'Did the head teacher congratulate you on your success?'

She replied, 'No.'

I could feel my stomach churning. What could I do to help people see the significance of this young person's achievement? I knew I had to stay silent. I would achieve nothing by losing my temper.

But as time passed, I felt the anger and frustration deep inside my gut continue to grow. Eventually, I awoke one morning and asked myself. *What is the point working in the classroom if I am not allowed to collaborate or have input into decisions about the education of deaf children?* I knew that if I continued like this, the anger would eat me up and make me ill.

I thought about the years and years I spent campaigning to become a teacher. I was now a chartered teacher, but I felt that all my efforts were in vain. My ideas and suggestions about educating deaf children seemed to have no value to those around me – I might as well just throw them into the dustbin.

I would watch the pupils in the classroom. They were so full of energy and fun, excitedly chatting and asking questions in sign language. But when the bell rang? We left the classroom and entered a different world, a world where we were considered 'impaired' and unable to achieve. I thought about all the medical and educational professionals who believed that priority must be given to listening and speaking and that sign language should not be encouraged or, at best, used only as a last resort to communicate with a deaf child (when lipreading failed).

I would walk along the corridor and see two different worlds in our school: the staff talking to each other while the pupils were communicating with each other in sign language. It seemed that sign language (the natural language of these deaf pupils) was regarded as having no value.

Although I was a fully trained deaf teacher, I was never asked for my views or advice on deaf issues. There was no joy in my life at school. I felt like a prisoner in jail looking through the bars of his cell to the world outside. But for me, the bars of my cells were communication and oralism, and the outside world was that of the hearing professionals who taught deaf pupils.

The legacy of Milan 1880 lived on in deaf education and I knew that there was no way I could fight it on my own. Deaf people were considered disabled. Being deaf was still treated as a learning disability because we could not 'speak' and 'listen' like hearing people. Every day the teachers checked that the pupils were wearing their hearing aids and that their hearing aids were switched on. The teachers covered their mouths with paper while speaking to check that the pupils were 'listening'. Deaf children were not expected to achieve in the same way as their hearing peers and were being 'saved' from disappointment by making their life easier at not having to worry about exams. There was only one thing I could do – try a new challenge to make people wake up and see that deaf people **could** do it.

The thoughts swirled around in my head. I looked back over my life and my dad's decision to move me to a boarding school for the sake of my education. I knew it had torn him apart inside sending me away to another country to attend school. And then there was eighteen years of campaigning to be allowed access to teacher training in Scotland. At one point, the General Teaching Council suggested that I should move to England and pursue a career in England, but I was determined to teach in Scotland. Still, despite my upset and disillusionment, I believed there was future for deaf education.

I thought about the snowdrop in early March. I love snowdrops. They are so tiny and beautiful but very strong and resilient. The snowdrop draws strength from its core and signals to us that the harsh winter is over and spring is on its way. Watching the snowdrops had taught me to think about how I lived my live. I knew that if I drew upon my inner strength to endure the pain and frustration of the barriers put in front of me, I would achieve my dreams. I knew that I had to do something to make the world think differently about deaf people and demonstrate that, given the opportunity, deaf children could achieve as much as their hearing peers.

I was tired and frustrated by the low expectations of deaf children. And I believed deep in my gut that the key to success for deaf children was fluent two-way communication in their native language: sign language. I thought back to my promise to myself when I was fifteen and the note I scribbled to Dad on the newspaper featuring Sir Francis Chichester: *'One day I will go like Sir Francis.'* I knew what I was going to do. I would sail around the world via the Five Great Capes. It would be tough, but I knew I had the skills and ability to do it.

I contacted the head of education with my proposal but was refused a leave of absence. I tried a second time but got the same response: I must stay at school to sign with the deaf children. I thought about other (hearing) teachers who were given leave to play sports, such as hockey and rugby. I became more and more frustrated, asking myself, *where do I go from here?* I felt unable to contribute anything to the school. It seemed my only value was to sign to deaf children, but I could not try to influence how deaf pupils were educated.

I spent months and months thinking over what I should do. Should I remain at school and become a deaf activist? Should I start a political campaign to secure the human rights of deaf children? When I was in the classroom, I watched pupils, busy working on their studies and unaware of the challenges that lay ahead of them when they left school.

Sometimes I looked out of the window towards the trees that lay beyond the flat-roofed building. I loved to watch the changing seasons but, more and more, I found myself contemplating the world that was waiting for the pupils when they left school. Life is very tough for deaf people in a hearing world. They would face discrimination and barriers every day.

It broke my heart to think of how difficult their lives would be. But I also had my own family to think about. I knew I might have to give up my job if I wanted to sail round the world. We had a mortgage to pay. Kay, Nicola and Ashley understood how dangerous sailing can be. Was it fair on them to put them through such stress?

I thought about Nelson Mandela who endured years of imprisonment to fight for his beliefs. There are seventy million deaf people in the world[17]. If I fight for justice in Glasgow and in Scotland, how many years of fighting and campaigning would it take until it made a difference to the lives of deaf children? But I have my sailing skills. I love the sea. It has always been my best friend. Only 200 yachtsmen and yachtswomen had ever succeeded sailing past all Five Great Capes since records began, when Joshua Slocum solo circumnavigated the world in 1895. So many had tried to sail this route but failed; what were the odds that a deaf yachtsman could do it and become Number 201 on the list? If I was successful? The seventy million deaf people could see that they can do anything they wanted as long as they believed in themselves and their abilities. My family believed in me and Robin Knox Johnston had said that he saw no reason why I could not sail round the world.

---

[17] Source: World Federation of the Deaf

As I reflected upon all these issues, I came to the conclusion that I had no future in the school. I knew that if I stayed, I would be betraying not only myself and my principles, but also the deaf people around me. So, with a heavy heart, I drafted my letter of resignation.

I held onto my draft resignation letter while I looked for a suitable boat for my challenge. I managed to track down an Open 50 based in Dartmouth. It was built by Mike Plant (in the USA). I knew the boat would be suitable for ocean sailing. I paid the deposit with an agreement to pay the balance in the New Year, subject to a satisfactory surveyor's report once we had travelled to Dartmouth to inspect the boat.

Just as Kay and I were getting ready to leave for Dartmouth, we received news that the boat had been sold. I was furious! Apparently, the owner had received an offer he could not refuse. In a few minutes, my dreams were shattered. I was going to have to start my search for the right ocean yacht all over again.

I spent weeks and weeks thinking about what I should do next. Then, one morning, I woke up and I suddenly thought about Bill McKay. Bill McKay is well known across the west coast of Scotland for his sailing skills. Bill competed in the 1979 Fastnet Race on his yacht *Pepsi* and survived the most ferocious storm.

Bill worked at the boatyard on the River Clyde, where my dad had wintered his boat. I loved it there. I was free to scramble about amongst the boats and would often see Bill and Dad chatting to each other. I wasn't sure if Bill was still working, so I jumped out of bed and checked the internet to see if I could find any information about him. I was delighted when I saw that he was still working and decided to send a quick email to him before work.

I typed something along the lines of: 'I do not think you will know me, but my father always talked about you. I need your advice on buying a yacht that is suitable for round the world ocean sailing and will meet my budget.' Bill replied that afternoon saying that he knew me very well and he would be very happy to help.

I didn't want to waste any time so I contacted Eddie Foley (a sign language interpreter), asking him if he was free to come to my house to interpret a telephone call to Bill.

I chatted to Bill, explained that I was aiming to solo-circumnavigate the world via the Five Great Capes and told him my budget. Bill suggested a Beneteau 42s7. I couldn't believe what I was being told. Beneteau are famous for the cruising yachts that are popular for recreational sailing. I thought he must have been joking!

'No chance!' I replied. 'That is a boat for sailing around the Greek Islands, not sailing round the world.'

Bill disagreed with me, saying that the 42s7 were very solid and fast and capable of sailing around the world. I refused to believe him. We argued back and forth. I just could not believe what he was saying. A Beneteau? No chance!

So, I was no further forward in my search for a boat. But I could not stop thinking about what Bill said to me. I mulled things over for weeks and weeks, and thought about what my dad had told me about Bill. My dad was in the Royal Navy and a skilled sailor. He really admired Bill's skills and knowledge of boats and sailing. I knew what my dad would say to me if I asked him what I should do. So, knowing that Dad would have told me to follow Bill's advice, I took a leap of faith and let Bill know that I was looking for a Beneteau 42s7.

Bill advised me that there was a 42s7 for sale in La Rochelle, France. Kay and I would have to fly to Paris and then get the TGV to La Rochelle. It was a cold, miserable February day in Paris as we boarded the train. I still had a nagging doubt in my mind about the suitability of the boat. I kept thinking, *can this really be the right boat for a sailing round the world?* When we arrived at La Rochelle, the broker took us to look around it.

She was on the dry dock but she looked so beautiful: strong and seaworthy. We climbed up the long steep ladder so we could look inside. Kay stepped on board and down the stairs into the cabin exclaiming, 'It's very nice.'

I couldn't believe my eyes. I had never seen anything like it! There were two toilets and showers and even a fridge. We didn't have anything like that when I was learning to sail.

While Kay busied herself checking the cabin, I climbed onto the deck. I placed my hand on the helm and cast my eyes beyond the deck. I had never sailed a boat like this (forty-two feet). She had a massive bow and there were large winches on either side. But, as my hand rested on the helm, I felt a connection with the boat and I knew we would work well together.

I thought about my childhood plans to build up my skills by sailing round the British Isles, then across the Atlantic and eventually around the world. I knew I had no chance of sponsorship because I would need to book and pay for sign language interpreters if I wanted to approach companies to seek sponsorship. That would take a huge chunk out of my budget. It would be wiser to use any funds to modify the boat to meet Ocean Safety Standards.

The only sponsors I had were Stephen and Debbie Gratton, who had kindly given me a cheque for £3,000 for my round the world kitty when I met them at the OSTAR reunion in 2009. Stephen raced in OSTAR 2005, in his boat *Amelie of Dart* (a Contessa 32). I thought about all those books I read that were written by solo circumnavigators. Most of them had managed to gain sponsorship for the voyages but Sir Robin Knox Johnston was different. He did not have any sponsorship. Sir Robin was not afraid to take a risk and do everything from scratch and keep trying until he succeeded. I was ready to do the same. I looked up at the mast and said to myself, *there is no going back now.*

After returning from La Rochelle, I had to attend a committee meeting for the 8th World Deaf Golf Championship, which was due to take taking place in St Andrews, Fife. I was waiting for the surveyors' report on the Beneteau 42s7 and was relieved when the surveyor contacted me to say the boat appeared to be in good condition.

The next thing was to organise a berth or mooring in the west coast of Scotland. I had been a member of Royal Gourock Yacht Club (RGYC) about twenty years before, when I had an East German Folkboat called *Faraway III*. I really enjoyed being a member of RGYC so emailed asking if they would accept my application for membership. The Commodore replied to say he would be happy to accept me as a member.

The Firth of Clyde can be very rough during winter, so I also needed access to a winter berth as well as a dry dock for working on the boat. I contacted Stephen Bennie, who runs Troon marina. Stephen offered me a special discount on the berthing fees at the marina as sponsorship on my project. I was delighted because it meant I would have more of my budget to spend on modifying the boat to meet Ocean Safety Standards.

With the mooring and berthing sorted, all I had to do was sail the boat back to the Firth of Clyde. My two friends, Mark McQueen and Erelend

Tulloch, agreed to be my crew. Both Mark and Erelend had sailing experience and had crewed for me before. The weather was not great when we arrived at La Rochelle. On 5th April, we sailed out of the marina to the Bay of Biscay and onwards to the Irish Sea, heading for the Firth of Clyde and Troon. I could see that the boat sailed well.

Bill McKay came to meet us when we arrived in Troon and smiled happily as he looked over the yacht. I had to acknowledge to Bill that he had been right all along and told him, 'It is very nice boat. From now on she will be called *Quest III*.'

I put my plans for sailing on hold for a few weeks while I focussed on the golf competitions that I had been selected to play in. We had a great time at the World Championships. Scotland won first place for the first time ever and I was very pleased with my own golf (I played as a senior and came fifth). But after the excitement of the summer, we received some devastating news.

On 6th September 2010 it was announced that our school for the deaf would close in October and the pupils moved into a mainstream environment in a secondary school near Glasgow City Centre. The deaf pupils would be placed in a 'Hearing Impairment Unit' within the school. I knew straight away that there was no point in challenging this decision, so opted to focus my efforts on ensuring that deaf pupils would have the right access to education and information in the classroom. I was really worried about what would happen to our pupils in a mainstream environment.

There were many long meetings to discuss the move. We were informed that that not all staff would be able to move and it was suggested that some may want to apply for voluntary redundancy, or apply to be transferred to schools elsewhere. At every meeting, I asked the same questions: what about the rights of deaf pupils to be educated in the way that is best for them?

At one meeting I was told that if I carried on like that I would be moved to a different school. Eventually, a senior teacher came to my room and cautioned me that if I continued to challenge the decisions that had been made, I was risking dismissal.

Adjusting to life in mainstream education was very difficult. St Roch's Secondary School was a different world. I had to rely on the support of our deputy head teacher, Tommy Donnelly, to keep me up to date with news and developments in the school. Tommy would let me know if there had been news announced on the TANNOY system, because it was impossible for me to hear it. Only a few of the staff in the Hearing Impairment Unit could sign, so I had no contact with the other teachers in the school. Sign language interpreters were booked for school meetings but, like all interpreters, they had to leave immediately after the meeting. I still had my letter of resignation but I was learning to work in a new environment so told myself it was best to give myself a few years to adjust.

Through time, I began to see that our head teacher (Gerry McGuigan) had a very clear vision for the school. Gerry believed that all pupils (including the deaf pupils) should be encouraged to achieve their ambitions. I could see the new opportunities were becoming available to our pupils, so I thought it best to discuss my plans with him before making my final decision and submitting my resignation.

We had always had BSL/English interpreters in school for 'in-service' days so, during one of these in-service days, I introduced myself to Gerry McGuigan, saying that we passed each other every day in the corridor but had never had a chance to talk. Gerry nodded. I asked whether it would be possible to book an appointment with him. He replied, 'of course' and a date was put in the diary.

I was very nervous, hoping that he might listen to my ideas. I prepared an outline of what I wanted to say to him and hoped that I would be able to convince him of the merit of my project: that it would provide young deaf people the opportunity to see that being deaf should not be a barrier to achieving ambitions.

I hardly slept the night before that meeting. I tossed and turned as I asked myself, *what will he think of me? What will he say? What if he felt the same way and refused permission?* On the morning 21st August 2011, my eyes kept darting to the clock. My meeting was at 09.15. I had spent so much time rehearsing what I wanted to say that my mind had gone blank.

I sat down opposite the head teacher. He sat back in his chair, with one leg folded over the other, his head lightly resting on his hand at the side of his face. His face was very, very, stern. When I saw how serious his face was, my mind went completely blank. I forgot what I had planned to say and began to wonder if any of the teachers had been talking to him about me. (I later found out that he was lost for words and was waiting for me to say something.)

After a short pause, I told him why I had asked for a meeting with him. I explained that I would like to ask for six months leave of absence for a sailing project.

'Where are you going?' he asked.

I replied, 'non-stop single-handed round the world via the Five Great Capes.'

His eyebrows shot up his forehead in surprise and he placed both hands firmly on the arms of his chair. 'Are you a sailor? That is unbelievable!'

And, for a minute, I did not need an interpreter. His face told me everything as he gave me a big *'thumbs up'*. From there on, we both relaxed and he explained to me that he had never had a one-to-one discussion with a deaf person via a sign language interpreter, and that this was a totally new experience for him.

He said that nobody had told him I was a skilled sailor. So, I explained my story and my love of sailing and how sign language was banned in schools across the world in 1880. I explained that under 'oralism', like many other deaf people, I struggled to read and write and about my years of campaigning to be allowed to train to be a teacher. He was shocked.

Gerry McGuigan agreed to give me a leave of absence saying, *'This is not about the deaf it is about the whole school seeing you sail around the world. This is fantastic.'* He told me that both he and our deputy head (Tommy Donnelly) would give me their backing. And so, on the 10th October 2011, Tommy emailed to tell me the good news! The Senior HR Officer had emailed to say I was granted my leave of absence and our head teacher, Gerry McGuigan offered congratulations and best of luck.

Then Tommy said, *'It is great that you are living your dream. I am happy that I know you will be coming back.'*

I threw my letter of resignation in the bin and thought about our head teacher: a man with no knowledge or experience of deaf issues but who could understand why this was so important to me. How could this man see what others could not? I was told that there had been an announcement via the loud speaker that Gerry Hughes was going to sail around the world non-stop, alone! With support from our school and the education department, I began to plan for the biggest and most dangerous challenge of my life.

My family (Nicola, Ashley and Kay). This photo was taken about a year before my solo circumnavigation.

Sally Morris (left) and Demi Stevenson during the test sail from Troon to Portugal, 2011. This was Sally's and Demi's first experience of being in a sailing crew.

Chapter 10: Remember me, to Bring Two Fishes Alive

I felt much more positive after I was granted a leave of absence because I had something to look forward to. There was a lot of work to do. I sat down at my kitchen table, opened an A4 notebook and started my action plan. By that time I had got to know *Quest III*, although she was a strong and solid boat, she was a cruising yacht designed for cruising from port to port and had been fitted with standard equipment for this type of sailing. I would need to modify *Quest III* to ensure she was ready to meet the challenges of the Southern Oceans.

I had already done some test sails with *Quest III* by sailing her home from La Rochelle and to Portugal so I knew that she had a comfortable and compact cockpit that had good foot bracing. This is essential for sailing on heel. I examined every inch of *Quest III*, taking notes to ensure I really understood the boat. Now that I had sailed *Quest III* and begun to understand her; I could see what Bill meant when he said she was strong and capable. But I had to be very honest with myself. I had never sailed at this level before. I knew that, no matter what boat I sailed, it was down to me, and my sailing skills, if I was going to complete the solo circumnavigation.

I didn't want to put a strain on *Quest III,* or force her to sail at speeds that were beyond her limit just to suit me. This would only cause damage (especially to her rudder). I would need to research what was required before making any decisions about the modifications. However, there was one large question I had to ask myself before starting: *Do I have the time to do all the work on my own*? The answer was a simple, *No*.

There was so much work to do that I knew I would need to ask people if they would be willing to volunteer their time to help me. The deaf community is very tight-knit and I know deaf people in Glasgow and across Scotland. Craig Speirs and Demi Stevenson kindly agreed to help me. That was great because communication was in British Sign Language. Craig and Demi are devoted Glasgow Rangers fans and I am a Celtic man so there were a lot of jokes about the best colour to paint *Quest III*.

Craig and I drove to Troon straight after school every day of the week. Every modification had to be completed step by step. I contacted Saturn Sails (a local company) and the Mast Rigging Service and showed them my plans for the masts and riggings. After many lengthy 'discussions', via passing written notes back and forth to each other, I was satisfied with the plans.

John Highcock (from Saturn Sails) gave me a discount on all the sails on board *Quest III* in exchange for me displaying the Saturn Sails logo on my sails. The next stage was to set up *Quest III* so the work could be done. I asked Troon Boatyard to prepare for the mast to be taken down. This would allow the Mast Rigging Service (MRS) to install new riggings that had a thicker diameter with a chain plate and new spreaders. I would need to be able to climb to the top of the seventy-foot mast if there was a problem while I was at sea, so I had twenty-seven composite steps fitted to the mast. I decided on for a Furlex 208S furling system for the staysail and Trysail track assembly. Selden Mast Ltd gave me a 50% discount on a gennaker bow spirit with CX25 Code 0 furler. Saturn Sails made a new small volume cone-shaped spray hood for *Quest III* free of charge. The batteries were secured by braces and a completely new set of electronics was installed: GPS, chart plotter, auto pilot and self-steering. The lockers inside *Quest III* were secured to ensure they could withstand the heavy seas (I knew I had to be prepared for the possibility of a knock down or even a capsize). *Quest III* was now prepared for the very worst conditions in the heavy seas.

When I wasn't working on *Quest III* or at school, I used my time to research my route and study maps. I investigated what foods I would need and how my nutritional requirements would change throughout the duration of the sail. I tried the freeze-dried food that a lot of sailors use when they are sailing.

My pupils had lots of questions about my plans. One day they asked me about the food I would be taking with me on my voyage and why. I decided to let the pupils see for themselves so I took in some samples and asked them 'whether they would like to taste for themselves'? The pupils agreed with me – it was horrible!

I pinned a Kelvin Hughes World Chart on the classroom wall and plotted the routes from the Vendee, Global and Velux Races from 2006 to 2010. As well as analysing the routes, I researched why these routes had been chosen (but, at the same time, bearing in mind that they had used much bigger yachts, such as an Open 60, Open 40 or 50). I also studied the routes taken by previous round the world yachtsmen. I collated all this information and used it to plan my route and calculate timings. As I did this, I took note of what to expect in terms of sailing and weather. This allowed me to create a schedule of what I would eat every day, taking into consideration sleeping patterns, when I would be able to rest and eat, and how my energy requirements would change with sailing and weather conditions.

I calculated that I would be using up to roughly 3,000–5,000 calories a day, and I also had to think about how I would store the food and the additional weight it would add to the boat. I had already changed my diet to match what I would be eating at sea. The starting point was pasta, potato, garlic, ginger and onions, then I added tinned tomatoes, baked beans, vegetables such as carrots, peas, runner beans, beetroot. The meat in my meals would be either corned beef or chopped ham. Fruit would be pear, apples, grapefruit, fruit cocktail, peach and pineapple. I added rice pudding, custard and, most important of all, porridge. I would also have water, coffee, soup and oatmeal and fruit juice on board.

I needed a stock of sugary foods for times when I would need a quick energy burst, so decided upon chocolate digestives, Mars bars and sweets. I would also take a stock of small cartons of apple juice and Ribena, knowing that I could put them in my pockets and drink them while at the helm and maintain my fluid intake in heavy seas.

While I was researching my food and nutrition, I came across ready meals called *Look What I Found*. They were delicious. I decided to take some with me and use them as a treat while I was away.

I had to prepare myself for the ferocious storms that I might face. After a lot of research, I decided to buy a Jordan series drogue. The series drogue was designed by Donald Jordan. If I needed to slow the boat, I could throw the series drogue and it would trail from the stern. It looks like a line with a lot of small cones woven into it and has a small length of chain at the end of it that acts as a weight. The number of cones needed is determined by the yacht displacement. The cones cause drag on the boat, preventing it from surfing the waves. This means that the yacht will accelerate down the face of a wave, but it will slow it enough to pass through it without dropping in to the trough. The drag force is applied softly, allowing acceleration until enough cones bite.

I sent a text message to my golf mate, Craig Rayment. Craig is deaf, a BSL user and the secretary of Glasgow Deaf Golf Club and played for Scotland in International Deaf Golf Championships. I asked Craig if he could come over to Troon and build strong and secure stainless-steel brackets for the series drogue at both sides of the stern hull. Craig also set up the satellite and wind vane mount. It was great to be able to discuss what was needed in sign language. It made communication so much easier. Craig did a beautiful job. I was very pleased with it.

I was really busy and making progress but, by the end of February, I was feeling tired and I could feel my energy levels dropping. I knew this was partly due to the long, damp, dark winter months but also because my pupils at school were preparing for their exams. My pupils were constantly on my mind. I began to wonder if I would be able to complete all the modifications in time. I decided to ask for more help. Erelend Tulloch and Graham Craddock agreed to assist me.

One of the biggest decisions I had to make was about the power supply while I was sailing. I discussed this in detail with Robert Hogg at his Autofreeze garage in Cambuslang. I met Robert shortly after I bought *Quest III*. The heater was not working. I had asked my mate Erelend to have a look at it but when he checked it he advised it would be best to ask a qualified engineer.

I checked online to see if I could find an engineer who could deal with the heating systems on boats. I was surprised when I spotted a company in Cambuslang (just a few miles from my house) that specialised in commercial refrigeration and heating systems. I contacted them and asked if they could fix *Quest III's* heating system. I was really impressed by Robert and his straight talking and we developed a really good rapport. It turned out he had worked on boats and his father worked on cargo ships. We spent hours and hours in the cold damp garage, surrounded by engine parts, wiring and equipment lying around the workshop on the concrete floor, discussing the power supply requirements during the sail.

I had four options to maintain my power supply while I was at sea: solar panels, wind vane, hydro generator, or generator. I also had to think about which batteries to use and how best to preserve the power. I calculated the total power consumption on the chart plotter, autopilot, radar and AIS. The demands on the power supply were adding up very quickly. This meant I had to think of ways to minimise energy usage and also about how much fuel I would need on board *Quest III*. I read about solar power, towed generators and the latest developments in marine engineering.

Robert's experience meant that he understood power usage and fuel consumption on boats. Although Robert did not know sign language, he understood that it was difficult for me to understand him via lipreading so he drew diagrams of wiring and positioning on his white board. This made it much easier for me to understand his opinions on this.

The chart plotter and autopilot would be in use at all times; they could be switched off to save energy but they had to be switched on while the auto helm was in use. This meant it was essential to ensure that there was enough energy/fuel to power them. Our conversations went on for hours and hours. Eventually, after weeks of research and discussions with as many people as I could find who had knowledge of this, I decided to follow Robert's advice and buy a diesel generator. This would allow me to use the autopilot, but crucially, also preserve power for communicating via my laptop. I cannot use a VHF radio so I had to prioritise the laptop to allow me to communicate. I could always resort to self-steering and I would use an oil lamp at night to save power.

A portable generator is risky in heavy seas – even if they are secured by braces. In addition, the fuel tank for a portable generator cannot be used when a boat is at heel 30° or more. I was also concerned that a portable generator would not last the full duration of the journey. We agreed a plan to install the Fischer Panda generator on a welded frame for strength and safety.

Quest III was taken out of water for few days and my mates agreed to help me with the installation. The design generator mount was set up in March. Robert and I inspected it closely before going ahead with the welding. Craig Rayment fitted new handles inside to allow me to brace in heavy seas. These would provide security during heavy weather sailing because I could hold onto them when my balance was affected and would help prevent being knocked down by waves and injured by high waves. Craig Speirs, John Church and Demi made a great job of anti-fouling the hull.

I bought the equipment I needed for ocean safety and survival: a sea survival suit, Ocean Safety Katadyn water maker (for converting sea water to drinking water) and I made up my emergency grab bag. I was planning to take *Quest III* on a test sail over the Easter Holidays, but it was impossible because there was one delay after another. I became more and more frustrated with each delay; time was tight and I couldn't afford to lose time.

One morning in mid-March, I woke up, switched on my bedside lamp, and decided to have a quick look at the text messages on my phone before having a shower. At the back of my mind was one nagging doubt: was I asking too much of my family? I began asking myself, *what on earth am I doing? I have spent two years preparing for sailing round the world: driving to Troon every day after work (and weekends) to make sure I am home for 10 p.m. every night to be ready for teaching in the classroom in the morning? Should I just forget sailing and focus on golf? There is far less pressure. I wouldn't need to worry about how to make phone calls, all the expenses of sailing and all the money being spent with no sign of sponsorship. What had got into my head?*

It was time to install the generator. Robert brought his van down to Troon. The new generator was bloody heavy! It took four of us (including Robert's father) to move the generator. It just managed to stay on the wheelbarrow as we gingerly maneuvered it along to pontoon. All eyes were on the generator. It was worth over £6,000 and could easily slip off the wheelbarrow and off the narrow pontoon into the sea.

When we arrived *Quest III*, we lifted the generator from the wheelbarrow onto the deck. Next, we shuffled the generator down into galley and into the berth. It was a real struggle. But eventually, in April, the new generator mounting was established and fitted, with the generator fixed on top with strong thick black rubber. It looked good and professional.

On 10th May, I had another setback. I was struck with a bad flu virus. It meant I was stuck in the house and unable to work on *Quest III*. I had only three months left until I planned to set sail, and I had to fit a test sail into the schedule. I didn't want to waste time so I sent a text message to Eddie Foley asking if he was free to come over to my house to interpret a few phone calls. I continued my research and preparation by examining the Piracy and Armed Robbery Map of 2012. The symbols on the map showed actual pirate attacks, and attempted pirate attacks. There was a recorded risk of piracy between Brazil and west of Africa. I plotted these attacks (recorded and attempted) on my charts to ensure I could avoid sailing into these areas.

On 21st May, Graham Craddock, his teenage son (Sean) and Craig Spiers came down to Troon to set up satellite fleet broadband, check the wiring and make sure that everything was working properly. At the same time, I wrote to my GP to ask if there were any specific health risks that I should be aware of overseas. I had to ensure that I had the right items in my first aid kits. I also asked my dentist to check my teeth and asked him to advise me what I should do if I had any trouble with my teeth during my voyage.

I spent every spare moment on *Quest III*. One day while I was inside the boat (everyone was busy securing new hatch lockers), I looked at the washboard. I wondered to myself what would happen if I capsized? It could open slightly and I realised that if I capsized, the water ingress would mean that the weight of the water could pull the boat deep into the sea. I decided to install a special lock on the washboard.

By 31ˢᵗ May I could feel that I was losing weight. My trousers were loose around my waist and I had to tighten my belt another notch. I could now see my cheekbones clearly when I looked in the mirror to shave. I checked my weight. I had lost just over one stone in a few months. My weight dropped from 13.5 stone to 12.3 stone. But I was not surprised that I was losing weight. I spent every spare moment working on *Quest III* and travelling between Glasgow and Troon.

I decided on PredictWind for weather and sea data. I had a number of reasons for this. PredictWind provides data for wind speeds, direction and also the swell height and the directions. It also has an emergency alert facility but, most importantly, PredictWind can be connected to email at a lower cost than satellite fleet broadband. This would allow me to keep in touch with Kay. I could press an SOS Alert button and it would send out an emergency signal to Kay's family and the coastguard with details of my location and position. The other big advantage is that PredictWind provided regular weather forecasts (essential for a deaf person who can't use long range radio) and routing information. I used this for customised GPS tracking, which was linked to the homepage of my website so people could follow my progress. I knew this would be important for deaf pupils to be able to follow my route visually without having to worry about language barriers.

I knew that PredictWind was the best option for me, but I had one big problem: I have never really understood technology. So I asked my mate Jim Colhoun if he could help me. Jim had also played for St Vincent's Football Team when we went to Rome for the European Cup. Thankfully, Jim agreed to teach me a few things so I would be able to manage the technology while I was at sea.

I was making progress with my preparations for sailing round the world but progress was slow. There were so many delays that my plans were in danger of becoming a mess. By 6ᵗʰ June 2012, I was becoming increasingly frustrated. The new riggings were delayed. It seemed that every time I tried to communicate with people, I faced another delay because I had to rely on email. Hearing people can just pick up a phone to talk to someone. The delays meant that I had to cancel my plans for a test sail to the Azores via the Scilly Isles. I could feel my mood changing. I was depressed, angry, and struggling to stay focussed on my goal. And then my mind would turn to my family. I was worried that I was not spending enough time with Kay, Nicola and Ashley while I was busy in Troon preparing *Quest III*. In addition, my funds were disappearing and I still had food, sailing gear and some more equipment to buy. I became more and more annoyed with myself for failing to gain sponsorship and asked myself why I was doing this. I had been advised that I would need to have a budget to pay a sign language interpreter if I wanted to spend time for public relations (e.g. meeting companies to ask for sponsorship). Paying an interpreter would take a huge chunk out of my budget (my life savings) so I was forced to decide between booking an interpreter or using what money I had left to make sure *Quest III* was ready to leave on 1st September. As my mood darkened, I became bad-tempered and caught myself swearing regularly. I was ready to cancel the whole thing.

But then something remarkable happened! Late one evening, Kay and I were alone at home chatting. My mind was not fully focussed on the conversation because I was busy thinking, *when should I tell Kay that I might have to postpone my round the word sailing for another year or so?* Our lights flashed in the dining room, letting us know that someone had pressed the doorbell. I wasn't expecting visitors so thought, *Who can that be?*

It was Joel Kelhoffer. Joel is well known in the deaf community for his media business AC2.Com Productions. I had known Joel for many years but was wondering why on earth he had come to our house. Joel told me that there was talk across the deaf community of Glasgow that Gerry Hughes was getting ready to sail around the world (news travels very, very, quickly in the deaf community!).

I told him that the rumours were true. At that point I needed some support in setting up a webpage that I could update while I was at sea so people could track my voyage via PredictWind and read my online log. Joel agreed to help me by setting up my new website. It would be expensive but it was still less than I would have had to spend on booking a sign language interpreter to work with me on PR to raise funds. Crawford Carrick Anderson (a deaf friend from Dunbar) designed my logo. Crawford is very well known in the mountain biking world.

I felt my spirits lift as we chatted in sign language about my plans for my website because I knew that the deaf community were happy to back me up. I was keen to ensure that my website did not reveal too much information until I was ready to leave. After all, there might be another deaf person who could find out about my plans and try to beat me to being the first deaf yachtsman to sail via the Five Great Capes.

And then I had some more great news. Eddie Foley volunteered to back me up. He interpreted phone calls, and then a meeting at Duncan Yacht Chandlers. That was great because they agreed to discounted prices. Finally, the new spray hood was installed and the life raft arrived. My mate

Erelend bought me a new oil lamp, very similar to the one that I have on the bulkhead. This meant that I had one on 'stand-by' for when the light went low and needed a refill.

By that time, my Garmin electronics had been professionally installed, but for some reason it was not working. The AIS was not transmitting my position. I tried switching it on but, when Robert checked his mobile, there was no sign of *Quest III*. I had to think what to do. I called Garmin directly from *Quest III* while she was at her mooring in the Firth of Clyde at the Royal Gourock Yacht Club (RGYC). I had no option: I would need to book a sign language interpreter again.

On 21st June, I drove to RGYC with Jim and Stephanie McQuillan. Stephanie can communicate via sign language and was volunteering at St Roch's Secondary School. Stephanie agreed to interpret a call for me. There were four things that needing to be sorted: AIS Garmin, Garmin Homeport on to Garmin Chart plot, set up the satellite fleet broad band, and then connect PredictWind to my laptop for weather routing and connection to the chart plotter. The AIS would not function.

I asked Stephanie to interpret another phone call to Garmin. The Garmin equipment would not accept the MMSI number. The software was set up so I should have been be able to click the image of the boat and get a pop-up message asking for my password. It wouldn't work. I was advised to take this to Duncan Yacht Chandlers and exchange it for a replacement. There was still a problem with the chart plotter. It was showing error messages and depth readings kept flashing. I had no alternative but to take it back to Duncan Yacht Chandlers for inspection.

I still had to take *Quest III* out for a test sail. I had been forced to cancel my plans for a test sail to the Azores so decided to try a test sail to Barra, via the Mull of Kintyre. Erelend was not able to crew for me but Sally Morris and Demi wanted to come along. Both Sally and Demi had been sailing with me before and made a great crew.

Demi sailed with us to Portugal and I could see her eyes were skilled and sharp and that she was sensitive to changes in the wind. Sally is well known for her skills in keeping the boat ship-shape and tidy and looking after the rest of the crew by doing things like making us a wee mug of coffee. I was delighted to have Demi and Sally crewing for me because I knew I could rely on them and it would be a great opportunity for them to see whether they would like to do more sailing for themselves later in their lives.

I felt much better when I returned from our test sail to Barra. There were one or two things that needed sorting out, but I was delighted with the series drogue after I tested it in the Atlantic Ocean. The sails performed well and I was satisfied that they would cope with the voyage. I was happy with my electronic equipment and the layout inside the boat. I felt happy knowing that I could now move on to thinking about buying the food supplies, books and charts that I would need for my journey. I had to have charts ready so I could still navigate if the electronics failed. I also contacted a company called Team Hado Ltd who specialised in translating between BSL and English, and vice versa. I asked if they would consider sponsoring me by providing back up for my blog. They agreed that in exchange for free advertising on my website, they would proofread my blog so it could be published online.

On 18th August, my friends held a fund-raising party to support my solo circumnavigation. I couldn't believe it when I was told that the committee at St Vincent's Centre for the Deaf decided to support me by donating £2,000 to the costs of my project. It was fantastic news. I had spent so much money so it was great to have something to help reduce the amount of debt I was building up. My friends raised £1,310 at the party so that meant in total I was given £3,130. What a great night!

On 20th August, I received an email from the Maritime and Coastguard Agency (MCGA) to tell me they were aware of my intention to solo circumnavigate via the Five Great Capes and that they wished me all the best for my journey. Then I went over to see my lawyer and hand in my will. I knew I had to have this sorted out if the worst should happen while I was at sea.

I started stocking up on foods, but on 21st August my mum was admitted to hospital because she had been unwell. I could feel the pressure mounting as I waited for a full report from her doctor. Mum had become very frail and I worried about leaving her. But I also knew that, even though she did not like my sailing adventures, she would never try to stop me.

When the BBC broadcast the *See Hear* programme about OSTAR 2005, Kay and I had flown to Plymouth for the OSTAR reunion. Helen Dunipace came with us to interpret. Mum telephoned us after watching the programme and Helen interpreted the call for us. Mum told us she was so proud of her son but was horrified when Sir Robin Knox Johnston said he saw no reason why I should not attempt to sail round the world. She warned us, *I have my handbag ready for that man if I ever meet him!*

I had already announced my departure date from Troon via a BSL video on my website (1st September) and I could feel the clock ticking. At least ten deaf people came down to Troon to finish off what still needed to be done to ensure *Quest III* and I were ready for departure. They helped with stowing the food supplies, first aid etc. Robert managed to get the water lock and get the generator fixed as smooth as possible. I checked through all my lists to make sure I had everything I needed. I knew I could leave toiletries until a few days before leaving. My priority was to make sure *Quest III* was ready. Then I could spend time with Kay and the family before leaving.

On 23rd August, we drafted a press release for the *Scottish Yachtsman*, telling them that I was aiming to be the first deaf person to sail single-handed non-stop around the world. On 27th August, Robert came on board *Quest III* to do the final checks of the oil, belt and engine. It was great to know that the generator was working well because I needed this to feed the batteries. But the AIS was still not working and it was impossible to trace my boat. *Quest III* was berthed in Troon. I had set the AIS to transmit but, according to the technology, *Quest III* was in Largs. I could not believe it. I also checked the satellite and emergency equipment such as flares and lifejackets.

On Tuesday 28th August, with just a few days left before setting off on 1st September, Erelend, Jim, the two Craigs, Demi and Kay came on board *Quest III* to help with checking over the boat and equipment. We sailed *Quest III* out of the marina to have final check for AIS, and then returned to fill up with fuel and water. Jim was standing nearby me and I asked him to lower himself so I could see. But when he lowered himself, his new iPhone dropped out of his tracksuit pocket, bounced straight off the deck and into the water at Troon marina near the fuel bay. Poor Jim! I can still see his face. He was devastated at losing his phone but was trying to reassure me that I shouldn't worry because it wasn't that important – after all, I was about to sail around the world.

Friday 31st August 2012 arrived. It was my last day on dry land before joining *Quest III* to meet great seas and oceans of the world. I relaxed in my bed for a few minutes before getting up. I thought back over the previous two years of driving back and forth to Troon every day to make sure *Quest III* was ready for the challenge ahead. I didn't know how I had managed to summon up all that energy for the months and months of work that needed to be done. I felt blessed to have the support of Kay, my family and all my friends. I got up knowing I had just had my last sleep in my own bed and that, for the next six months or so, I would be sleeping on board *Quest III*. I knew I would be comfortable while I was at sea.

Every morning, Kay and I drove to school together via Glasgow Green. On that morning, like many mornings before, we stopped at the traffic lights, waiting for them to change to green. Kay was sitting next to me, busy on her iPhone, reading and answering text messages. I turned to look at the trees in the Green, noticing that the leaves were starting to change colour – autumn was approaching. I love watching the changing seasons and the mellow colours of autumn. I looked at the trees again. They were the same trees that I had been looking at for many, many years, (sometimes on our way to and from school, and all those years ago when we did our football training at Glasgow Green). A thought drifted into my head: *I wonder if I will see these trees again? Will I come home?*

There was a wee surprise farewell party in the classroom to wish me good luck and I gave a short speech. I told the deaf pupils not to be afraid to speak their minds and follow their dreams. At the end of the speech, one first year pupil put up his hand and asked if I could bring him one or two live fishes when I came back to school. I was told that, just before the school bell was due to ring, an announcement came over the school TANNOY

Pray for Gerry and Good luck.

When the bell rang, Gerry McGuigan and Tommy Donnelly came down to the car park to say cheerio and good luck to me. Then Kay and I drove home to get ready to leave for Troon later that evening. We loaded everything into my car. I checked everything.

Kay was in the front room packing a box, but she wouldn't let me into the room. Every time I asked her what was in the box she replied that it was just a few things for Christmas. I smiled to myself thinking of how lovely it was that Kay had wrapped up presents for me to open on Christmas Day, but I could not help wondering how I was going to fit the huge box in the tiny forward bunker. I asked again about the contents of the box, explaining I needed to know if there were any bottles in it because I would need to look after them in stormy weather. Kay just ignored me and asked me to lift the box and put it into the car. It was really heavy.

We arrived in Troon and I prepared myself to make my final checks. I knew a few of my local deaf mates would be there to help me, but I wasn't expecting to see so many deaf people from outside Glasgow. It was lovely to see them. They were very excited and asked to see the boat. I couldn't say no but, at the back of mind, I could not stop thinking of the long list of checks I still had to make.

Scott Campbell explained to me in BSL how to set up my digital camera. My mind was buzzing while I tried to concentrate and follow his instructions. Jim was busy trying to set up the laptop. I had three laptops with me, to make sure I always had one on standby for communication and then, out of the blue, my sailing pals from England 'the three crazy men' (Matthew, Mike and Andrew) appeared. I wasn't expecting them but it was great to see them and it took me back to our days of sailing in the Bay of Biscay. Craig, Demi and Scott emptied the car boot and followed my instruction on where to put everything. I told them just to put everything in the forward berth because I would have time to sort through everything when I was sailing.

Eventually, one by one, people drifted over to the Harbour Bar across the road from the marina. We had agreed to meet there for a farewell drink. I am well known in the Harbour Bar. It was where we met for a farewell drink before I set off to sail around the British Isles and also before setting off for OSTAR. Now I was getting ready to sail around the world.

Finally, I was ready to disembark from *Quest III*. But as soon as I did this, I got straight back on board and returned to the skipper's desk and picked up the book with all my checklists in it. I needed one last look to make sure I had not missed anything. I climbed up onto the deck and placed my hand on the wheel and thought about what lay ahead and it hit me: this is really happening! For forty years, I dreamed of sailing round the world, and now I was really going to do it. I spent years and years reading, and watching documentaries about great sailing adventures, and now my time had come. I felt as if I had been given the greatest treasure – the opportunity to experience for myself the magical world of the great oceans.

The last two years had been so busy. And now? For the first time, I was completely alone with *Quest III*. My mind was quiet. I cast my eyes up the towering strong aluminium mast soaring into the peaceful early evening sky. It was dusk and it was twinkling softly as the remaining light from the sun dipped over the horizon. I made a final inspection of *Quest III* and calmly told myself, *I am nearly there.*

I felt warm and content inside as I slowly walked up the pontoon towards the gate. I turned to look back at *Quest III*. She was gently resting at her berth. Her hull shone gleaming white under the soft light from the flood lights on the pontoons. This would be *Quest III's* final rest before we faced the great oceans of the world together.

The automatic gate of the pontoon closed behind me, and I made my way across the car park, through the gates of the marina, and across the road, to the path that leads to the Harbour Bar. I could see through the porthole window on the heavy wooden door that the bar was full of deaf people excitedly signing to each other. I stood at the bar, lifted my pint of Guinness, looked at the ship's clock on the wall and, for a few seconds, asked myself: *I have fifteen hours until departure. Will I have the strength to leave my family?*

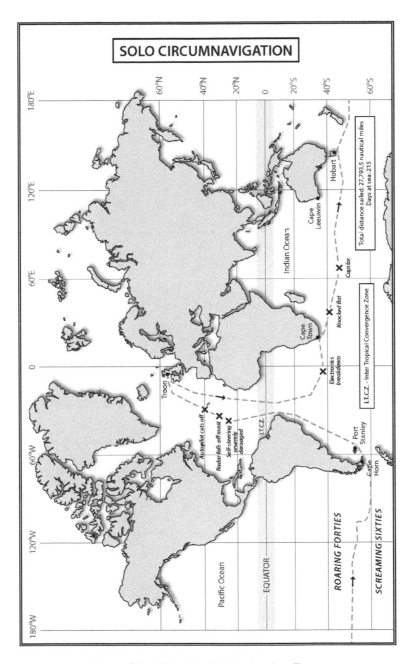

Map of the World with Navigation Route

Final goodbye with my family (photo courtesy of Heidi Koivisto Robertson)

Chapter 11: Let it begin! Round the world non-stop!

I was woken by the vibration of the mast on 1st September. I felt cold, wet, damp and slightly hung-over from the farewell drinks. I looked around *Quest III*. It was a mess inside the cabin. I still had to organise everything before leaving at 12.00. I still had a few nagging doubts whether I could leave my family but my gut was telling me I had to go. *This is it*, I said to myself. *This is the day. There is no turning back now.*

I took my last hot shower for the next few months at Troon marina and climbed the stairs to Scott's Restaurant to join my family and a couple of deaf friends for breakfast. I ordered porridge, rather than a full English breakfast. While I waited for my breakfast, I looked through the huge window of Scott's Restaurant towards the Firth of Clyde. Strong, fresh mid-level clouds were racing towards the shore. I studied the motion of the waves. The very strong, black and high-crested waves crashed towards the shoreline. I knew it was going to be a very tough sail to Mull of Kintyre.

It was departure time before I realised. To my surprise, a crowd of people (deaf and hearing) had turned up to wave me goodbye and good luck. I wasn't expecting anyone other than my family and a few close friends. Rev Richard Durno gave *Quest III* a blessing and said a short prayer in sign language, telling me: 'Don't be nervous, don't be disheartened. Be strong. Have faith and you will round the world safely. In Jesus's name. Amen.'

Everything was so busy and there was a camera crew on deck. As I worked my way through my final checks, I realised that I had forgotten to buy eggs. Thankfully, our friend Kay Hughes (this Kay is hearing, a sign language interpreter and has the same name as my wife) arrived with dozens of fresh eggs from her own hens. I would look forward to enjoying them while I was at sea.

I put on my ocean oilskins and switched on the engine. Sally and Demi came on board *Quest III*. We had agreed that they would help me pull up sails and secure the warps before I passed the break water. Scott Trewern (Troon Haven Master) came along the pontoon, ready to clear the wraps and to let me know that there were gales on the way.

Scott shook my hand wishing me luck before taking control of the wheel to allow me to say my final goodbyes. Then it was time to say goodbye to my family. Kay, Nicola and Ashley did not say a word but I could tell from their eyes that they did not want me to go. I thought about how strong and self-sacrificing *they* were. They were prepared to forgo their own fears to allow me to follow my dreams. I hugged the three of them to me tightly to me. Tears streamed from my eyes. It was much more difficult than I ever thought it was going to be. I took a deep breath and prepared to depart.

Quest III freed herself from the pontoon and we headed towards the harbour entrance under engine. Walter Clelland's speedboat left the launch and followed us. Demi took the helm while Sally helped me pull up the mainsail. As we approached the breakwater, I instructed Sally and Demi to prepare themselves to step down from *Quest III* onto the speedboat. I looked at it and spotted James Anderson at the wheel. I was surprised to see Jason Clelland there too. I had taught Jason at school and hadn't seen him in six or seven years. Then I realised that Kay, Nicola and Ashley were on the boat. I waved to Kay, Nicola and Ashley, knowing that there was a chance that I might never see them again.

As *Quest III* and I headed towards the south of Arran, I spotted a crowd of people on the rocks at Troon beach waving a Scottish banner. Gradually, the banner and the small figures drifted out of sight as *Quest III* pushed against the strong southwest winds.

A few hours later, after passing the south of Arran, I opened my log book to record my voyage: time, position, course, nautical miles, speed, direction of wind, barometer reading and remarks.

Gerry's online log 1st September:

> *It's been a hell of a day! We've faced a tough sail through strong, fresh, facing winds, which meant we had to keep tacking port and starboard all time. While I was at the helm, all I could think of was getting out of the Firth of Clyde and past the Mull of Kintyre. At the moment it seems impossible.*
>
> *The strong southerly westerly winds have started to veer to an Easterly wind and the heavy seas are against us. The changing tide made the sea confusing. The strong tide coming from the Firth of Clyde to the open Atlantic suited us and allowed us to sail fast and get out of the Mull of Kintyre.*
>
> *While Quest III was close hauled, I leaned over the coach roof from the cockpit to fasten ropes. Quest III broached from port to starboard to side. The boom shot across the boat. I felt a gust of air as the boom narrowly missed me but caught my favourite blue Musto woollen hat*

and lifted it right off my head. I watched my hat fly through the air and then disappear into the heavy swell sea.

I returned to the cockpit, grasped the steering wheel and thanked God that the boom did not knock me unconscious. Every part of Quest III vibrated as she shot through the sea like a torpedo diving deep into the bottom of the swell and shooting upwards into the air. Quest III sailed beautifully fast under full 3rd reefs with inner fore stay. I braced myself, thinking: this is only the start. The roaring black waves were topped by white horses. I could see them crashing against the cliffs of the Mull of Kintyre.

I woke before sunrise on 2nd September. Like every morning, I turned to chat to Kay. That was when it hit me. Kay was not there. Kay and I are always chatting. I looked over at a photo of us on our wedding day. I felt lost without her.

The sun was rising and lighting up the sky by 06.30. I had a 360° view of the horizon. There were ships and fishing boats dotted around. I decided to have a good breakfast – sausages with some of the fresh eggs Kay Hughes had given me. I mixed in curried baked beans. It was then that I realised that I had forgotten to pick up fresh bread. I must have left it in the car boot! I checked the Navtex weather forecast. There were warnings of gales coming from the Atlantic Ocean.

I was beginning to really understand *Quest III* and could feel that my mood had changed. What a difference! After a difficult start, I was looking forward to the voyage that lay ahead. It was me, *Quest III* and the sea. There was nobody to tell me what I should do. I would be solely responsible for every decision I made. *Quest III* and I would look after each other and work as a team.

By 12th September Portugal was on our Port side (380 miles away). The conditions were so different: blue sea, no clouds and a warm breeze. I went down below and opened all the hatches to let fresh air into the cabin and write up my log. The Barometer risen to 1018.

For the first time since leaving Troon, I was able to take off my ocean-sailing oilskins, leaving me in the cockpit in my T-shirt and shorts and relaxing while I enjoyed the warm weather as I sailed along with the long swell. I opened a tin of fruit cocktail and tin of custard, mixed them together and relished the taste of the fruit while watching the waves towards the south.

The problems started on 14th September. I was awoken suddenly by unusual movement of the boat and the sea. It was very dark and misty outside and the cabin was still glowing by the light of the oil lamp. I had a strong feeling that the boat was heading in the wrong direction.

According to the navigation equipment, *Quest III* was heading south towards Madeira (about 150 NM and from the portside 540 NM across to the North of Morocco) but, despite the readings on the navigation panel, inside me was telling me we were headed in the wrong direction. I climbed into to the cockpit. It was pitch black and there was no sign of the sun rising on the east horizon at 07.00 UTC. It was then that I saw that the autopilot was not working. I had no idea why it had stopped but switched over to monitor self-steering, so *Quest III* could continue our planned course.

I searched the boat, looking for clues, but had no luck. Thankfully, the sea and wind were calm. If not, the *Quest III* could gybe (jerk suddenly from one side to the other) and possibly break the mast because she was sailing full sail as fast as she could.

I switched on the autopilot system from the square display panel near the steering wheel. It came back online. But just as I was leaving the cockpit, the autopilot steered the boat back in the wrong direction. I rushed back to the wheel to take control of *Quest III*. I had to figure out why this was happening.

I examined the equipment. Everything was fine but, when I pressed autopilot 'engage' button, there was no sign that it was taking over the steering controls of the boat. I waited a few minutes before pressing the button again. It worked and the autopilot was functioning again, and *Quest III* was heading in the correct direction (direct to Madeira). I decided that I deserved a treat after all that work, so made myself a small mug of coffee.

A few hours later, the internal compass in my head, told me that *Quest III* was off course again. I climbed back into the cockpit to check the equipment again. The lights on the autopilot were lit. I felt as if they were smiling to me as they said, 'I am still engaged', *but* I could see that the steering wheel was not in control. The depth finder on the monitor of the chart plotter was flashing and the AIS (automatic radio identification system) was not working.

I was becoming more and more frustrated. I had invested a fortune in this equipment, had a Garmin expert check it and it had failed only a few weeks after I left Troon. *I have had enough of the bloody Garmin!* I was furious because I knew if I couldn't resolve the problem myself, I might have to sail to Madeira and stop there for repairs.

I tried to stay focussed on the problem in front of me. I kept telling myself: *Think, think, think.* I worked my way through my checklist, ticking off each item on it as I tried to locate the problem. As I worked my way through the checks of the autopilot system, I noticed the small black fuse box. I opened and lifted out the fuse. The fuse had blown. I fetched a spare from the cabin and replaced the fuse. At last, *Quest III* was back on course and heading in the right direction towards Madeira.

My log at that time recorded: *Time logged on: 13:00, compass reading 180°, barometer 1015mb, wind Easterly 10 to 15 knots, full sails, position 34 35 26 N, 17 54 12 W, Temp. 23.2C, 88 miles left for Madeira.* I was so relieved to be back on course, but I was not happy with my electronics. It was too risky to trust them.

Quest III and I sailed between the La Palma, Gran Canary opposite to Tenerife on 17th September. There was beautiful blue sky. I looked across the islands and thought about our family holidays to Tenerife.

By 20th September, I was about 500 miles from Cape Verde. I pressed the button to switch on the generator to charge the batteries. It failed to start. I was puzzled. Why wouldn't the generator start? I picked up the generator handbook and read through the instructions, trying to identify the problem. I opened the generator box and checked for leaking, overheating or a loose wire. I couldn't see anything wrong. I tried the switch again. No luck.

My spirits plummeted as I said to myself. *This is hopeless. One problem after another. What's going to happen next?* I sat, thinking it over and over. I checked everything again and pressed the button. It was not working. My best option was to email Robert the engineer.

Quest III was sailing well but everything else seemed to be breaking down. I tried to work out how I would manage without both the self-steering and the autopilot. I calculated that I would need to spend between eight to twelve hours at the helm (on each shift). The sun was so strong that I would have to start sailing late in the afternoon and sail through the night. I would stop sailing when the sun was above my head.

An email from Robert popped into my mailbox. It contained step by step instructions on how to check the generator. I examined the starter motor and the solenoid fuel switch. Then I changed the relay switches. I tried the generator again. It failed. A few hours later, Robert sent another email:

'Let's start from scratch and try to work this out until we find out what is wrong.' Another few hours later, after following Robert's instructions, the generator was in working order. It was a glorious, warm evening, so I celebrated by treating myself to a *Look What We Found*[18] Norfolk Chicken Tikka with the golden veg rice mixed with chopped ginger.

Quest III was rolling downwind very fast from the Northerly wind at 18 knots, under Goosewing with third reefing and second reef from the genoa. We were making good speed at 8 knots as we headed towards Cape Verde (297 NM).

By 23rd September we were very close to Cape Verde. I felt wonderfully relaxed. *Quest III* was sailing well. The sea temperature was 23.8° at 02.30 UTC. I stayed in the cockpit most of the time and observed the stars. At 09.14 UTC, I switched on the generator to charge the batteries and went to the galley to boil some water for a mug of coffee.

About twenty minutes later, I felt a strange vibration. It wasn't coming from my feet. I glanced over to the generator to see if could detect any motion from it. There was no sign of any movement. I placed my hand on the bulkhead. I could feel a slight vibration from the straining of the riggings, sails and mast, but there was no vibration from the generator. I checked the switch panel for the generator: *Bloody shit! It has stopped!*

By midday the temperature risen to 27°C plus and it was getting hotter and hotter inside *Quest III*. I opened a tin of rice pudding. It was lukewarm and liquid. I poured is straight into the bowl, planning to top it up with blackcurrant jam that had turned to liquid. There was no place to keep food cool (especially my Guinness). I opened my laptop, connected to PredictWind and emailed Robert to let him know about the generator (knowing that he would also say, 'oh bloody shit!').

Robert replied immediately with instructions. I spent the whole afternoon reading and following his instructions, still no luck: the generator would not start. The last stage was to consider whether the fuel switch might be faulty. I spent so much time trying to identify the problem with the generator that it was impossible for me to eat or catch up on sleep before dusk. That evening I looked up the sky, as *Quest III* slowly rolled side to side; as she sailed along with long swells, I kept thinking over and over and over again: *what do to do now?*

---

[18] http://www.lookwhatwefound.co.uk

Cape Verde island was in sight just before sunrise on 24th September. I had to decide what to do next. I had two options: keep sailing and ignore the generator, or sail to Cape Verde and stop for professional repairs to the generator and Garmin equipment. Ignoring the generator and relying on the main engine was a risky strategy because of the fuel capacity. If I stopped at Cape Verde, it would mean giving up my dream of a non-stop solo navigation. But if the generator could not be fixed at Cape Verde, I could refill the fuel and sail to Cape Town. I made my decision. I would stop at Cape Verde. I was fed up with the technology and generator problems. I emailed Kay to let her know of my situation. By mid-afternoon I pulled up full sails and altered course, heading twenty-two miles to the Cape Verde.

Another email arrived from Robert. He asked me to check the wire near the relay switches, then take the square plug out of the solenoid valve by unscrewing the valve, open it and check the wires inside. I read his instructions very carefully. My body began to shake as I hoped that this might solve the problem.

It was so hot inside *Quest III* that my whole body was soaking with perspiration. I opened up the case of the generator and lay down in the tiny compartment below the portside berth. It was pitch black inside the compartment. Using my head torch, I located the relay switch, unscrewed it, and carefully removed the top side. The tiny screw slipped out of my fingers and quickly rolled away and out of sight. I could feel panic rising in my body. Where had it gone?

It seemed to take forever to find that screw but, at last, I spotted it. It was in a really tight space. There wasn't enough room to put my hand in and lift it. I picked up a screwdriver and used it move the screw until it was within reach. Now I could take the square plug out and inspect the wires. One of the wires had disconnected! I reconnected it, rolled away, and then pressed the button. The generator started and was running healthily. At last, after thirty-two hours with no power, the batteries were charging. I laughed out loud with joy saying, 'Good old Professor Robert!'

I emailed Kay and Robert to let them know my good news: I would not be stopping at Cape Verde. I altered my course, heading past Cape Verde and towards St Paul's Rock, near the doldrums. I decided to eat another of my treats to celebrate fixing the generator (stew casserole with tinned vegetables) and I ate my meal outside in the cockpit and washed it down with a large red wine.

During a most beautiful evening, I sat watching the sunset as the moon rose into the sky. *Quest III* was enjoying herself, sailing under full sail along with the northeast trade winds and riding the long swell. I relaxed in the cockpit, leaning over starboard side and enjoying the warmth and light from the brilliant moon. Suddenly something (or someone) tapped from behind me on my shoulder. My heart leaped into my throat. *What, or who, was that?*

The area between the Brazilian coastline and the west coast of Africa is well known for piracy attacks. I was terrified. What if there was a pirate on board? My heart was racing, and I could feel that my eyes were wide open as I tried to steady my nerves. I sat absolutely still, waiting to feel vibrations that would let me know if someone was climbing on deck. All I could see was the reflection on the moon glimmering on the surface of the ocean. I took a deep breath and turned my head as quickly and as far as I could.

There was nobody there. My heart stopped again as I felt a vibration close to my bare feet. Something was moving on the deck. I slowly looked towards my feet. It was a tiny flying fish. Its silver scales glistened in the moonlight as it flapped around, desperate to get back to the sea. I picked it up and put it back into to the sea. I would have cooked the wee fish for Kay if she was with me. Kay loves fish.

On 7th October 2012, nearly five weeks after our departure, *Quest III* and I passed through the equator. It felt amazing but strange at the same time – not what I expected. I imagined that it would be hot, but the air temperatures were mixed, and it became cooler towards the evening. This area is called the Inter Tropical Convergence Zone (ITCZ). This is where the northeast trade winds meet the southeast trade winds. Air is forced upwards by the converging winds and clouds form, resulting in heavy rain and frequent thunderstorms. It also causes the Doldrums. These are the famous regions of calm where boats can be becalmed.

The conditions were so changeable in the ITCZ. A strong gust of wind blew hard against *Quest III*, then there were powerful thunderstorms. Later, during the early sunrise, the sea was calm but there was a heavy downpour of warm rain. It was still dark because of a heavy mist. It was too good an opportunity to miss, so I grabbed my shower gel, jumped out of the cockpit, took my clothes off and enjoyed a warm shower. It was my first shower in over a month. It felt great to be clean and fresh again. I celebrated passing the equator with a special equator menu:

Boiled new potatoes, carrots, drizzled with olive oil served with chopped ham, cooked wee fry over garlic, ginger, topped up with soy sauce, Worcester and Kikkoman, pour baked beans over the top – it tastes delicious.

The electronics broke down again on 27th October. *Quest III* and I were on the same Latitude as the Cape of Good Hope. The autopilot was not functioning. I replaced the fuse and switched it on. The fuse blew. I tried with another fuse. No luck. I decided it was best to leave it. I was only 870 miles from Cape Town. I had not planned to stop there, but I needed to have the autopilot checked out. In addition, the AIS was not functioning correctly.

Things went from bad to worse on 29th October. Something had happened to the steering wheel. I could feel it vibrating and clicking when it turned as I held the wheel. I could feel it as I held the wheel. I suspected that either the rudder bearing or the steering wheel itself was faulty. I checked down below but it seemed fine. The problem persisted and after a few days *Quest III* was not on course accurately.

On 5th November, I spent a long time thinking through my options. *Quest III* had done very well so far, but it was too risky to enter the Southern Oceans without repairs to the electronics and the steering. I remembered an email I had received from someone in Cape Town congratulating me in attempting to sail round the world and that I should contact them if I experienced any problems.

I decided it would be best to stop at Cape Town for repairs so sent an emergency email to Jim Colhoun in Glasgow, asking him to contact the deaf person who had emailed me. I was delighted when I received an email from Ralph and Paloma of Cape Town Sailing Academy. They kindly offered their support to help me get the repairs done as quickly as possible. It was then that I also found out that I was mistaken. Ralph is not Deaf. He is hearing. I had assumed that the email from Cape Town must have come from a deaf sailing school.

On 6th November, I logged my position at 12.00 UTC Lat 34 11S Long 17 17E. I was about sixty nautical miles from Cape Town. The wind was developing with much stronger gusts from the east and visibility was poor. *Quest III* and I were sailing against the wind so had to tack for hours and hours. It was very difficult sailing. The weather turned calm in the early evening, and I could just make out the shape of Table Mountain shrouded in mist.

I was expecting to arrive at the port at roughly 22.30 that evening. Ralph and his crew arranged to meet outside the busy port and guide me into Royal Cape Yacht Club (RCYC). It was pitch black and the port was full of lights. It would be difficult to identify Ralph's boat. I knew there was a rocky pier so I had to be really careful.

Just as I was looking at a chart to check my position, a text came from Jim Colhoun to tell me that Ralph was waiting for me outside on the shore. I prepared for my approach. I put lots of fenders on the starboard (just in case) and I slowed down the engine as I approached the shallow waters. I watched the depth reading begin to go down slowly. I could not identify Ralph's boat. The depth readings continued to drop, telling me that it was getting close to the keel.

I decided to go back and start it again. I steered *Quest III* to a different area. It was then that I spotted a tiny flashing light moving from side to side, and up and down. It was Ralph. I revved up the engine and motored to meet Ralph's boat. Ralph was at the wheel, indicating to his crew to standby on the starboard side deck and be ready to jump on board *Quest III*.

I hadn't seen another human being in just over two months so it was lovely to see them and be welcomed to Cape Town with a warm hug. Then I had the most amazing surprise. There was a deaf crew member! He gave me my instructions in sign language. It was brilliant. It turned out that Ralph had been looking for someone who could sign and communicate with me. And that day he met a deaf man walking in the marina – marvellous!

Three of Ralph's crew jumped on board *Quest III*. We followed Ralph's boat but the strong gusts meant we had to rev up high on engine to control our speed and it took ages to make our way into the marina. The rest of Ralph's crew were waiting on the pontoon. The strong squalls made it difficult to enter the pontoon and berth *Quest III* so it was great to have a strong crew on standby, ready to throw the ropes and secure *Quest III* alongside the pontoon of the RCYC.

Everyone at Royal Cape Yacht Club was amazing. They were all so friendly and welcoming and made sure I was settled for the evening. They even gave me a pizza and a bottle of Guinness. I settled down and opened my log book:

6th November 2012 22.25. Arrived at Royal Cape Yacht Club safety with no regret.

Chapter 12: The Southern Oceans

I spent two busy but wonderful weeks in Cape Town. I worked every day from 08.00 to 18.00 to get *Quest III* back in order. She had sustained more damage than I realised. When *Quest III* was taken out of the water to allow inspection of the rudder, I found out that the rudder was not fitted to the sail. The autopilot was replaced, and the self-steering and the steering wheel were repaired.

Ralph joined me for breakfast every morning at the Royal Cape Town Yacht Club. Ralph does not sign, so we communicated via written notes. He would ask me what work needed doing that day then pick up his mobile phone and contact various workmen and ask them to come over and help.

Ralph made phone calls for me and helped arrange the repairs. He was great. When the repairs were complete, I asked for an invoice but to my surprise, I was told the bill was already paid. The staff in the marina pointed towards a man. I looked over at him and he nodded towards me. Bernard Monteverdi paid the bill for my repairs to sponsor my solo circumnavigation. I couldn't believe the generosity of this man who had never met me.

While I was at Cape Town, Ralph also introduced me to Nick Leggatt. Nick sailed round the world three times competing in the Global Ocean Race. He explained his experiences of sailing in the Indian and Pacific Oceans, showing me charts and photographs of his routes. I really appreciated Nick spending so much time with me, especially as the next leg of my journey would be in the Indian Ocean. I have to record my thanks to everyone who I met in Cape Town. They all worked so hard and made me so welcome with invites to spend time with them and their families.

Quest III sailed out of Cape Town before sun rise on 20th November 2012. We were heading towards Cape Point (the southernmost point of Africa). The sea was calm. *Quest III* and I were only few miles from the coast of Cape Town when I caught sight of a pod of whales. I could not believe my eyes. There must have been about fifty whales blowing water up into the air and turning somersaults with joy. It was amazing. I stood at the helm, enjoying watching them when suddenly I spotted massive dark log shape a few metres from the starboard side of *Quest III*. It looked like a submarine breaking the waves and coming towards me. It was a whale and she was swimming towards *Quest III* at tremendous speed. The whale was swimming so fast that there was not enough time to manoeuvre *Quest III* out its path.

I remembered that Ralph had advised me that if I saw whales, simply to switch the engine on and let it run. He reckoned the noise would cause the whales to move out of the way. I held my breath and pressed full throttle to give the maximum speed as I helplessly watched the whale swimming towards *Quest III*. I braced myself and held the wheel tightly as I could see that the whale was within a few seconds of knocking the hull.

Suddenly, the whale dived deep into the sea, her huge tail towering above us. I knew that if the whale knocked the rudder she would easily snap it, but she disappeared out of sight without touching *Quest III*. By this point, my legs had started to shake so I slowed down the engine and pull up the sail again.

By 22nd November, we had sailed past Cape Point, South Africa and were heading for the Southern Oceans. The Barometer read 1012. The sea was calm and peaceful. We sailed under full sails in a west-southwest wind. I had the emergency forestay for storm jib on standby.

The next morning, the barometer had dropped to 1009. *Quest III* and I sailed through the long slow swell on the sea, enjoying the blue sky and the gentle wind. I was looking forward to experiencing the challenges of the Southern Oceans. I was heading south to avoid Agulhas Bank. Agulhas Bank is the western boundary of the Indian Ocean and has a reputation for strong winds and currents. The barometer continued to drop, and the winds were picking up strength. I knew that conditions could change very quickly so prepared myself for the potentially severe weather.

The wind continued to pick up strength and reached Force 8 in the early morning of 24th November. I decided to drop the mainsail and use storm jib alone. *Quest III* sailed much faster and was surfing the waves. By 05.00 the Barometer had dropped to 991.4 and the wind continued to gain strength.

As I sat at the navigation station table, the pressure of the wind against my eardrums, I could feel the table vibrate under my hand from the riggings as they juddered under the force of the wind. I decided to go on deck to check the mast and riggings. The sea was pitch black and the waves were topped with white horses as they pushed towards the east. But *Quest III* was sailing comfortably under the storm jib at a speed of 10 knots.

It was my responsibility to regularly check the boat while at sea: check all the riggings; the shackles and keep watch for any sightings of ships and yet, from my understanding, the waves were very high, much higher than a one storey building. But this time, when I did my checks, I forgot to close the hatch and a freak wave came over the cockpit, splashing into the galley and soaking my laptop. It was ruined. I was furious with myself. My laptops provided my only means of communication – emails. I quickly checked the other two laptops in the cupboard to make sure they were safe and working.

The wind continued to get stronger. By 14.25 UTC wind speed had reached 57 knots and rising. It was a full-scale Force 10 storm. I took the helm to reduce the risk of damage to *Quest III*. *Quest III* and I needed to work together to stay safe. The wind was furious. I had to push hard against the wheel to keep my body from being rammed into the wheel by the wind raging against my back. It felt like doing push-ups. I had never experienced anything like this before, but it was fantastic. Real sailing!

Quest III surfed fast over roaring storm waves under the storm jib. By late that evening, the wind had slowed to Force 8. I was so pleased with *Quest III*. She sailed beautifully during the storm, reaching speeds of 17 knots (and more) in the driving wind and rain. The waves were enormous. I couldn't allow *Quest III* to heave to because she would have capsized easily with the height of the waves. While I was at the helm, I focussed on reading and checking the compass bearing to keep *Quest III* steady. I had no time to look around and take in the seas of the southern oceans. I knew that, if I lost control, she would roll over in seconds. At one point, I thought I would have to call it a day and throw the series drogue to slow the boat and go down below and wait for the wind to ease off, but somehow *Quest III* kept going; we were both relishing the challenge.

Quest III had her first knock down just before sun rise on 25th November. I was lying down in the bunker and could see through the hatch the mast was almost flat against the surface of the sea. I climbed on deck to check *Quest III*. The Ocean Safety lifebelt and rescue harness that I kept on the port side had gone. Only the cover bag remained. It had been ripped wide open. Fortunately, there was no damage to the mast.

When I was in Cape Town, Nick Leggatt had informed me of the possibility of knockdowns by rogue waves in the Southern Oceans and advised me to tie up the mainsail and use the storm jib. Thankfully, I had followed his advice. I tried to figure out what had happened, but my best guess was that *Quest III* had been hit by a rogue wave from the direction of the starboard side of the hull.

At 06.00 UTC on 25th November, the Barometer had risen to 1010. Good news. The wind was had dropped to Force 5/6 and was coming from the southwest. I dropped the storm jib and put up a reefing genoa (but no mainsail). *Quest III* made good progress sailing at speeds between 8–11 knots. I took advantage of the break in the weather to have a cooked breakfast and ate my last two sausages, with tomato and baked beans.

After breakfast, I checked the barometer again and observed the sky – we had a good day sailing ahead of us. Later in the day, I slept for a couple of hours and woke up to a breath-taking full moon shining across the ocean. My mind drifted back to the days when my dad and I sailed the old 36-foot gaff ketch at Rothesay pier alongside the old fishing boats. I could vividly remember the smell of fish, oil and petrol, and the masses of seagulls circling the boats. But at the same time as these memories played back in my mind, I was thinking about all the people who helped me out in Cape Town, even though they did not know me, but gave up their time to get *Quest III* back to sea.

The good sailing conditions lasted less than a day. By 02.50 UTC on 26th November Barometer reading had dropped to 1006 and the winds were gaining strength. Within a few hours we were battling a strong gale (Force 9). I made sure I paid attention to securing the boat by locking and closing all the valves for fuel, toilet, engine, water tank, generator etc. We were sailing eastwards but the powerful waves from the south were clashing against the westerly waves.

Quest III lurched to and fro. I could feel that she was not making good progress. Then *Quest III* shuddered and shot over the waves at the wrong angle; she kept turning toward the wind, at extreme speed, with waves crashing right over her. I couldn't understand why she was doing this. I had no time to waste. I jumped into the cockpit and took the helm until she was steady again and content.

Once *Quest III* was settled, I examined the self-steering and saw that one of the line ropes had snapped. I switched to auto pilot and rushed back to replace the temporary line attached to the drum of the wheel. Repair done, I switched off the auto pilot and let the self-steering take control. I didn't want to take any chances, so I stayed at the helm for a while, watching the self-steering until I was sure that *Quest III* was steady.

The wind continued to gain strength and was storm force (Force 10) by 07.42 UTC. The barometer was still dropping. I could smell something. It smelled like leaking fuel. I rushed to check the bilge but found nothing. I checked the fuel tank and found that the screws that connected the fuel tank to the generator had rusted. I wasn't 100% sure if this was the source of the leak, but I could not see any other problems.

Later that afternoon (12.00 UTC), I had to take the helm again. The waves were huge. *Quest III* was being tossed around in them. The surface of the sea was obscured by spray – the only thing I could see was white. After four hours of steering, I needed a rest from the forces pulling and pushing *Quest III*. I switched on the autopilot and went down below to get some rest.

At 16.45 UTC *Quest III* was knocked down by a breaking wave which caught her beam-on. I gripped the rail hard and looked out of the porthole, waiting for the sea to clear away. After a few seconds, *Quest III* was upright again and I scrambled into the cockpit to check all was OK. All the sheets were on the portside at right angles.

At 17.00 UTC I had to let the self-steering take control and go down below to rest. But I was only able to get a couple of hours sleep. *Quest III* was knocked down again.

Gerry's log
22.16: Quest III has suffered a 3rd heavy knock down. I believe this was caused by the southerly waves. I was lying asleep. My sleeping bag was on top of me. This meant in an emergency I can shoot out without having struggle and open the sleeping bag.

I felt a heavy knock from the starboard hull. All I could feel was my cushion lifting. I grabbed the rails above me and braced my feet on the bunk. I was really lucky. I narrowly missed landing face-down on top of the cooker. Everything from the navigation table was thrown to the other side of the cabin. Thank goodness I had stowed my laptop in a safe place. I stayed awake until sunrise.

Quest III heading for the roaring 40s in the Indian Ocean

On 27th November the temperature outside dropped to 8°C. I ate my first porridge since leaving Scotland. I felt like I needed it. We were heading south to the 40s and then we would steer east towards New Zealand. I emailed my daughter Nicola to wish her happy birthday.

The weather improved slightly on 28th November. The wind had slowed to Force 5/6 and *Quest III* was sailing well, so I enjoyed some lovely hot tomato soup with bread that I had bought in Cape Town. My rest didn't last long.

By 18.00 UTC, the rain was becoming heavy and there was very little wind. At 19.30 UTC, I was down below when I felt *Quest III* shudder and thud. I could feel vibration from the hull, but I didn't know what was causing it. I rushed out to the cockpit. It was dark and pouring with rain. I switched on my head torch and searched for the problem.

Quest III was not sailing correctly – she was veering off course and backing up. I prayed to God that it wasn't another problem with the self-steering. I checked the self-steering. Everything seemed fine but there was slack in the rope from the self-steering to the wheel adapter drum that fastens with clamps to the spokes of the steering wheel. I looked toward the steering wheel, wondering if it had come off. The steering wheel was still there, but the clamps fastening the wheel adapter drum to the spokes of the wheel had come off. One of the clamps was broken so I went and got a spare to replace it and fitted it.

On 29th November, I got a shock when I looked at the clock at sunrise. It said 01.13 UTC. I just couldn't understand it. I thought I must have made an error with my calculations but, after checking again, I realised I was sailing longitudinally towards the east and every fifteen degrees east adds one hour. The distance travelled meant adding +3 hours, giving a correct sunrise time of 04.30 in Britain. I had two clocks – one showing UK time and the other clock following my longitude, so I made a note to remember to change clock one every time I passed another fifteen degrees in longitude.

I spent a while deciding what to have for my breakfast. I decided on grapefruit. I hadn't had grapefruit for ages. A very nice, refreshing breakfast it made too!

I received a report from Jim and Ralph, to tell me that the Vendee Globe competitors were on their way and would be passing me soon. The Vendee Globe is a round the world, non-stop race for Open 60 yachts. Open 60 yachts are very fast and powerful boats that can sail much faster than *Quest III*. On average, *Quest III* sailed about 145 to 170 nautical miles in twenty-four hours, whereas an Open 60 averages between 200 to 350 nautical miles every twenty-four hours.

That evening, I saw my first Roaring Forties sunset. *Quest III* had already had three knockdowns. I felt chills down my spine, thinking about what challenges the weather might throw at me in the Roaring Forties.

By 30th November (St Andrew's Day), I was in the Roaring Forties. The sky was brilliant blue and white horses were scattered across the tops of the waves. It was beautiful but freezing cold.

On December 1st 03.45 UTC the wind was rising to 38 knots plus. It was too much for the genoa, so I decided to change to a staysail. To my horror I could not furl (close) the genoa. I didn't know what was wrong, but the waves were rising, and *Quest III* was sailing much faster behind the wind. I had to find out what was causing the problem with the furling drum.

I pulled on my heavy ocean oilskins, lifejacket and lifeline and inched my way across the deck. *Quest III* was a roaring through the waves under the genoa. The deck was awash with waves. I identified the problem with the furling drum: the rope was left too close the genoa. I couldn't understand how this had happened and I was also furious with myself. I should have checked it before darkness fell.

I was running out of time. I had to fix it before it was too late but the pressure from the wind was so strong that I just couldn't take it down. *Quest III* was riding high and diving low, following the waves. There was no time to go back down and think about what to do.

I went into the cockpit, let go of the genoa sheet and let her free. The genoa flapped furiously in the wind as *Quest III* plunged through the waves. I lay down flat against the deck to avoid the jib sheets slashing at my face and to protect against the risk of breaking a bone. I gripped the pulpit and used my left leg to brace myself whilst holding the stanchion with my other as *Quest III* rolled down and dived toward the ocean.

Sea water was washing over the deck, over my head and down my neck. I stayed there for over an hour, trying to fix the drum and wrap the furling rope round the drum as many times as possible. Thank God that I did not drop the huge genoa down because at nearly 40 knots of wind, it could have easily been thrown overboard.

I finished fixing the rope round the drum and then I slid/walked my way back to the cockpit. I could feel the heat inside my body starting to rise and my heart thumping as I told myself, *you must get this job done, there is no other way to do it*. I braced myself as firmly as I could, said a few prayers (*please God, let the furling gear turn clockwise*) and started to pull the furling rope hard. At last, the genoa started to furl closed. I put up the storm jib and altered course, steering away behind the wind. I stayed at the helm while *Quest III* flew faster and faster. The barometer continued to drop.

I was pleased at how solid *Quest III* was. She proved she was capable of sailing in strong winds and almighty waves at the highest speed. At one point, the winds hit Force 11 (violent storm). My immediate thought was that I would need to slow down *Quest III*. The power of the wind meant that *Quest III* was roaring through the waves at maximum speed under the storm jib.

I had to ensure that she did not suddenly drop into the troughs of the waves, because if the nose of the boat caught under the water from the top of the waves, the mast could easily have been broken. I was ready to throw out a series drogue, but she didn't need it. *Quest III* sailed amazingly well, zig-zagging her way downwind under the helm.

The storm raged for hours and hours. Thankfully, at about 22.30 UTC after eight hours at the helm, the wind started to slow down. I watched the readings drop from 58 knots, to 54 knots and then down to 48 knots. I was so proud of *Quest III*. She responded well under the helm.

The waves were enormous, and visibility was poor, so all the time I was the helm, I had to constantly focus on the angle and pattern of the waves. If I missed only a few seconds, *Quest III* would head abeam, facing huge waves which could have very easily crushed her or could pitch pole and capsize. *Quest III* steered brilliantly behind the waves and, as the wind dropped down to about 38 knots, I was finally able to leave the helm to check the shackles, riggings and ropes. I went down below after completing my checks and fell fast asleep.

I was woken by the sunrise on 2nd December. I felt good knowing there were no strong winds. *Quest III* was sailing well, in Force 5/6. I looked up to the sky, dropped the storm jib, pulled up the mainsail and genoa in full and soon we were sailing nicely along Latitude 40S. Later that morning, I could feel the wind start to drop. Then *Quest III* stopped moving. There was no motion at all.

I could not understand it but, when I looked out, I saw that the sea was so flat that it looked a mirror. I couldn't believe how different the conditions were from the day before but took advantage of the calm to examine the sails, catch up inside and have a good big breakfast.

I picked up the pressure cooker, filled it with potatoes and chopped onions, cooked them up, then put them into a bowl and mashed in some butter. I topped it up with baked beans and black pepper. It was delicious. I checked the barometer. The barometer was starting to rise but there was no wind, so I used the break to clear away and tidy up in the cabin.

We were still heading south. I was about 550 nautical miles to the south of Kerguelen Island and it was freezing cold. I dropped the mainsail as the wind rose to over 30 knots, leaving the reefing genoa alone and sailing behind the wind. It was so cold that I wasn't surprised to receive news that the Vendee Globe route had been altered slightly because of the positioning abnormal cluster of small icebergs. The route was 300 nautical miles from Kerguelen gate to the Crozet gate.

By 5th December, the waves were becoming more aggressive with massive speed. I woke up, feeling thankful that I had been able to have had my first good three-hour sleep in ages. I could feel the wind pushing hard on *Quest III,* so I got up and changed to the storm jib to allow her to keep in good pace, with a good steady speed. I decided to have a quick breakfast and named it the Roaring Forties Menu: sliced ham and fried sliced potatoes with onion, heated up with short spaghetti in cheese-flavoured tomato sauce, served with coffee.

After breakfast, I wrote my web reports and then watched a DVD that Kay sent to me in Cape Town. It was called, *Gerry Hughes Sails Around the World.* The DVD was made by Gerry Malley and included photos by Heidi Koivistoi. Kay sent this to me in Cape Town. I also received a USB stick from Lee Robertson and Heidi. It was full of wonderful messages from my Facebook page. I had no idea how much interest there had been on Facebook about my solo circumnavigation attempt until after I arrived at Cape Town. It made such a difference to see my fans cheering me on and sending me messages.

There was email from Jim letting me know that Mike Golding in Vendee Global Race was on the very same track as mine (Mike was at Lat 42S Long 30E and we were at Lat 42S 57E) so it might be possible to see his mast in the far distance. There was also an email from Neil Lennon (Manager of Glasgow Celtic) saying, *'Well done and keep going'.*

By midnight on 5th December, the wind had increased to Force 8/9 and changed from southwest to west-southwest increasing to gale force.

Early the 6th December, at 09.30 UTC, the waves were much higher. *Quest III* was heading much harder downwind carried by the storm job, and was in good spirits, carried by the storm jib alone. The southwest wind was Force 7/8. At 12.00 UTC, the autopilot blew its fuse. After four attempts at getting it working again, I switched to self-steering to keep her going. The self-steering responded well under the storm jib. Quest III was sailing at a good pace following the rhythm of the four to five metre waves. An albatross followed us on the port side flying deep into the v-valleys and then soaring high to meet the crests.

I was sitting at the back of the cockpit watching the albatross and looking around to make sure there were no ships. Everything was under control. *Quest III* was looking after herself so I decided to make myself a quick mug of coffee and start thinking what to do about the autopilot. I went down below, closing the hatch behind me. Just as I was about to make my coffee, I realised that my jar of Coffee Mate was empty, so went another cabin to fetch other jar.

As I opened the cupboards, looking for a jar of coffee mate, I could feel the force of gravity pulling against me as *Quest III* sailed deep into the troughs of the waves. I found the coffee mate and made my back to the galley.

As my foot stepped into the galley cabin, I could feel the motion of *Quest III's mast* change. She was heeling at 55°, then 65°, then 75°. I was sure *Quest III* would right herself but the mast continued to descend towards to sea. I grabbed the pole to my right to keep myself steady, facing toward the navigation table. As I continued to walk, my feet briefly brushed against the top edge of navigation table. I looked down. My legs were now dangling in the air. I feel a heavy strain on my right arm.

The strain on my arm became so great that I had to let go of the pole. As I looked down towards my feet, I realised that I was standing on the cabin ceiling. The cabin was dark but I could see the green water of ocean through the Perspex glass hatch. Sea water was gushing into the galley cabin through the hatch beneath my feet and from the other cabins. It already above my ankles and rising quickly. *Quest III* was capsizing. My heart pounded as my mind turned to the massive keel that was now above my head and I saw my life *This is it* I said to myself. *There is no way I can escape. Quest III is about to sink to the floor of the Indian Ocean.* There was only one thought in my mind: Kay.

My life flashed before my eyes. Items from the cabin were now floating in the rising sea water. I stood perfectly still, trying to think of a way to get out of the cabin. Suddenly the boat moved. The sea water gushed to one the side and the navigation table returned to its original position. *Quest III* was righting herself.

I must have been underwater for just under one minute, but it felt much, much longer than that. *Quest III* had been in a 180° capsize.

As soon as *Quest III* was upright, I rushed onto the deck to check the mast. The mast was fine, but *Quest III* was hopelessly out of control. The self-steering was badly damaged and unusable. The pin and welded bracket on the wheel adapter had been shorn off. I had to devise a make-shift system, replacing the pin with ropes. It would mean that *Quest III* was not 100% on course and I knew the ropes would chafe and need replacing regularly, but at least I could still use the self-steering when I needed to work on *Quest III* or get some sleep. I would have to remain on the helm during heavy seas.

The wind sensor above the mast was damaged. *Quest III* was a shamble inside. The chart table had flown open during the capsize and the contents were strewn across the cabin. Everything was sodden. I logged my time and the position of capsize: Lat 42 34S Long 62 31E.

From that moment on, I was besieged by intermittent faults with the autopilot. There was no way I could rely on it. I had no choice but to plan ahead as if it was not working at all. From 6th December to 27th December I had to focus all my efforts on one thing: my own survival. *Quest III* was battered relentlessly by severe gales and storms. I had no time to eat, no time to rest, and my log entries were limited to very brief notes. I took advantage of any lulls in the storms to check my equipment and gulp down food straight from the can. It wasn't until 27th December that I had time to write an account of what happened.

I knew I was fighting for my life. I wrapped myself in my soaking wet sleeping bag, bracing myself in the bulkhead to wait out the worst of the storms. *Quest III* was pushed hard by the waves and rolled violently from side to side but something deep inside me told me I had unfinished business. I was not prepared to give up.

On 7th December, I was devastated when I realised that my spare laptop was broken. That left me with only one laptop for communication. I thought about Kay, Nicola and Ashley. I had to stay in touch with them. Now I had only one laptop, and if anything happened to it, I would be completely cut off from them. I had to plan what to do next. *Quest III* needed repairs and I had to reach Cape Horn before February.

I weighed up my options – where should I sail to for repairs? Then on 9th December I received an email from Ralph in Cape Town suggesting that I sail to Australia for repairs. I decided that my best option was to sail to

Hobart, Tasmania. I had another 3,560 nautical miles of tough sailing ahead of me before arriving there.

As soon as the wind started to drop, I checked the engine and the generator. I had locked the valves before the capsize so they were both working.

From 17th to 24th December, the angry black sea roared with white horse waves. *Quest III* was travelling at tremendous speed directly towards Cape Horn. She was being hammered so hard by the waves that it felt as if she was tumbling around inside a washing machine. On the morning of 17th December, the GPS blew again, and three clamps were broken on the self-steering. I tried the electrics again but had no luck. I still had 2,366 nautical miles to sail before reaching Hobart and I had no chart plotted, no wind speed and no autopilot.

I thought about Kay. I hadn't replied to her latest email. I knew she was waiting to hear from me, but what could I tell her? I knew she had invited a few friends round for a meal to celebrate Christmas. If I told her how bad things were, it would just cause stress and worry and ruin their celebrations.

By mid-afternoon on the 17th December, I managed to fix the GPS and get it working again. On 18th December I fixed the self-steering and the autopilot had started working again. But the repair to the self-steering did not last long. The ropes were chafing again by the next day. And the autopilot blew again! All I could do was stay down below and brace myself as hard as possible against the forces battering *Quest III*.

I kept my eyes on the barometer as it continued to drop slowly. Very often I asked, *God, when are these gales going to stop?* My whole body was at a very low ebb. I was bitterly cold, had no energy, no appetite, and feared that worse was yet to come.

By Christmas Eve, the autopilot blew again with a terrible thud and shudder. I rushed out to the cockpit, not knowing what it was. I had no idea until I felt the steering wheel and thought, *My God, the steering wheel is broken. That means I don't have a steering wheel now.*

I went over and touched the steering wheel and steered to starboard, to see if it was turning, which it was. I wondered why, and where the noise was coming from (I could feel it coming from the steering wheel stand), then of course, I realised that it was the autopilot vibrating right through. So, I switched the autopilot off and steered her until it was all set and there were no problems. I then switched the autopilot on again to strong thuds and bangs, so switched it off again immediately and just left the autopilot alone.

I knew I had to do something to lift my morale. So, on Christmas Day, I took advantage of a short break in the weather to open my Christmas box from Kay.

It was soaking wet and I was worried that the contents may have been damaged during the capsize. I waited for the wind to go down before opening it.

I was delighted to have lovely cards from Kay, Nicola, Ashley, Sally and Demi. They also gave me some Musto socks (which I really needed). I could not believe my eyes when I saw the bottles of Guinness, whisky, and wine that Kay had packed were still intact. I was so glad and knew that I would look forward to enjoying them when the weather calmed enough to allow me to switch off and let *Quest III* look after me.

For a very short time that afternoon, I was amazed to see the sun again. The sea became blue and wee birds were flying behind me. My mate Jim emailed me a photo of Kay, Nicola and Ashley, which was taken as they were about to eat their Christmas dinner at home. They were so lovely, and I was delighted to see them in a photo again.

I decided I needed to boost my morale so set about planning my Christmas dinner. I decided on an Indian Ocean inspired menu of Staffordshire chicken and sage soup, then fried onion, garlic, soy sauce and a drop of mustard mixed with West Highland wild venison stew. I then had a tin of pears, washed down with red wine from my Christmas box.

More gales arrived on the evening of the 25th December. I was feeling really fed up with the weather. I could not believe how fast the clouds covered the whole sky and the sea rose. I was ready to throw in the series drogue to slow the boat down as the enormous waves rolled at great speed. *Quest III* struggled to maintain control in steady down wind, she was going at extensive speed, like she was heading downhill! I took the helm for eight to nine hours until my time was up, managed a temporary repair by winding ropes round it and hoped it would last until I arrived at Hobart.

Things changed dramatically on 27th December. The clouds parted and I could see a circle of bright blue sky. The winds dropped and it was so calm that the sea was almost flat. It was the first calm weather since *Quest III* and I sailed onto the Roaring Forties nearly a month before.

I pulled off my oilskins, opened three hatches and all the portholes to let fresh air into the cabin. I cleaned *Quest III* from top to bottom, then gave myself a good wash. I climbed into the cockpit and breathed in the air of the Indian Ocean while watching the birds flying around at the stern of *Quest III* as she rested in the calm sea. I patted *Quest III* to tell her well done. *Quest III* had refused to abandon me during the most ferocious storms and seas.

The gales and storms were worse than anything I had ever imagined, but *Quest III* sailed on under the storm jib. My dad was also on my mind throughout that time. I thanked him for all the sailing skills he had taught me. I had never been in the Indian Ocean before, but faith and the spirit in me helped. Together my dad and *Quest III* helped me through the toughest sailing of my life.

The respite from the storm did not last long. Within a few hours, the clouds had gathered again and the gales returned. *Quest III* was sailing at 5–6 knots when I altered course to Hobart. But I was happy and relaxed knowing that *Quest III* and I would soon be in Hobart for a rest and repairs before facing Cape Horn together.

On 4th January, on my forty-fifth day at sea, I could see Mount Wellington, Tasmania. Hobart is located in the foothills of Mount Wellington. Jim Colhoun, Linda Richards and Debbie Aitken had been liaising with the office at Prince of Wales Bay marina at Hobart and explained my situation. I felt great knowing I would soon be sailing into Prince of Wales Bay marina, and sorting out essential repairs to *Quest III*.

It was a very bright sunny day, but I was puzzled by the strong wind that was blowing from Bruny Island. The wind was blowing very hot. I had never experienced anything like it. It felt like hot air blowing from a hair dryer. It was completely dark by the time I arrived at Prince of Wales marina. I sent a text message to Pieter to let him know I had arrived. Pieter was on the shore near to his house. Using a powerful torch, he flashed the light to identify the location of the mooring. I approached slowly, following the light from Pieter's torch. Pieter guided me exactly to the right area. I picked up the buoy and secured *Quest III*, knowing that I was safe for the night.

The next morning, Pieter Van Der Woude (co-owner of the Prince of Wales marina) arrived on his speedboat, along with a sign language interpreter. Pieter guided me into the marina. It was then that I found out the cause of the strange hot wind I had felt the day before: there was a huge forest fire in the hills surrounding Hobart. I secured *Quest III* alongside the pontoon at the marina. She looked awful after her experiences in the southern oceans. I was looking forward to bringing her back to her usual self as soon as possible.

Kay, Demi, Sally, Nicola and Ashley waving goodbye from the speedboat. You can also see James Anderson (left) who was steering the boat. (photo courtesy of Walter Clelland)

An unexpected visitor to Quest III

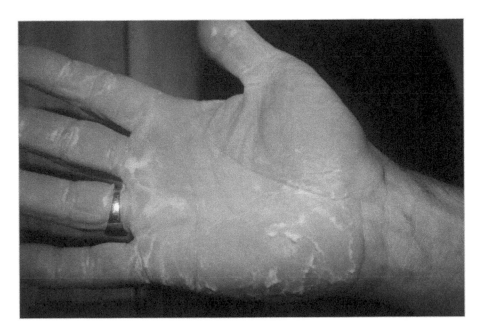

1st October 2012: my hands were beginning to feel the effects of the salt water

The Inter-Tropical Convergence Zone. Staying dry was a challenge.

Quest III berthed at Royal Cape Town Yacht Club

Quest III being removed from the water for repairs to her rudder.

Repairing the rudder.

The Roaring Forties

V-valley wave in the Roaring Forties.

White horse waves in the Roaring Forties

Stormy seas in the southern oceans.

Damage to the self-steering during the capsize. The stainless steel knobs have been shorn off and the metal plate bent out of shape.

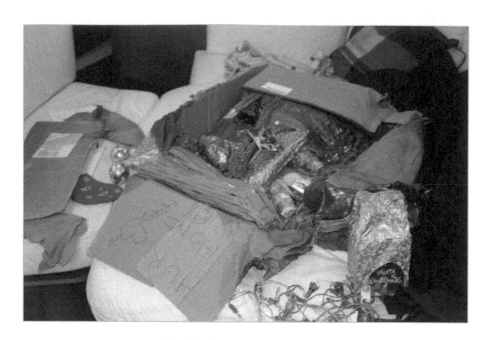

My Christmas Box from Kay

My 'repairs' to the self-steering after the capsize.

Hobart Marina: drying out Quest III after the capsize.

The self-steering is repaired – you can see the welding.

Massive swell in the Indian Ocean

Few more days before we reach Cape Horn

Passing Cape Horn

The Falkland Islands.

The stainless steel tube connecting the self-steering to the rudder is broken off in the North Atlantic. I still have 2845 miles to go

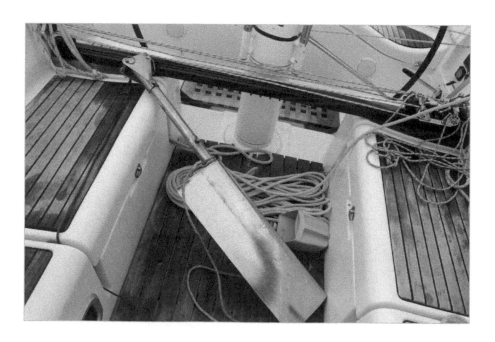

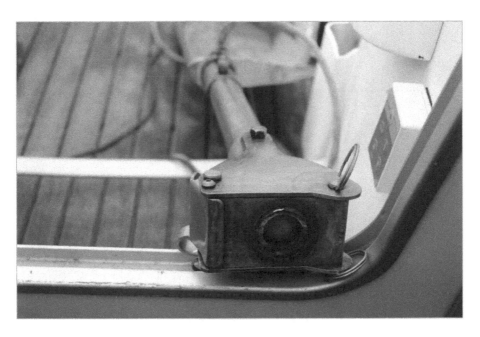

Close up of the broken stainless steel connecting tube

Four days after the self-steering fell apart, my radar thumped onto the deck
(despite being secured by sixteen rivets).

One of the speedboats that came to meet me. Erelend Tulloch and Jim Colhoun are at the front and were communicating to me from the boat via sign language

Entering Troon Harbour

Jim Colhoun welcoming me home. Jim was my main email contact while I was at sea.

Home with my family

Chapter 13: Rounding Cape Horn

My spirits were at an all-time low by the time I arrived at Hobart. *Quest III* and I had been devastated by the capsize and we were exhausted. *Quest III* was a mess – everything inside was wet and damp and covered with salt. It was difficult to see how she could recover from this. There were 5,670 nautical miles between Hobart and Cape Horn and it was essential that I arrive there between February and March and while it was still summer in the Southern Hemisphere. The seas and weather would be too unpredictable and dangerous for *Quest III* by mid-March.

To this day, I am still so grateful to Noel Richardson and Pieter Van Der Woude for the wonderful support they gave me while I was at the Prince of Wales Bay marina. Noel is the general manager and gave up much of his time to come to my boat every day to find out what needed to be done before going back to his office, making phone calls on my behalf.

From the start, everyone in the Prince of Wales marina was determined to make my stay as pleasant as possible. Noel and Pieter had never met a deaf person before, but they made a great effort to communicate with me. Pieter arranged for a sign language interpreter to come to the marina the first day I was there. I can't explain how relieved I felt when I met the interpreter because I had been worrying about trying to understand people by relying on lipreading.

Most of the time, Pieter, Noel communicated via written notes – it was easier for all of us. I was very busy every day working with professional engineers, sail makers, riggers and welders, but there were also people who came along to say hello to me and *Quest III*. Bill and Julie Harkins were a great support, showing me around Hobart as well as giving me the best breakfast I had eaten since leaving Cape Town. They also gave me their Wi-Fi USB so that I could communicate with my family. Bill and Julie knew Gerald Doonan's family. Gerald and I were at St. Vincent's School for the Deaf together.

My mate Jim had the brilliant idea of asking Karalyn Church (John Church's daughter) to make a special delivery to me. Karalyn is a sign language interpreter and lives in Australia with her partner, Susie. They were flying from Scotland to Australia and agreed to fly to Hobart carrying three laptops for me to replace the laptops that were damaged in the capsize. The laptops were donated by Erelend and Joel. Erelend donated a brand-new laptop whilst Joel gave me two second hand laptops, both in perfect working order. I was so grateful to Erelend and Joel for their generosity.

Karalyn also interpreted an essential phone call to Garmin. Karalyn and Susie stayed for a couple of days and thoroughly enjoyed themselves, staying comfortably in *Quest III*. I was very sad and emotional when they had to leave. It was hard to say goodbye to them after the wonderful time we'd had together. Once they had gone, I focussed on working out how I could keep my three new laptops safe. They now had protective waterproof covers and a special place in a secure cupboard, in the hope that it would keep them in good order during gale force winds and heavy seas.

I also got to meet up with Phil Malm, one of the world's greatest deaf golfers. Phil plays for Australia and we had met several times over the years at the World Deaf Golf Championships, but never actually spoken to each other. I was amazed to learn that he lived in Tasmania and was delighted to be able to meet up. It was so nice and easy to be able to communicate in sign language. Phil knew that I would need to be ready to leave at any time and kindly agreed to be on standby to give me a lift to Coles to do some food shopping when required.

I was also thrilled to meet Angela Maclean, lecturer at Victorian College for the Deaf, Melbourne. Angela is hearing but a fluent sign language user. Angela came to do a short thirty-minute interview with me and brought her two daughters, Ruby and Lily. I was interested to learn about Victorian College for the Deaf and their policy of focussing on meeting the needs of students through a bilingual philosophy, supported by an innovative curriculum. Their approach really seemed to challenge students to achieve their personal best. It was very similar to the philosophy in place at St. Roch's Secondary School in Glasgow. Angela brought me a gift (a cap and sweater with the Victorian College for the Deaf logo on it) and showed me a short video on her phone. It was a video of some of the students and Ramas, a deaf teacher, signing, *'Go, go, go, Gerry!'*

I completed a long list of repairs to *Quest III* while I was in Hobart. The top of the mast Garmin wind speed sensor and WINDEX vane for wind direction were both damaged in the capsize, so they had to be replaced. The stainless-steel framework on the self-steering was cracked and needed welding. The wheel adaptor for the self-steering also need welding. Initially, the welding had to be abandoned due to unbelievably strong winds. The winds were so strong that *Quest III* was heeling at nearly 40° at the pontoon.

I added plenty of fenders to protect *Quest III*. Some of the fenders were burst by the force of the wind. Thankfully, the winds and the welding were completed three days after it started. The self-steering had been repaired and the wheel adaptor for the self-steering was now attached to the steering wheel with new clamps. I ordered twelve new clamps as a standby, as they were broken during my time in the Southern Ocean.

The storm jib and genoa were ripped and needed to be repaired to ensure they were secure for the next leg to Cape Horn. The jib sheets, furling rope and self-steering rope line needed replacing due to wear and tear. The riggings also needed to be checked after capsize.

Garmin Headquarters recommended switching from a Class A autopilot kit to a Class B kit. They told me that an engineer would fly from Sydney to examine my set-up and bring a Class B kit with him. They agreed to replace the autopilot as a straight exchange. They also agreed to replace the wind vane and wind speed sensors at the top of the mast. This was done when all the riggings were checked. The spinnaker pole was broken in half in the Southern Ocean so had to be replaced.

On Friday 18th January, I took *Quest III* out for a test sail to check that the autopilot was still working. Noel and the engineer from Garmin joined me on the test sail. The new equipment was working well so I prepared myself to leave Hobart as soon as possible and head south of New Zealand and onwards to Cape Horn, then back into the Atlantic Ocean and homewards to Troon.

I woke at sunrise on 20th January 2013 and gazed at the sun peeking above the horizon. My mood had completely changed since arriving in Hobart. I had thoroughly enjoyed myself. I was feeling positive, confident and determined, and my mind was fixed on only one thing. Like me, *Quest III* was ready to meet Cape Horn.

I showered then made a Skype call to Kay and my mate Jim before heading homewards. I knew that if things did not go to plan, this might be the last time I ever chatted with them but something inside me told me that I would see Kay in Troon.

Noel and a customs officer joined me on *Quest III*, and I completed all the paper work and customs checks necessary before leaving Australia. *Quest III* and I departed the marina by 10.00 UTC. A few hours later, there was enough sea room to pull up the sails.

As I sailed towards the Tasman Bridge, I spotted a rib speedboat approaching *Quest III* from behind. It was Pieter! He had caught up with me to say 'Cheers' and wave me on my way. Then he gave me a message via gesture: *'Stay Brave'*. I gave Pieter a 'Thumbs Up' signal and I wondered what lay ahead in the South Pacific Ocean.

On 22nd January, I updated my log at 03.15 UTC. There was light rain and a strong wind. My position was Lat 44S, Long 149E and I was heading south to New Zealand. *Quest III* was sailing well and I had got back into my regular routine of eating, sleeping, checking and updating my log. But at 07.45 the intermittent faults with the autopilot started over again – and the autopilot failed.

I was exasperated. I had been at sea for only two days! I sat looking at the steering wheel in utter disbelief asking myself, *what next?* The autopilot had been professionally installed and worked so well during the test sail. Should I return to Hobart? Or, should I keep coping and try to figure out what was wrong. I checked all the wiring. Then I pulled the plug from the ECU and put it back. The autopilot came on but it broke-down again at 08.20 UTC. I was at my wits' end with it. I was so infuriated by the constant problems that I was ready to throw the autopilot into a black bin bag and get rid of it.

On 24th January, at 06.30 UTC, the wind changed to north-northeast Force 5 and there was a lovely blue sky. I decided to try the autopilot. Holding my breath, I switched it on. It was working again. I couldn't figure out why it had suddenly started working again but decided not to touch anything and make the most of it. I switched from self-steering to autopilot. Gales had closed in by 18.30 but *Quest III* was making good speed between 7 to 10 knots.

By 27th January, *Quest III* and I were heading between Stewart Island and Auckland Island, south of New Zealand. The Tasman Sea, between Australia and New Zealand, was almost behind us. At 18.00 UTC, I logged my position: Lat 49S Long 166E. We were 550 NM from the International Date Line and due to pass the South Cape of the Stewart Islands (the fourth Great Cape) in a few hours. The weather was miserable. Visibility was very poor with very thick fog with mist and the wind was blowing hard.

I spotted something odd. The voltage of the batteries had dropped. Normally, the batteries held the charge for longer. I gave the batteries a boost from the generator. After writing my log, I studied my chart for the South Pacific Ocean and planned my route from New Zealand to Cape

Horn. I researched the Atlas Pilot Chart and the Admiralty Ocean Passages for the World, making notes.

My plan was to pass either south of New Zealand 48S or thirty miles south of Snares Island 48°S. Then steer to the east between Bounty Island (47S 179E) and Antipodes Island (49S 178E). Inclining slightly south, the plan was to follow a mean track of 51S from about 150W across the ocean to 120W. I had to keep at about 50S to reduce the risk if encountering icebergs. From 115S, I would incline gradually S to round Islas Diego Ramirez (56S 68W) and Cape Horn.

At 17.00 on 28th January, I noticed that the voltage reading on the batteries was far too low to keep the autopilot running. I had run the generator for about three and a half hours the previous night to boost the batteries but now the batteries needed boosting again. This was worrying because it used up a lot of fuel and I had to ensure that I had enough fuel left to keep me going until I arrived at Troon, Scotland.

I switched to self-steering to preserve the fuel and tried a few experiments to try to work out what was wrong with the batteries and the autopilot. I tried charging the batteries for five hours. The autopilot seemed to benefit from this and worked well, but I was disappointed when the charge didn't last long. I was beginning to wonder if this new autopilot (which had been recommend to me) was the right choice. I needed advice from someone who was skilled in electronics so decided to contact Robert in Cambuslang. I sent Robert a photo of the new autopilot via Satellite Fleetbroad Band. A few hours later two emails arrived from Robert with his reply:

'Gerry, I saw the pictures of the autopilot it looks like a hydraulic system.

'Remember, I phoned about the two different types when I was on the boat? Garmin told me there were two types. A linear motor for Sail boats and hydraulic for motor boats. Hydraulics use a lot more power because they are pumping hydraulic oil. This is ok on my boats cause the engine is running all the time. I wonder why they changed it to hydraulic, probably more stuffing in it.'

Then…

'Gerry, I was correct. They have fitted the heavy-duty kit. I spoke to them and there are a couple of things to do, although you can't use it twenty-four hours a day as it will discharge the batteries very fast. The

original kit drew 1.5 amps, the new kit will draw between 6&8 amps normal use and 12 amps in heavier weather! The lad emailed me instructions, I can foreword this if you like. Let me know. Cheers, Robert

'I have to admit when I got the battery message from you having seen the photo of the new gear my heart sank! I thought the batteries won't last! At least we found a solution quite quick :-)). How long do you think to Cape Horn? Remember you are being watched every day :-). Keep in touch! Watch the fuel! Cheers Robert. Ps you still owe me a sail around the Clyde.'

I was gutted. I had spent a fortune on this equipment but all it had done was cause problems. What was the point of it? But I had no choice now. I had to accept the situation and carry on.

By 30th January 2013, I had almost reached the International Date Line. I still had 3600 NM of open sea ahead of me before reaching Cape Horn. I was completely on my own, with no visible signs of human life. I passed time watching the two albatrosses who had kept me company swooping down and skimming the surface of the sea with the tips of their wings.

It was summer in the Southern Hemisphere, but it was bitterly cold. I put on extra thermal clothes to keep me warm. It was so damp and cold that it was difficult to prepare meals, so I kept myself going on Mars bars and fruit juice. I tried making a cup of coffee to warm myself up but it went cold quickly, only a few minutes after I boiled the water.

I needed some rest so wrapped myself up to go to sleep and I gave myself a break from focussing on the *Quest III* by passing time thinking about golf and the World Deaf Championships I had competed in. Finally, I fell into a deep sleep but I was jolted wake by the juddering of *Quest III* and a loud crash on the deck above me. It could mean only one thing: the mast had collapsed onto the deck.

I raced up onto the deck but the mast was still upright. What a relief! It had been a vivid dream. The next night I experienced another disturbing dream. This time *Quest III* was sailing fast through an enormous swell. *Quest III* bounced hard against the waves cracking her hull. A three-inch crack in *Quest III's* bow exposed the cabin and water was rushing into the boat. I woke suddenly and grabbed my torch to check for water in the cabin. The cabin was fine but the dream had been so intense that I was feeling a bit unnerved and anxious.

I decided the best thing to do was to get up and do some routine jobs to keep me focussed. I checked the generator, sorted out the winches and then checked the fuel tank. The tank was completely full when I left Hobart but now there was only three quarters of the fuel left in the tank. The new autopilot was very good but it was depleting the batteries very quickly and using up a lot of fuel because I had to run the generator every day to recharge the batteries. I began to consider whether I would need to stop somewhere to refuel.

From 30th January to 3rd February, conditions in the South Pacific Ocean deteriorated and sailing became much harder. The weather was very unpredictable. When the poor visibility cleared, it was dull, miserable and overcast. The swell was now much higher than anything I had experienced before so I decided to reduce sails, leave reefing and stay sail to keep pace along the waves with very strong gusts.

More trouble arrived on 3rd February. There was water leaking into the engine room. I couldn't understand where it could be coming from. I checked every sea cock and looked for cracks, but there appeared to be nothing at all that would explain the leak. I waited until the next spell of calm and checked everything again. Still nothing. It was really puzzling.

I couldn't afford to have anything happen that might take my focus away from sailing. It was beginning to feel as if I had been in the South Pacific Ocean forever but I had to keep going and stay focussed. I still had roughly four weeks hard sailing before reaching Great Cape Horn and the weather was becoming more and more unpredictable: very deep depressions and high waves suddenly became calm. But when it was calm, sudden strong gusts could easily knock *Quest III*.

As soon as the fog lifted, I stood behind the mast to scan the horizon: miles and miles of ocean with no visible signs of life. I was on a tiny yacht in the middle of the South Pacific Ocean and was thousands of miles from anything. It felt amazing! I felt so tiny that I wondered if the International Space Station would be able to see *Quest III* in the midst of the massive expanse of the Southern Oceans. When conditions were like this, *Quest III* strolled along and surfed towards the east under the No.3 reef mainsail and reef genoa.

On 11th February at 18.00 UTC, I logged my position at 50 31S 140 09W and checked the barometer. There had been warning signs of gales for a few days. The barometer had dropped to 998.3 mb and by 22.30 UTC the seas were high with very confusing swells. I had the feeling a deep depression was on its way.

It was very uncomfortable sailing. *Quest III* would be sailing at 12 knots over the waves, the wind dropped, and we were suddenly sailing at 8 knots; the winds were changing so quickly that I had to change sails every few hours. *Quest III* and I made a good run over the next few days but then the self-steering rudder tube broke again. I had only one tube left so decided to switch on the autopilot. By now, Cape Horn was on my mind every day. I was constantly checking and planning ahead. I knew there could be a mishap at any time. Conditions could change very quickly. Lots of sailors in bigger boats than *Quest III* had failed to pass Cape Horn because of the sudden and unpredictable changes in the weather. I was determined that there was no way I was going to let this happen to me. There was a high risk of damage to the mast and rudder in these conditions. Other boats had been dismasted while attempting to reach Cape Horn. I reduced the sails as much as possible, but enough to still allow me to maintain speed and keep my eye on the barometer for any changes.

Finally, on 12th February, after nine days, I located the cause of the leak. I had gone down below at the stern to check the steering wheel mount. It was then that I spotted that the deck fitting bolts were loose, meaning that water was getting in from the deck. I tightened all the bolts and hoped that there would be no more leaks until I reached home.

By this time, I could also tell I was getting much thinner. My T-shirts were now too big for me and my pants and trousers kept dropping down. I had to tighten up my trousers by using ropes as a belt.

On 19th February at 20.46 UTC, after nearly three weeks of grey and overcast skies, the sun appeared. I sat at the cockpit wondering when I had last seen the sun. It felt as if *Quest III* had been tossed and turned by the monster waves and powerful winds for almost a lifetime. The respite from the gales lasted only a couple of hours. By 22.50 UTC, the clouds and gales had returned. The sea was black and rising with white horse waves.

On 21st February the barometer dropped 4mb between 06.00 and 18.00 UTC as the wind rose to Force 7 to 8 blowing north-northwest. I checked my weather reports and the seven-day forecast. If I continued on the same course, *Quest III* would hit a high-pressure system that was approaching the land mass of South America. It was risky. I began to wonder if I should alter my course to head towards the South Pole, rather than straight to South America as planned. I changed course and headed south. My friends at home must have thought I was going mad! I received lots of emails asking, 'Where are you going?' But they didn't have access to the same weather information as me.

The sea was getting higher and higher and more powerful. The swell was almost as high as the mast. *Quest III* roared bravely through the swell, diving into the deep troughs of the waves and then climbing upwards over the crests at an average speed of ten knots under the storm jib. *Quest III* was almost losing her balance as she approached the top of the waves, and she was heeling far too much out of control. To make matters worse, the autopilot seemed to be having difficulty getting a signal. Conditions were getting frightening, but this was only Force 7/8. I knew it was likely that *Quest III* and I could face winds of Force 10 as we approached Cape Horn.

Conditions continued to deteriorate and, by 22nd February at 02.00 UTC, the barometer had dropped to 995.7 and the wind had increased to Force 8 varying north-northeast to north. I logged my position: 55S 108W. I stayed down below, tightly bracing myself on the starboard side bunker while waiting for the barometer to rise. I could feel the monster waves brutally pounding the deck from all directions.

My feet were locked tightly against the base of the seat across from me, when suddenly and without warning, I shot across the cabin. Within a faction of a second, my head hit the galley and my feet were in the sink. My tongue was covered in blood and the pain in my neck was so severe that I thought it must be broken. I had bitten my tongue so badly that it was completely numb, but it was extremely painful to close my mouth. I tried to straighten my neck, but the pain was excruciating.

Quest III was sailing at high speed. I tried pulling myself upright but was being pulled backwards by the force of gravity. I waited for *Quest III* to start climbing the next wave then ran as quickly as I could to the cockpit to check for damage. *Quest III* was fine but I would need to take the helm to ensure she survived the storm. Under these conditions, it was too risky to use the autopilot. There was a strong chance that something could go wrong with the autopilot and *Quest III* would quickly be out of control.

By 04.20 UTC, wind had increased to 40 knots. Luckily, I had already put up the storm jib, so I sat tight the corner of the bulkhead. The barometer continued to drop. At 06.00 UTC the wind was 47 knots and rising. This was far worse than any of the storms I had experienced before. All I could do was believe in myself and keep *Quest III* going. At 11.50 UTC I altered course to south 138°T. The wind changed to north-northeast and increased to 48 knots plus.

The wind continued to increase and had reached 57 knots and rising by 14.50 UTC. The barometer had dropped to 978.9 mb. Conditions were getting treacherous. I had to keep control of *Quest III*. By now, the series drogue was on standby in case I need to throw it to prevent *Quest III* sailing so fast that she became unmanageable, broached, and capsized. The pressure of the wind was frightening and the waves were so enormous that it was hard to believe my eyes – almost 200ft long (almost the length of a football pitch). The wind strength continued to increase; it was nearing Force 10. I remained standing at the helm to ensure I had full control of *Quest III*. In my heart I knew that in conditions like this, I would be better with a tiller. *Quest III* was a sailing at 17 knots. We would experience catastrophic damage if she capsized at such high speed. I glanced back and forwards towards the series drogue on standby on the starboard side, wondering whether I should throw the series drogue and go down below to give myself a break. My gut told me to hold on and stay at the helm but, at the same time, I asked myself, *when will this wind go down?*

By 19.15 UTC, the wind changed to west-southwest and, at last, the barometer had started to rise. The barometer was now at 980.1 mb and the wind had dropped to Force 7/8 from the southwest. The deep depression had passed, meaning I could go down below to give myself a break and catch a few hours' sleep. But I didn't sleep long. I woke after only a few minutes.

My oilskins were really uncomfortable and covered with sea water. I decided to take them off for a while. The cabin was freezing cold (1.6°C) so I put on as many layers as possible to try to keep warm: three fleece jackets, three pairs of fleece trousers and two pairs of socks. I didn't want to use Eberspaecher heater because I had to save fuel. The other option was to use the gas cooker to add heat to the cabin. It didn't make any difference.

By 25th February *Quest III* and I were 800 NM from Cape Horn. I pulled up full sail and altered course to 097°T, heading towards Cape Horn. It was my last week of sailing in the Southern Pacific Ocean. I thanked God for my safe passage so far but could not afford to relax – there was still a long way to go before we faced the challenges of my final Great Cape.

Over the next few days, I began to lose my appetite – possibly because of the anxiety about what lay ahead. Visibility was poor and the waves continued to increase in height. The waves were hammering *Quest III* so hard that I felt like a piece of clothing being thrown about inside a washing machine.

At 00.70 UTC on 27th February, I logged my position (Lat 59 22S Long 87 04W) and checked the barometer. The barometer was now reading 999.3

mb and the northwest wind was registering at Force 7/8. It was bitterly cold inside the cabin and the glass of the portholes was covered with frost. I rubbed the frost and peered outside. A three-quarter blue moon shone over the surface of the ocean. I gazed at the stars and thought about those nights in boarding school when I lay in my bed, gazing through the dormitory window at the stars and dreaming of sailing round the world.

Quest III and I were now about two days from Cape Horn. Visibility was poor and the waves were over four metres high. And, there was a storm approaching from behind us. I didn't feel like eating. I was too tense. We had only a few hundred miles to go before reaching Cape Horn and there was another storm approaching from the west. To make matters worse, my fuel reserves were now just below half. The new autopilot was using so much power that I did not have enough fuel to get me back to home to Troon. I had force myself to accept that that I had no option but to stop at the Falkland Islands to refuel.

The barometer eventually rose to 1005mb on 2nd March 2013. The wind and sea started to ease but there was still a heavy swell from the west. *Quest III* made a good run of 188 NM. For the first time since leaving Hobart, I had time to watch the ocean's waves. I was 89 NM from Islas Diego Ramirez. This meant I had only 140 NM to go before reaching the most treacherous cape of all: CAPE HORN. It was then that I began to realise that I had almost achieved my life-long ambition and wondered if I would ever see the southern oceans again.

Quest III and I rounded at Cape Horn on 3rd March 2013. I recorded our position at 12.40 UTC: Lat 56 15.558S Long 67 16.315W at 12 40 UTC, course Bearing 060T, Barometer reading 1008mb, Temperature 8.7°C, Wind from west Force 5/6. I was 16.7 NM from the Cape Point, but it was grey and overcast and the poor visibility meant that I could hardly see anything. I refused to be disappointed by the poor visibility. I was thrilled to be there.

I went down below to prepare the special treat that I had been saving for Cape Horn. I unpacked my Bialetti Espresso maker and brewed my first espresso coffee since I left Troon. I saluted Cape Horn with my coffee saying 'cheers' and congratulated *Quest III* as the roaring white horse waves pushed as eastwards. And I said 'thank you' to Kay, Nicola and Ashley for letting me go on this once in a lifetime opportunity. At last! Forty years after I first dreamed of sailing round the world, I had safely rounded Cape Horn.

At 17.45 UTC on 3ʳᵈ March, the land mass of Cape Horn was visible from the portside. The light from the sun picked out the aretes and valleys that had been carved out of the mountains by glaciers millions of years ago. That was when it really hit me. I had done it! I had achieved my lifelong ambition. But I was on my own with nobody to celebrate with me. I thought about Kay and our two beautiful daughters and wished they could be there with me.

Quest III and I were heading northwards towards the Falkland Islands. The wind changed from west to northwest and the sun shone in an amazing blue sky. The Chilean island of Isla Lennox was visible. I opened up the portholes and hatches to let air into *Quest III* and dry out the cabin. I took off my oilskin jacket and trousers and warmed a tin of tomato soup. The calm sea meant it was the first time that I had been able to cook without difficulty.

Three albatrosses paddled contentedly in the water around *Quest III*. I felt like the spring was coming. Suddenly, the wind dropped to 4 knots and all was calm. I looked south and could see huge waves travelling towards Scotia Sea. It was so different from the peace surrounding *Quest III*. I felt a wonderful sense of achievement, but I had one more task to complete before I could claim to be a round the world yachtsman: sail through the equator and cross from the southern back into the Northern Hemisphere.

On 4ᵗʰ March, I received a lovely surprise. It was a message from Sir Robin Knox Johnston:

> *Tell Gerry, the easy things are not worth doing. Where is the satisfaction from achievement? It is the difficult things we take on that bring us pride and is real achievement.*

> *Reading Gerry's blog brings back some cold, wet and uncomfortable memories. It is such a relief when you clear Cape Horn and turn north.*
> *I shall look forward to adding Gerry to the list of solo circumnavigators south of the three great Capes when he gets back.*

I was delighted when I received this. It was so unexpected. Sir Robin is always very busy so it really encouraged me to know that he had taken the time to write a message to me.

Shortly after receiving the message from Sir Robin, the autopilot failed again. I switched to self-steering and sailed hard closed haul with fifty miles left before reaching southern Falklands. I emailed Port Stanley Customs to see if I could communicate with them but got no reply.

Fortunately, Jim in Glasgow managed to make contact via the Embassy and, after much discussion, I was allowed entry to the Falkland Island and given the details of the route for entry to Port Stanley.

At 18.30 UTC that day, the forestay collapsed. I went up to the coach roof to examine it. I could see the halyard flying horizontally in the air. Without thinking, I started to climb the mast. I didn't stop to clip on my safety harness. *Quest III* was rolling from side to side due to the strong gusts of wind. I climbed about thirty-five feet, to half way up the mast, caught the halyard and brought it down with me. I replaced the shackle, attached it to the stay jib, and pulled it up under Force 7 winds as she roared fast on hard heel.

There was still no sign of the Falkland Islands until 21.00 when I caught sight of Barren Island, south of East Falkland. It was really difficult sailing into Port Stanley. The wind blew hard under the nose of *Quest III*. I had to tack at all times and stay well away from the breakwaters nearby on the coast, at the same time as keeping an eye out for kelp (seaweed), which can get tangled up under the propeller shaft and could affect it when it comes up to speed with the throttle.

Quest III was heeling so I reduced the mainsail to No.3, until we passed the Cape of Pembroke on port side. I had been given very strict instructions on my route into the Harbour because of the possibility of unexploded mines left by the Argentinean forces during the Falklands War of 1982. Strictly no landings were permitted other than other than those directed by the Custom and Immigration Service or Port Control.

I was so shattered – I was worn out, cold, wet and damp – and was focusing on things bit by bit, looking at the sails and wondering if they could hold through, gust after gust. In no time, the wind rose from Force 4 to 8, making sailing closed haul very difficult, tack after tack, as I dreamt of arriving.

Visibility was poor so I had no idea where to berth. It was getting darker with time dragging on, so I decided to put up the Q Flag (the yellow flag for Customs) before it was dark, just in case the harbour patrol boat came. I was anxious to make it and had the anchor chain on deck on standby, in case I failed to get there as scheduled.

Quest III and I arrived at Port Stanley harbour at 6th March 21.30 UTC. I was so relieved, knowing I could go to sleep without worrying about dropping the anchor – you need to be on standby and to watch out for the weather – if the wind rose at it strongest peak, it could drag the bit away and you could potentially hit rocks, which I did not want to happen that evening.

I was amazed to see how many local people had come to help me to secure the boat. I met the customs officer and we worked through the paperwork. After checking that all the paperwork was in order, the customs officer shook my hand to congratulate me on my arrival.

Then a local couple (Bob and Janet McLeod) indicated to me to go with them to their car. I wondered what was going on. It was impossible for us to communicate because it was very windy, and my notepad was wet, meaning I could not write on it. I realised that they were inviting me to their home for a meal.

I checked *Quest III*, making sure I had switched off all the power before leaving her to rest, then disembarked. My legs were not used to walking on land after so long at sea, so I felt a bit unstable as I walked along the shore to their jeep.

Bob and Janet drove me to their house. When we arrived, they offered me use of their home to have a hot bath. It was wonderful! Then Janet treated me to a home cooked meal of two chicken breasts, with home grown potatoes, cauliflower, broccoli, carrots and white sauce. For dessert, I enjoyed homemade scones washed down with beer.

I thoroughly enjoyed spending my evening with Bob and Janet. If they hadn't offered me the hospitality of their home, I would have had to go out in a wet and windy evening to search for a proper meal. Bob and Janet drove me back to *Quest III* after dinner.

It felt so damp with condensation inside. I wrapped myself up in my wet sleeping bag and drifted peacefully off to sleep, looking forward to waking up with the sunrise the next morning. I would take the opportunity to have a few days' rest, knowing that I had sailed around Cape Horn. All I had to do now was think about getting fuel for that bloody Garmin autopilot!

Chapter 14: Paterson's Rock

It was freezing cold when I woke up the next morning. The bulkhead and portholes were covered in condensation and I could see my breath in front of me. I switched on the heater and the gas cooker to heat up the cabin and then made myself a mug of coffee. It was good to be able to enjoy my coffee without the worry of having to brace myself against the high seas.

I had a look outside at Port Stanley. It was very, very quiet, with no sign of any local people. But it was just after sunrise so I thought perhaps I was up too early for the residents of Port Stanley. I started planning my next few days to ensure I could leave as soon as possible. I climbed the mast and checked all the shackles, securing them and replacing them where needed. The heavy rain meant that it was slow work.

While I was half way up the mast, I noticed a man looking at me. He had a notepad in the pocket of his waterproof jacket, so I assumed he must be a reporter from the local newspaper. I climbed down to say hello. It was then that I found out that he was not a reporter. He worked for the RAF base in the Falklands. He had brought a notepad so he could communicate with me. He asked if I had time to go with him to a local café for breakfast.

The man bought me a full English breakfast and what a breakfast it was! I thoroughly enjoyed it after weeks and weeks at sea. I washed it down with two mugs of coffee. The man wrote his name on his notebook: Paul Rhodes. I was a bit puzzled by him: *how did he know who I was?* He explained that Richard Ellis (who had crewed for me in the Bay of Biscay) had been in touch with him. I was amazed – *what a small world.*

Paul told me that he had to go back to work but asked if I needed help with anything. '*Yes,*' I replied, explaining that I needed a diver to check *Quest III's* rudder, keel and propeller. I wanted to make sure that everything was OK before setting off on the last leg of my voyage. Paul wrote that that would be no problem and that someone would come over first thing the next morning.

It poured with rain for the rest of the morning. And it was freezing. I was struggling to get any work done so decided to pass some time at the local pub. I was delighted to find out that the Juventus v Celtic game was on the TV, but disappointed that they had no draught Guinness because they were waiting for the delivery. I 'made do' with a can of Guinness and returned to *Quest III* when the pub closed at 14.00.

That afternoon, Jane Barber, who also worked in Customs, kindly asked if I needed any laundry done. I replied, '*Yes please, that would be great*' but told her there was no need to iron anything. I just needed my clothes to be clean and dry.

I awoke early the next morning with the sunrise. The weather wasn't too bad but it was too early to go to the shops. I waited until 8.30 a.m. to have breakfast at the café.

After a good breakfast, I was ready for mug of coffee only to discover that Paul had brought his workmate Paul Holland along, as well as three engineers from the RAF/Marines. They were happy to volunteer to change the oil, impeller and fuel filter. They were highly skilled and worked really quickly. I could have done these jobs myself but it would have taken much longer.

A few hours later, the diver (Warrant Officer Chris York) arrived, along with his mate, Sergeant John Holden. Both Chris and John were marine commandos in the RAF. Chris dived underwater and discovered that kelp was tangled up in the propeller. The propeller was supposed to be closed when under sail, but it came open and dragged a wee bit. I had felt the propeller vibrating but had been unsure what had been causing it. Chris confirmed my suspicions.

After checking the rudder, propeller and hull, the team invited me to visit the RAF campus that afternoon. Then the fuel truck arrived. It stayed on the main road but reversed as close as it could to get to the pontoon rail. A heavy rubber fuel pipe was connected to the *Quest III*. The minute the fuel tank was full I was thinking about leaving and heading home to Scotland. I checked the weather forecast – it wasn't good.

That afternoon, Paul Rhodes and Paul Holland arrived in a jeep to take me to the RAF base. I was a bit taken aback when they asked me if I was OK. They both had very concerned looks on their faces. I asked them why they were so worried. They had seen me standing on my own, signing to myself.

I explained that I was fine and that I was not signing to myself. I instructed them to look up at the roof of a nearby the building. There was a webcam on top of the building. People in the *Quest III* Fan Club had spotted the ship at Port Stanley via the webcam, so I was signing an update to the fan club to let them know *Quest III* and I were having a wee rest and that this afternoon I would be visiting the RAF base. The two Pauls shook their heads (they didn't know there was a webcam there) and we got into the jeep.

It took forty-five minutes to get to the RAF base along slow bumpy roads through low mountains. I was astonished to learn that there were still thousands of live mines left from the Argentinean invasion in 1982. I could imagine the fierce fighting that took place in this area.

When we arrived at the RAF campus, Mount Pleasant Airfield, I was taken to look at a Typhoon FGR4 war plane that was about to leave. A few minutes later, I could feel the engine running as the plane passed by about a hundred metres away on the runway. The pilots waved at us. The plane turned right on the runway, and less than a few minutes later, the ground shook as the jet engine roared into life. My feet shook with the strength of the vibration under my feet and hot, strong smelling fumes filled my nose. Powerful red-hot flames shot out of the exhaust. I could feel the pressure on my chest from the noise from the engine as the plane shot up vertically into the sky. Within ten seconds, the plane had disappeared from sight.

After that, I was taken to see another war plane in the hanger. Young RAF men and women were working on it, checking the engine and wings with sophisticated computer equipment. Sergeant John Holden gave me the opportunity to sit in the pilot's seat. I couldn't believe how complex the electronics were.

Warrant Officer Chris York asked if I would like to see the meteorology officer and check to see if there were any icebergs north of the Falklands. What a relief when I found out that I would not be encountering icebergs on my sail home, but there were also warnings that the weather was not good. By the time I had finished up in the meteorology office, the plane had returned to the base.

I met the pilot (Squadron Leader Matt Peterson) and we had a chat about the plane he was flying. The RAF Team gave me a poster of it and each of the team signed their name on it. I posted that back to Glasgow. I didn't want to risk it being damaged by the dampness on board *Quest III*. That evening we all went to the local pub. I had great time with them all but, by then, I had made my decision – I would be leaving tomorrow (10th March). The weather forecast was not good but I was going to risk it. I couldn't really afford to spend any longer in the Falkland Islands.

The following day, I went through the customs checks at the local police station. My plan was to leave at 17.00 UTC. I sent text messages to all the local people who had helped me during my stay to let them know my plans. They all came to bid me farewell. Janet McLeod even brought me some homemade fruitcake. I would look forward to eating that before the *Quest III* and I reached the doldrums.

The wind was strong, blowing hard against the starboard side of the hull, making it tricky to get out of the pontoon. Luckily, some local yachtsmen came over to help us to take off. *Quest III* and I were heading towards Kidney Island and then we would sail clear of the Falkland Islands.

I was heading for Kidney Island before clearing the Falklands when I discovered that there was kelp trapped around the propeller shaft. I could see the kelp below the rudder from my position at the stern. It took hours to remove it. After completing the job, I took a break. I switched to self-steering, closed haul, No.2 reefing, with the stay sail up, in Force 6 in a strong heavy swell from the southeast wind, and relaxed with a beer and whisky. I glanced at the thermometer and the barometer. The barometer had dropped to 997.4mb. My position was Lat 49 45S Long 55 43W. The weather looked like early spring in the west of Scotland, but it was autumn in the Southern Hemisphere. It was very cold but the sky and ocean were brilliant blue. I altered course to the north, heading for Ilha de Trindade Lat 20 30S Long 29 20W.

On 15th March, the temperature started to rise. It was now 6.1°C. I began to feel slightly different. *Quest III* was sailing comfortably under full sail. I sat on the coach roof, watching the sun rise above the horizon. When the sun had risen, the sky was brilliant blue and, far off in the distance, I could see clouds forming. I felt good as I thought about the horrendous conditions *Quest III* and I had battled in the southern oceans.

The temperature rose to 11.9°C that afternoon. We were heading towards the 30s latitudes and would soon leave the Roaring Forties behind us. The barometer rose to 1016mb, wind speed was variable from 8 to 15 knots. But the good weather didn't last long.

On 16th March, strong gusts of wind were blowing hard with torrential rain. I had to pull the head sail down as fast as I could and reef the mainsail. Then the autopilot lost its network. I switched to self-steering so I could sort out the electronics.

The strong gusts from the south-southwest continued into 17th March but the temperature continued to rise. It was 13.5°C and, for the first time, I felt warmer. I had kept a keen eye on the sails as *Quest III* roared through the waves.

The electronics problems started again that afternoon. This time the chart plotter reading was very different from the one from in the cockpit unit. The chart plot from the navigation area said GPS heading 106T, the autopilot compass from the cockpit said heading 030T, but the original compass was reading 150T. I was sick and tired of the constant problems and couldn't understand why it kept happening. I decided to reduce to the third reef and put the inner forestay up.

The temperature had risen 14.8°C by 18.00 UTC. It was a magnificent evening; a beautiful orange sky as the sun began to set. The weather changed very quickly, and the next thing I knew the wind was much stronger and squally, reaching to Force 7/8. But *Quest III* was magnificent, sailing strong and fast, covering 186 NM from noon to noon.

The evening of 17th March to 18th March was a very uncomfortable night. I was up all night sailing. I couldn't sleep because I felt very unwell – my joints were aching and felt really nauseous. I felt so bad that I wondered if, perhaps, I had drunk some contaminated water. I had recently switched from the water tank astern to one at forward, but I boiled all my water so that should have thoroughly killed any nasties.

By late afternoon, the sea was still very rough. *Quest III* sailed between 6 to 10 knots under speed with a No.3 reef mainsail with inner forestay. It was very uncomfortable inside the boat. I felt like I was on a carnival ride as I braced myself over and over while *Quest III* shot out over the waves and thudded down. By 17.00 UTC the temperature had risen to 14.9°C and the wind had started to gradually go down, so I took off my jacket and tried to catch up on some sleep.

I felt a lot better the next day but still felt as if I had something wrong. I checked the temperature from the chart plotter reading and it said the air temperature was now 16.7°C. I could really feel the heat inside the boat so I took off my T-shirt (my commemorative T-shirt from the Scotland v England Golf International Match in 2007 at Cardrona Golf & Spa Hotel (Peebles), Scotland). By 18.00 UTC the temperature had risen to 17.7 at Ilha de Trindade Lat 35S Long 39W.

On 20th March, *Quest III* sailed close-hauled, hard against the wind, riding over the waves and diving down the troughs, still with a very uncomfortable hard heel with high speed. I couldn't cook or sleep. I tried to nap but couldn't manage it. *Quest III* was bouncing too hard. I wanted to maintain the progress so ate Mars bars and drank cans of Coke to keep me going. It felt like being on a speedboat with full throttle. By now we were on the same latitude as Cape Town 33S (and, on the other side, Uruguay West) and about 800 NM from Trinidad.

On the evening of 22nd March, I put away my extra sleeping bag. It was so warm inside the cabin that I no longer needed it. Even when it was raining, I felt much warmer. At 18.00 UTC, I updated my log: '*18.00, temp 19°C, 023T barometer 1023mb, wind E/ESE, Lat 33 16S 38 19W*'.

The wind had dropped slightly so I closed my log book and started thinking about preparing a meal. I couldn't think what to cook so I decided to have a look at the tins in the other cabin. Just as I was about to go to the other cabin, I felt something was wrong outside. I couldn't believe my eyes when I went outside to check – torrential rain was pouring down so hard that I could barely see.

Quest III was heeling well over and sea water was washing over the deck and into the cockpit, but inside the cabin it felt calm. The mast was being pulled towards the sea. I tried to close the genoa by pulling the furling rope, but it was an impossible task. The genoa was flapping so wildly that I could feel the vibrations from the mast.

By now, it was dark and I felt I could lose either the mast or the genoa at any time. I tied the furling rope using all my strength to turn it as fast as I could. Thankfully, as I turned, I could feel the vibrations beginning to lessen and I glanced up to see the genoa beginning to close completely. I sat and looked up at the black sky as the torrential rain poured down my face – it was lovely and warm.

After inspecting it, I could see that the genoa had torn itself from the clew for about a metre. I was really concerned there could be more rips elsewhere, but I would have to wait until daylight before I could check properly. Just before I cleared the cockpit and tidied up the halyards, etc., thunder rumbled and lightning flashed so bright it was like something out of Second World War. It was so bright I could see the horizon of the ocean. I figured I'd need sunglasses to protect my eyes from going blind completely, so I went down below immediately. I left the third reef and inner forestay up, knowing she would be OK.

I checked the chart plotter to make sure she was on course, and I could not figure out what was wrong with the wind direction, as it was the opposite of what I could actually see. Our yacht was sailing port tack, yet the reading from the chart plotter said the wind was from the starboard side!

I was ready to call it a day – I had had enough with the Garmin! I decided to take a wee whisky, closed my eyes and took a nap. I forgot about the food that I had and went to sleep wondering what I should do. The genoa needed to be repaired, but it would be best to wait for light winds to come before attempting that, and that could mean a delay; failing that, I'd have to think of something else.

I was also wondering what to do about the bloody stupid electronics. I fell fast asleep and, a few hours later, I woke up to see that the lightning was still raging. Everything inside the boat was lit up with the flashing, just like watching a horror movie!

I rose before sunrise on 23rd March. The thunder and lightning were still visible far off on the horizon. My first thought was to look at the genoa, before I ate or drank. The tear I had found the night before was repairable. That would be no problem, but I was concerned there might be further rips. The sky seemed nice and calm, though it was still a bit windy, but I decided to open the full genoa and inspect it thoroughly. Thankfully, the metre-long tear from the bottom tack of the clew was the only damage.

That afternoon, when the wind went down, I started the repair work to patch up the sail using the sail cloth that I got from Saturn Sails in Largs, Scotland. Thank goodness I had taken it with me. When the repair was complete, I inspected my handiwork, reckoning that it would be able to withstand conditions until I arrived in the North Atlantic Ocean. I decided that I deserved a beer to celebrate my handiwork.

As walked around the deck, carrying my beer and examining the shackles and ropes, I found that the furling rope was damaged and could snap easily – only one pull would have resulted in disaster. I forgot about my beer for the time being and replaced the furling rope.

I rose before sunrise again on 24th March. I went up to the cockpit to drink my coffee and look at the stars that were still lingering in the sky. The sky on the eastern horizon was filled with yellows and blues as the sun began to rise. The sea was calm, with waves coming from the southeast. The temperature was now 23°C, water temperature 27°C and wind Force 2/3. I was heading toward the west of Ilha da Trindade Lat 20S Long 29W. By 11.25 UTC, flying fish were everywhere, leaping up out of the sea and onto the deck. I lifted them as quickly as I could and threw them back into the ocean.

On 26th March, the wind changed to north-northwest Force 4. The barometer was steady at 1024mb, and we were on course for 028T, Lat

21S Long 35W. I closed haul and stayed inside because it was too hot outside. I decided to fix the winch as it is noisy when it turned. I had only 1,350 NM to go before reaching the equator.

On 5th of April, *Quest III* and I passed the Brazilian of Islands Fernado de Noronha. Our position was Lat 03 27S Long 32 51W and we were heading 348T. The barometer remained steady at 1008mb. After months of being cold and wet, I was now constantly soaking in perspiration. It was 31°C inside the cabin. Outside, the air temperature had risen to 28°C and the temperature of the sea was 30°C.

Sailing in the southeast trade winds was glorious – especially at sunrise and sunset. During the evening, I sat in the cockpit watching shooting stars. It was so hot during the day that I stayed inside to protect myself from the sun. When there was a good wind and *Quest III* was heeling, I could go out on deck and work under the shade of the sails.

It was impossible to keep my food supplies cool. I tried stowing my tins in a shaded area but it was no use. Even the bilge was very warm. At one point I was thinking of having rice pudding and jam. When I picked up the tin I could feel the warmth from the rice pudding before I opened it. I opened the tin and looked inside. Both the rice pudding and the blackcurrant had turned to liquid in the heat. I mixed them together and drank the rice pudding straight from the tin – at least it filled my stomach.

Quest III and I still had a few hundred miles to sail before crossing the equator into the Northern Hemisphere and entering the North Atlantic. Although it was very warm, it was time to start preparing my body for the colder conditions and rough sailing conditions of the North Atlantic Ocean.

I needed to do something to try to perk up my appetite. It was very poor and I had to increase my food intake to maintain my energy levels in the cold weather. I love freshly baked crusty bread so decided to take advantage of the good sailing conditions to bake a couple of loaves. I prepared the dough, kneading it for ten minutes before leaving it aside to prove. Usually, when I bake bread at home, I leave the dough for one to one and a half hours, but it was so warm in the cabin that it doubled in size in just thirty minutes. When I opened over door to check the loaves, the cabin was filled with the aroma of freshly baked bread. I put the loaves aside to cool. When the loaves were cool enough to eat, I made some Italian tomato soup, eating it straight from the pan and dipping my homemade bread into it to soak up all the flavours. It was delicious. I felt so different after my meal that I managed to a good quality forty-five-minute nap afterwards and, for the first time in ages, I awoke feeling rested and refreshed. From then on, I began to very slowly build up my food intake.

In the evenings, I took advantage of the full moon to go on deck to check the sails, tidy and put away the ropes, and then do a 360° check of the horizon for any ships that might be in the area. One brilliant starry night, I climbed on deck to do my routine checks and then I returned to the cabin, planning to my get some more sleep and to be ready to start sailing at sunrise.

Just as I was about to get into my bunk, I noticed something at the end of it. It was long, black and cigar-shaped. Assuming my book was jammed at the very end of my bunk, I reached over and picked it up. I shuddered with fright when I felt something soft and slippery in my hand. I quickly picked up my torch to find out what it was. It was a flying fish! I looked up and realised that I'd left the hatch wide open. The flying fish must have flown high enough to drop through the hatch and fallen down onto my bunk while I was dozing. Normally, I would be woken up by the vibrations of something landing on my bunk, but not this time. I threw the flying fish back into the sea and cleaned up the bunk before getting back in, remembering to close the hatch this time.

On the morning of 7th April, the sky was cloudy and overcast and strong Force 5 wind came from northeast varying to east-northeast. *Quest III* was approaching the inter-tropical convergence zone and would soon be heading for the North Atlantic Ocean, so we had to be ready for the tough sailing conditions ahead of us; I switched to self-steering and close hauled to get some rest. I sat at the navigation panel with my eye fixed on the chart plotter.

At 08.00 UTC (just before sunrise) the reading changed from 0S to 0N. *Quest III* and I had crossed the equator. I updated my log. I felt good knowing I was now on the last leg of my journey but the battle was not over yet.

Later that day, I sat with my mug of coffee looking astern. My plan was to sail home via the west coast of the Azores. From there, we would sail into the northeast trade winds and onwards to the Horse latitudes (25N to 30N). I could follow the wind towards the Caribbean before heading north-east towards Ireland, but I was worried by cracks that had appeared in the winch mount and further hairline cracks that had appeared along the edge of the U-shape of the frame at the stern.

I checked the chain plate for the riggings, the keel bolts. I knew that the keel and rudder were at risk but I had no idea how long they would hold. I had to get home as quickly as possible. Sailing towards the Caribbean would only add time to the journey.

As I watched the wake from *Quest III*, I looked out towards the horizon behind us. There was nothing but sea. The great oceans of the Southern Hemisphere were far beyond that horizon. The ocean was so vast. It was almost impossible to believe that *Quest III* and I had sailed so far and were now heading home. As I reflected upon my incredible experiences of sailing in the southern seas of the world's great oceans, part of me wondered if I would ever see them again. It was soon time to get back to work.

I looked up the mast to check the WINDEX wind indicator. The previous day a bird had tried to perch on top of the wind vane several times. At one point it managed to grab the wind indicator but took fright when the boat rocked and flew off.

The first four days after crossing the equator were very tough sailing. I was really struggling. The skies were miserable grey, the temperature began to drop and we were hammered by strong gusts from the northeast wind. It was exhausting and I was struggling to maintain my focus. *Quest III* was tired as well. She had been through so much. But she kept going, bouncing over the waves.

Quest III was heeling at roughly 40° under the force of the wind, even with reduced sails. Everything inside the cabin was moving. It was impossible to keep my balance without grabbing hold of the rails. It was hopeless trying to sit on any of the seats so I sat on floor. Normally, I would be able to keep going and stay focussed under these conditions, but I was finding it very challenging.

The intermittent problems with the chart plotter and autopilot continued to plague me but now *Quest III* was really feeling the strain of the batterings she had taken. Twice the rope snapped from the furling forestay drum, causing the genoa to open.

The genoa thrashed wildly as *Quest III* bounced through the waves, the mast shaking as it flapped uncontrollably. *Quest III* was at risk of severe damage. I knew that if I did not replace the ropes at the furling drum, it was very likely that the mast would break.

The rope for the jib was tightly knotted and the jib sheet was whipping furiously in the wind. I had to avoid being hit by it because it would likely cause me serious injury – a broken bone at the very least. I flattened myself as close as I possibly could to the deck and edged myself towards the furling drum.

Quest III was lunging through the waves at tremendous speed. I gripped the toe rail tightly as *Quest III* dropped into the waves. I was completely submerged in cold dark water and couldn't see a thing – over and over again, as I picked my way towards the furling drum. *Quest III* continued to bounce through the waves and the mast continued to shudder under the force of the genoa as it violently thrashed in the wind. I was terrified. It was a nightmare of a job trying to replace the rope in the furling drum, but I had no choice. It was a two-man job to bring the genoa down.

First, I had to pull away the furling rope from inside the drum. I was soaking wet and cold. Wave after wave crashed over *Quest III*, each time I rolled away in the hope of avoiding another drenching then rolled myself back to continue working on the ropes. It was painful and awkward, staying flat to avoid being hit by the jib sheet, so I had to keep shifting my position.

After removing the chafed section of the rope, I began the slow process of replacing it. First, I had to secure the rope to the furling drum. The rope was thin and fiddly in my cold hands. My fingers felt for the hole to thread the rope through. It was like trying to thread a needle with a blindfold on.

Then I wrapped the rope round the drum and pulled the rope to close the genoa. I pulled as the rope as hard as I could, but the drum wouldn't move. I decided to return to the cockpit and try from there by using the extra length of the rope as a lever. The furling drum wouldn't budge.

My last resort was to use the winch. I wrapped the rope round the winch and turned the handle. I could feel the tension on the rope as it tightened but still the furling drum refused to move. I kept turning the handle, using all my strength and screaming with effort. Gradually the furling drum began to move. Too scared to stop, I kept turning the handle until the genoa closed. After three to four hours of effort, I inched my way back to the furling drum and attached to rope to the stanchion to lock it.

I was wiped out, my body was cold, wet, and shaking from fear and exhaustion. I needed a whisky. The sea was still rough but *Quest III* was now sailing comfortably. I went down below, poured myself a whisky to steady my nerves, dried myself off and changed my clothes before enjoying rice pudding and jam with some fruit juice to follow.

By 13th April, we had reached Lat 13 33N Long 36 33W. The barometer read 1012mb and wind was Force 5 varying northeast to east-northeast. We were heading 350 T towards the Azores. That night I spotted the Pole Star – the first real sign that I was on my way home. The following day the NE wind rose to 30 knots. Dazzling white horse waves topped the miserable grey sea.

Quest III and I suffered another blow on 16th April. The self-steering was severely damaged: the stainless-steel tube that attached to the head of the rudder was broken. It was beyond repair and needed welding. I was devastated. I had about 700 NM to sail before reaching the Azores, before I could then head towards Northern Ireland. All I could do now was take the helm to steer *Quest III* home and hope, that by some miracle, the intermittent problems with autopilot would rectify themselves so I could catch some sleep.

Sometime before sunrise on 19th April, I felt the vibration from thunder and torrential on the coach roof above me. *Quest III* was sailing well and heeling at about 30°. It was still dark. All of a sudden, it was upright and stopped making progress. I looked through the porthole: everything was calm. The wind had suddenly dropped to 0.4 knots. The temperature dropped to 17°, from 22° the day before. I was feeling very chilled so I pulled on a fleece jacket for the first time since arriving in the Northern Hemisphere. The calm was interspersed with sudden gusts of wind that were constantly changing direction: west-southwest, then northeast.

By evening, it was completely calm without a gust of wind. *Quest III* was rolling gently with the long swell, so I decided to make to most of the calm and pass time by baking bread. That evening, flickers of light danced around the cabin as the rays from the sun was reflected off the surface of the sea and through the portholes. I had never seen anything like it. It was breath-taking.

We were still making very little progress the following morning. The autopilot was working again but I was keeping my eye on it. Conditions were varying between Force 0.5 to calm. I decided to have a quick nap. No sooner had I closed my eyes when I was jolted awake by a strange vibration.

I could see occasional flashes of lightning east of Madeira but it felt as if something was wrong outside. I stayed still, concentrating my attention on the vibrations of the boat. There were two different vibrations. The first I recognised: it was from the flapping of the sail. The other vibration was more like a judder. There was nothing on the boat that could cause thudding like that. There was very little wind so *Quest III* was gently rolling with the swell.

Thud! The whole boat was shaking. A few seconds later there was another thud. Something outside was bumping against *Quest III*. My heart was in my mouth. I knew of stories of sharks attacking boats. I placed my hands against the hull to feel where the vibration was coming from: nothing. I went out to the cockpit, switched on a torch, and inspected the deck, both sides of the hull, and then shone the beam of my torch out across the ocean. There was nothing there; just the light from my torch shining across the surface of the swell.

I returned to my bunk to get some more sleep. Thud, thud, thud! I got up from my bunk and started to feel around for the vibration all over again. I could feel the thudding under the forward bow but it was gentle, so I moved nearer to the mast area. The vibrations were much stronger. I was really puzzled. How could the thudding be coming from the mast? I went back outside to check the mast again. Just like before, I couldn't see anything wrong. I decided it was best to wait until daylight before investigating any further.

I wrapped myself up warm in my bunk and dosed off to sleep but before long I was woken by a loud bang just above my head. Something had crashed onto the deck above my head. I looked up at the ceiling. It was fine; there were no cracks. I rushed out onto the deck and I couldn't believe what I saw in front of me.

My radar was lying on the deck. The scan strut bracket that supports the radar mount had been secured to the mast by a total of sixteen rivets and now it was lying at my feet. The radar had fallen off the mast. The rivets had been shorn in half by the constant pressures from sailing against the wind. *Quest III* was falling apart. I still had 590 NM before reaching the Azores but I had no self-steering, no radar and the autopilot and chart plotter were unreliable.

I caught sight of the Azores Islands at 02.00 UTC on 26th April 2013. Faial and Pico Islands were visible under the light of the moon on the starboard side of *Quest III*. I could see waves roaring east to west and, far in the distance, I could see the twinkling street lights of the coastal towns. We were in a full-scale storm and *Quest III* was travelling extremely fast (11 knots) in a Force 8 wind. There were lots of fishing vessels in the area so I altered course to Faial and then to the north of the Graciosa Island.

Quest III and I were safely north of the Azores by 27th April. *Quest III* was heeling steeply under the powerful gusts from the east. Waves crashed over the deck. I needed a break from steering, but the winds were so strong that there was a high risk that *Quest III* would capsize if I heaved to. The autopilot and chart plotter were still playing up and had failed several times. This time it said 'power on wait'. That meant I couldn't use it. I pulled down the head sail, leave No.3 reef in the main sail, letting *Quest III* sit at about 55 degree apparent wind. I put the traveller right down to leeward with plenty of sheet tension, allowing *Quest III* to sail comfortably in winds of up to 40 knots but hardly heeling over.

While I was resting, I spent most of my time examining and experimenting with the electronic control unit and the T-Connections, trying to find the fault, but had no luck. The autopilot was still cutting out and giving a reading 'waiting for the controller'. I had eaten hardly anything for two days (just biscuits) and, according to the weather forecast, I could expect the wind to drop soon. I needed to eat something to ensure I would be ready to take the helm, so I made myself a quick meal of pasta.

The wind dropped to Force 6 (varying east-southeast to east) on 28th April. I took the helm, pulled up the inner forestay and headed on north on bearing 004T. The autopilot was working again but it was far too risky to rely on it. It could cut-out at any minute and without warning. My best option was to take the helm to steer *Quest III* home.

By then I was averaging between eight and twelve hours of steering before taking a short break, but with the prospect of roughly 1,300 miles at the helm ahead of me, I had to carefully plan my routine of sleeping and eating. I stayed at the helm twenty-four hours a day, leaving my positions only when absolutely necessary. During these short breaks, I would make coffee and collect tins of fruit, vegetables, corned beef and tinned custard to take back to helm. I ate them all straight from the tin, drinking down the juice for vegetables and fruit.

The next day, I started my investigations again, repeatedly checking the network cables, T-connectors. I also checked the wind speed indicator, GPS, depth/speed. I still could not locate the fault. Then I had the idea of pulling all of the T-connectors out and connecting them again, one by one. First, I attached the first GPS T-Connector network cable to the switchboard near the navigation desk – it worked. The chart plotter came on, along with the GPS and AIS. Next, I tried connecting the wind speed indicator. It worked fine but broke again when I tried connecting it to the depth/speed socket. I decided it would be better to disconnect in order to keep the chart plotter going. But not matter what I tried, the autopilot refused to work.

While I was steering, I tried pressing the button to switch the autopilot on from cockpit. The autopilot came on and was working again. But it was still unreliable; it was switching itself on and off again for no apparent reason.

By 2nd May *Quest III* and I were about 450 NM from the south of Ireland. I was averaging twelve to thirteen hours at helm before taking a short break. The tiredness was really kicking in, but I knew that I would soon be able to smell the landmass of Ireland and, all being well, I would be in Troon in five or six days. I could feel my mind racing at the thought of being home, so I had to pull my focus back to the task at hand.

I continued trying to figure out what was causing the problem with the autopilot. On 3rd May, I was steering at the helm when I had the idea to check the network panel in the locker at the stern of *Quest III*. Conditions were good and there was no rain so I didn't need to worry about water getting into the electronics network. So, keeping one hand on the wheel, I opened the hatch below the seat to access the network, and stepped down below.

My head and upper body were still above deck, allowing me to keep one hand on the wheel. I used the other hand to experiment with the connections. One by one, I removed each of the four cables from their socket and inspected it before plugging it back in. When I plugged on the fourth cable, the display panel lit up. I tried engaging the autopilot. It was working! I couldn't believe it; it was like a miracle.

The autopilot cut out again soon afterwards. This time I tried wiggling the cable. It came on again. What a relief. I now knew that the problem was due to a faulty cable and that if it should happen again, I could fix it (even if it was only temporary). I would forget the rest of the network and focus on keeping that connection working.

It was great to have the autopilot working again. It was not reliable and I would need to keep a close eye on it but, at least I could try to catch up on some sleep. I began to look forward to my last few days of my voyage and sailing home to Troon.

At sunrise on morning of 7th May, I could smell land. By 07.00 UTC, Tory Island, Ireland was visible about six miles from the starboard side of *Quest III*. I stood on deck, wrapped up against the cold, with a mug coffee in my gloved hands, and toasted Tory Island. I was nearly home and would soon be able to see the Mull of Kintyre. But I also knew the last 140 miles could be the most difficult leg of my journey so far.

The weather forecast warned of gales in Malin. The Malin area of the North East Atlantic can be very difficult sailing. There is a busy shipping lane, with cargo ships and other merchant vehicles and the occasional battleship. There are also lots of fishing trawlers. The sea around the northern coast is dotted with buoys indicating lobster pots. One of these could easily catch the propeller.

The weather in the Malin area change quickly and unpredictably – anything could happen. The best sailing in Malin is when the wind is from the west or southwest, but the weather forecast was for gales from the east. I breakfasted on porridge topped with honey and a wee shot of whisky to prepare me for sailing towards the Mull of Kintyre.

I know the Firth of Clyde and the seas around the Mull of Kintyre well, because I have sailed there many times. My plan was to pass the Mull of Kintyre, head towards to the south of Arran, then onwards to Troon. I checked my fuel. I had three jerry cans of fuel left. I would use these to fuel the engine if need be.

The gales around the Mull of Kintyre were ferocious and relentless. The hours between 10.30 to 04.40 UTC felt like the most difficult sailing I had ever done. *Quest III* battled, hard tack by hard tack, to pass round the south of Mull of Kintyre. The gales from the east piled the waves against *Quest III,* pushing her into the shipping lane and into the paths of trawlers. There are dangerous rocky outcrops near Sanda Island (off the Mull of Kintyre). I was worried that the waves throw Quest III against the rocks, so stayed at the helm. Finally, *Quest III* and I sailed past Sanda Island.

Before I had time to think about my next move, I saw what looked like a dim flashing light ahead of me. It quickly vanished from sight as *Quest III* bounced through the waves. I went to the navigation table to check my position. I enlarged the chart. Suddenly, terror was coursing through my veins. *Quest III* was heading for Paterson's Rock. I rushed to the cockpit.

The red light of the buoy sped past on the port side of the boat. Grabbing the helm, I tacked as fast as I could to avoid a collision with Paterson's Rock. I couldn't believe that I had made such dangerous mistake (in the

Firth of Clyde, of all places) but by now I was getting more and more fatigued and struggling to stay focussed.

Early on 8th May, I watched the early morning sun rise and breathed in the smell of the land and sea. It was the smell of my childhood: The Firth of Clyde. I felt as if I must be dreaming. I thought about that day when I wrote a message to my dad on the newspaper about Sir Francis Chichester. My dad kept that for the rest of his life today, and, now, here I was sailing home to Troon after completing the Five Great Capes and passing the equator from both directions. I was looking forward to being home with my family.

By 08.15 UTC, Holy Island off the east coast of Arran was visible. I was exhausted and drained of energy. But I knew that, within in few hours, I would see Troon harbour and Kay, Nicola and Ashley would be there waiting for me. I looked over *Quest III* as she sailed towards Troon under engine. She had been battered and bruised by storms and ferocious seas. But she was tough, determined and strong and kept going, battling hard against the wind and the oceans. Even when I thought she was about to fall part, she kept going. What an amazing yacht. I thought about everything *Quest III* and I had been through together and the months and years preparing for sailing round the world. I couldn't quite believe that I had done it. After years of dreaming about sailing round the world, it was suddenly over: finished. I was delighted but felt a hint of disappointment that my adventures with *Quest III* were over. I patted *Quest III* saying, 'Well done. Thank you.' My phone vibrated. It was a text message from Kay, 'Hello, you have done it. Am so proud of you and looking forward to see you in about three hours. Can't wait xxx.'

As I approached Troon, the local RNLI lifeboat and a rib speedboat from the marina sailed towards me. I assumed that the lifeboat must be on a call-out, but the lifeboat crew waved to me. They had come to escort me into Troon harbour. I could see well-wishers on the coast waving and cheering. Then I saw two men waving to me from the rib speedboat. It was Erelend and Jim! Just before we entered Troon marina, the rib came alongside and my mates jumped onboard *Quest III*.

The marina was filled with deaf people from all over the UK cheering and waving flags. The pontoon was full of camera crews and journalists *Quest III* berthed at the pontoon at 12.30 UTC on 8th May. We had sailed 215 days together and covered 27,793.5 nautical miles. I hugged Kay, Nicola and Ashley as close to me as I could. I was home.

... I returned to work a few weeks after arriving in Troon. Once I had settled back into my routine, I was invited to give a presentation about my solo circumnavigation to the school assembly. Tommy Donnelly interpreted my presentation into spoken English for the staff and pupils who did not know British Sign Language. Shortly afterwards, Tommy told me that he and Gerry McGuigan had agreed with Glasgow Education Department that the 'Hearing Impairment Unit' would be changed to the 'Deaf Education Department.' I could see the oppression of deaf pupils coming to an end. In the past, the focus had been a deaf pupil's ears and training them to lipread and speak. Now deaf pupils would be valued as individuals in their own right with inherent linguistic and educational potential. My spirits lifted and I felt a new sense of optimism about the futures of our deaf pupils.

Appendix 1: Quest III

QUEST III - Beneteau 42s7 1996

1 Code 0 - Gennikar with Selden bowsprit
2 Radar
3 Geona
4 Stay Sail
5 Storm Jib
6 Furling
7 Steering Wheel
8 Jordan Series Drogue (used during storms)
9 Self Steering - Monitor
10 Satellite Fleet Broadband
11 Liferaft
12 Trysail
13 Mast Step
14 Windspeed

Naval Architect Bruce Farr
LOA 42'6" (13.0m)
LWL 35'9" (10.9m)
Beam 13'6" (4.1m)
Draft 7'7" (2.3m)
Ballast 6,283lb (2,850kg)
Displacement 18,220lb (8,265kg)

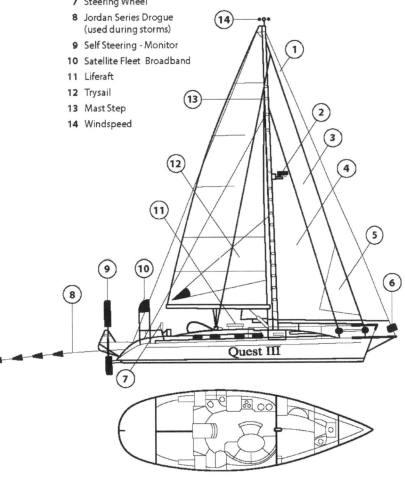

Quest III

Appendix 2: Glossary

Barometer
Atmospheric pressure is measured in millibars (mb) using a barometer. Atmospheric pressure indicates weather. A rapid drop in air pressure means a low-pressure system (depression) is on its way.

Beaufort Scale
The Beaufort wind force Scale measures windspeed on land or at sea.

Greenwich Meantime (GMT)
The time zone centred on the 'prime meridian' which runs through Greenwich in England.

Latitude
Latitude is a   measure of how far north or south you are relative to the equator. Latitude is measured in degrees, minutes and seconds north or south of the equator.

Longitude
Longitude measures how far east or west you are relative to the 'prime meridian'. Longitude is measured in degrees, minutes and seconds east or west of the prime meridian.

Nautical Mile
A nautical mile (NM) is based on the circumference of the earth and is equal to one minute of latitude. This means a nautical mile is slightly more than a statute (land measured) mile (1 nautical mile = 1.1508 statute miles). Nautical miles are used for charting and navigating.

Reefing
Reefing is the means of reducing the area of a sail. For example, reef the mainsail in strong winds

True Bearing (T)
True bearing is measured using true north (geographic north pole) rather than magnetic north pole.

Universal Time Coordinated (UTC)
UTC is a time standard and is used in sailing.

Appendix 3: Beaufort Scale

Beaufort Wind Force	Mean[1] windspeed Knots/ms[-1]	Description[1]	Sea[2]	Height of waves[2]
0	0/0	Calm	Calm (glassy/like mirror)	0 m
1	2/1	Light air	Calm (rippled, no foam crests)	0.1 m
2	5/3	Light breeze	Smooth (small wavelets, not breaking)	0.2-0.3 m
3	9/5	Gentle breeze	Slight (small wavelets, crests beginning to break	0.6 -1 m
4	13/7	Moderate Breeze	Moderate (small waves becoming longer, numerous whitecaps)	1-1.5 m
5	19/10	Fresh Breeze	Moderate	2-2.5 m
6	24/12	Strong breeze	Rough (larger waves forming, whitecaps everywhere)	3-4 m
7	30/15	Near gale	Rough-very rough (sea heaps up, white foam blown around)	4-5.5 m
8	37/19	Gale	Very rough-high (edges of crest break into spindrifts)	5.5-7.5 m
9	44/23	Strong Gale	High (sea rolls, reduced visibility)	7-10 m
10	52/27	Storm	Very high (very high waves with overhanging crests)	9-12.5 m
11	60/31	Violent Storm	Very high (exceptionally high waves)	11.5-16 m
12	-	Hurricane	Sea completely white excessive foam	16 + m

Sources:

1: Met Office
(https://www.metoffice.gov.uk/guide/weather/marine/beaufort-scale)

2: National Oceanic and Atmospheric Administration
(https://www.wpc.ncep.noaa.gov/html/beaufort.shtml)

CPSIA information can be obtained
at www.ICGtesting.com
Printed in the USA
BVHW021043031119
562777BV00016B/114/P